Enduring Grace

Living Portraits of Seven Women
Mystics

❧

Carol Lee Flinders

HarperSanFrancisco
A Division of HarperCollins*Publishers*

FIRST EDITION

Library of Congress Cataloging-in-Publication Data
Flinders, Carol.
      Enduring grace : living portraits of seven women mystics / Carol Lee
Flinders. — 1st ed.
            p. cm.
      Includes bibliographical references and index.
      ISBN 0–06–062645–3 (alk. paper)
      1. Women mystics—Biography. 2. Mysticism—Europe—History.
I. Title.
BV5095.A1F57 1993
294.2'2'09224—dc20   92–56399
[B]   CIP

05 04 03   ❖ RRD(H)   30 29 28 27 26 25 24 23 22

This edition is printed on acid-free paper that meets the American National Standards
Institute Z39.48 Standard.

Dedicated to
my teacher
Sri Eknath Easwaran
&
To my parents,
Jeanne Lee Ramage
and Gilbert H. Ramage

ENDURING GRACE

Contents

ix   Acknowledgments

xi   Preface

1   Introduction

15   ❧ Saint Clare of Assisi

43   ❧ Mechthild of Magdeburg

77   ❧ Julian of Norwich

103   ❧ Saint Catherine of Siena

129   ❧ Saint Catherine of Genoa

155   ❧ Saint Teresa of Avila

191   ❧ Saint Thérèse of Lisieux

221   Conclusion

229   Notes

239   Select Bibliography

244   Index

Acknowledgments

To Christine Easwaran, for her warm encouragement from the very outset, my deepest thanks. Also to my agent and friend Candice Fuhrman for initiating me into the subtleties of proposal writing, and to her daughter Carrie Jacobsen for her graceful editorial work on the proposal itself. And of course thanks to Candice for finding me a home at HarperCollins. My editors have been superb: Tom Grady, Caroline Pincus, Priscilla Stuckey all improved the manuscript substantially, bringing astute critical faculties to the task but kindliness, too, and tact.

Enduring Grace really began in the Sunday-morning sessions of retreats given by the Blue Mountain Center of Meditation in northern California, where for about five years I gave talks regularly on the mystics included in this book. To all of the participants in those retreats, I owe a great deal, for they gave me ample opportunity to develop my ideas and raised penetrating questions as well.

The members of my spiritual family at BMCM have helped me through this project more than they'll ever know: especially JoAnne Black, and also Laurel Robertson, Helen Cornwall, Sarah Dole, Julia MacDonald, Gale Zimmerman, Sumner West, Melissa Larson, Sandra Delay, and Sultana Harvey. Several friends read and responded to early drafts—Madeline Gershwin, Janet Niemi, Spring Gillard—thank you!

Undertaking a project like this, you never really know—and it's probably best that you don't—how much time it will take and how much of *you*. For bearing the brunt of my absorption with good cheer and full support, my greatest thanks go to my husband, Tim, and my son, Ramesh.

Wouldn't it show great ignorance, my daughters, if someone when asked who he was didn't know, and didn't know his father or mother or from what country he came? Well now, if this would be so extremely stupid, we are incomparably more so when we do not strive to know who we are, but limit ourselves to considering only roughly these bodies. Because we have heard and because faith tells us so, we know we have souls. But we seldom consider the precious things that can be found in this soul, or who dwells within it, or its high value.

— Teresa of Avila,
Interior Castle 1.1.2

Preface

It seems to me that our three basic needs, for food and security and love, are so mixed and mingled and entwined that we cannot straightly think of one without the others. So it happens that when I write of hunger, I am really writing about love and the hunger for it, and warmth and the love of it, and the hunger for it . . . and then the warmth and richness and fine reality of hunger satisfied . . . and it is all one.

. . . There is food in the bowl, and more often than not, because of what honesty I have, there is nourishment in the heart, to feed the wilder, more insistent hungers. . . . There is communion of more than our bodies when bread is broken and wine drunk. And that is my answer, when people ask me: Why do you write about hunger, and not wars or love?

> — M. F. K. Fisher, *The Gastronomical Me*[1]

> That prayer has great power
> which a person makes with all his might.
> It makes a sour heart sweet,
> A sad heart merry,
> A poor heart rich,
> A foolish heart wise,
> A timid heart brave,
> A sick heart well,
> A blind heart full of sight,
> A cold heart ardent.
> It draws down the great God into the little heart,
> It drives the hungry soul up into the fullness of God.
> It brings together two lovers,
> God and the soul,
> In a wondrous place where they speak much of love.

> —Mechthild of Magdeburg,
> *The Flowing Light of the Divine Godhead* (5.13)

FRIENDS who know me mostly as a food writer and one of the authors of *Laurel's Kitchen* were surprised by this book about women mystics: many wondered out loud what the connection was between these two realms and how I happened to pass from the one to the other. The lines I have quoted above—from a celebrated contemporary food writer in the first instance, and a revered medieval mystic in the second—are meant to suggest that my two worlds are not as remote from each other as they might seem. Whatever interest we have in food, the late and much loved Mrs. Fisher reminds us, arises out of the simple fact that we are hungry—hungry, albeit, for all *kinds* of things. Mechthild, too, recognizes how hungry we are, and for how many forms of nourishment, but she traces that hunger to the soul itself, and insists that nothing short of "the fullness of God" can satisfy it.

That is the short answer. I like to offer it because it hints at the rich possibilities of dialogue between women—no matter what their historical context—who know something of "the wilder, more insistent hungers." But demonstrating that those two worlds are not mutually exclusive doesn't explain how one might actually travel from the one to the other, and I think that is what friends and readers of *Laurel's Kitchen* want to know. Here, then, is the longer answer, a backward look, brief as I can manage, at how this project came to be—specifically, at the personal concerns and questions that shaped it, for these lives can be approached, and have been, from a great many perspectives, and the one I have adopted is admittedly idiosyncratic.

In the first place, I am not a Roman Catholic. I didn't grow up acquainted with any of these women as saints. None of them hovered in the background of my childhood, either as inspiring role models or as figures who might have interceded with the higher powers on my behalf. Not that I disliked the idea, because some form of intercession would have been in order. But at the rural Presbyterian church where my parents dropped me off on Sunday mornings, I got the idea that you were expected to lay your case directly before your maker—in person, or not at all.

They were absent, too—both Catherines, Teresa, all of them—throughout my growing-up years. At Stanford, in fact, in the early sixties, feminine voices and perspectives of any kind were a rarity. Not until late in the spring of my senior year was there even a hint of the great opening-out that was to come: this was when some of us organized a faculty-student conference on the topic "The Role of Women." Amazing now that it could have been stated as clumsily as that—"the role," indeed! But there it is; we didn't know any better, men *or* women.

About the same time, and as predictive of things to come, another group of us took advantage of a new university policy that permitted students to initiate courses and set up an informal seminar on Eastern mysticism. A sympathetic faculty member gave us a reading list and then left us to our own devices. It was the last quarter of our senior year, so our own devices weren't worth a whole lot, but we all felt gloriously Cutting Edge, and the readings were well selected; I still have the books.

In June of 1965 I graduated from Stanford and shot like a homing pigeon to Berkeley, first to a job on the campus, and within a year or so to graduate school in the comparative literature department. I loved the atmosphere, loved the sunsets over the bay and the fog that moved tenderly in over the hills at night. I'd never felt as completely at home anywhere as I felt in Berkeley. When I drive in of a morning to teach there now, the feeling still sweeps over me.

Since much of Berkeley's powerful draw for me was its political climate, I gravitated as a matter of course toward the antiwar activities that were taking place on and off the campus.

It didn't work, though. Try as I would, I just could not catch hold— not at the rallies, not at the planning meetings, not at the teach-ins. It was as if some kind of centrifugal force kept spinning me out and away.

Years later, looking back, I think I understand what was wrong. The women's movement was indeed beginning to stir, and the questions it was raising had real personal urgency for me. The men involved in the antiwar movement were not insensitive to what was going on with their women friends. They were willing to agree, in principle, anyway, that we were at the meetings to do more than just make coffee. Some could even go further and advocate equal gender representation on steering committees. But this didn't begin to answer the real need. What was missing—and we women still could not articulate it much better than the men—was a genuinely feminine perspective on the issues themselves. It was the absence of that perspective that I believe left me and many other women feeling so intensely marginal.

Let me add right away, for there were certainly women who felt as I did but who made heroic contributions to the antiwar movement anyway, that I was also discovering that I was not suited for radical politics. I was too easily overwhelmed by feelings of confusion, despair, or inadequacy to be of much use to any movement.

And so I studied Doris Lessing's *Golden Notebook*, and I pondered Virginia Woolf's *Three Guineas*, and I saw other women carrying them around and took heart at least in knowing I was not alone. I enrolled in graduate school and more or less buried myself in course work. The deeper, unresolved matters I just shelved for the time being.

Then, in October 1967, a friend took me to a noon lecture on meditation given by a man from South India, a slight, impressively erect, and professorial figure with silver hair and a smile of singular sweetness. His name was Eknath Easwaran. By way of introducing himself he said he had come to this country as a Fulbright scholar, that in India, he had indeed been a professor of English literature. He had grown up, he went on to say, in a matrilinear tradition. His surname was his mother's, and *her* mother had been his spiritual teacher. "I was, literally, born into her arms," he liked to say. Later he would add that in his native Kerala, women had had full economic, educational, and political rights for centuries, and that in Kerala, moreover, as in Bengal, worship of the Divine Mother is widespread.

The burgeoning feminist in me was captivated by Easwaran's references to his grandmother: this was one *strong* woman.[2] Each story he told about her shattered another cultural stereotype. And the ease with which he would reel off whole passages from Wordsworth or Shakespeare or Shaw dazzled me. Most of all, though, I had never felt myself to be in the presence of anyone for whom religion was a living reality as it was for him.

Within a few weeks I was attending Easwaran's classes regularly and practicing meditation under his direction. He provided clear, straightforward instructions that made complete sense to me, and far from trying to make ersatz Hindus of us, in his weekly talks he drew freely upon an almost endless number of mystics from every tradition I'd ever heard of: the *Bhagavad Gita*, to be sure, but the writings of Meister Eckhart, too, and Brother Lawrence, the Sufi Jalal'adin Rumi, and the Compassionate Buddha.

He was almost as conversant with women mystics. The irony was not lost on me that after years of religious studies course work and endless browsing in bookstores, my introduction to the great woman mystics of my own tradition, Teresa of Avila, Julian of Norwich, and others, came from a man—one who was Hindu, moreover, by birth and upbringing. He liked to compare the devotional poems of Mechthild of Magdeburg with those of North India's wandering saint Meera. He loved

Teresa best of all (I think that in her "very determined determination" she reminded him of the women in his ancestral family). Placed just behind him as he spoke, a constant reminder of his matrilineal background, was a portrait of his grandmother.

Easwaran also introduced me—and in doing so addressed a great many of my deepest concerns—to the life and works of Mahatma Gandhi. In Gandhi I found for the first time a powerful model for social change that did not merely accommodate women: Gandhian nonviolence, particularly with regard to what Gandhi had called the Constructive Program, seemed to me to be altogether steeped in what we would now call "the feminine." The true measures of India's freedom, he insisted, had to do with what people ate, and whether they ate; how they earned a living; the state of their latrines, and the level of literacy. Whatever might be going on at the political level, there would be no truly free India until all these problems were addressed. Gandhi had found that women intuitively understood what he was doing, and they brought immense love and creativity to the work of village uplift. Even women from wealthy backgrounds had been able to regard India's poor as their own family members, just as he did. They spun cotton, wove it into "khadi cloth," and clothed their families with it, destroying the Indian market for British textiles and reviving a cottage industry that had once kept whole villages employed. It thrilled me to learn that the home itself had been the very heart of India's nonviolent revolution and the women its driving force.

The relevance of Gandhi's ideas to the contemporary West became clearer and clearer to me. As Americans, I began to see, we had been colonized, too, not by a foreign government, but by something subtler—materialism itself and the competitive, painfully separate way of life it brings about. It followed, then, that in the West, just as in India, that lesser-known side of nonviolence, the long, slow, invisible, and unglamorous work of village (and city) uplift, might be as significant and useful as the nonviolence of the political demonstration—the sit-in, the fast, the march on Washington, D.C.

We wrote *Laurel's Kitchen*, accordingly, in a spirit of direct continuity with Gandhi's nonviolent revolution. My co-authors and I—and they numbered far more, really, than the three of us whose names appeared on the book—*did* want to save animals and promote healthier eating. But we also wanted to address the pervasive sense of isolation that characterizes the affluent West, and we believed that diet was a powerful way to do that. We felt that the way people eat can separate them from one another and pit them against the environment—a fast-food burger made from Central American beef and eaten on the run is a good example—but it can just as easily connect them to one another and the earth itself. A home-baked loaf of whole grain bread, shared with friends, seemed to us a sound mid-seventies American equivalent to the homespun cotton of Gandhi's India: symbol of both self-reliance and interdependence, but catalyst, too, a starting point for community.

All those years of food writing, then—the two editions of *Laurel's Kitchen,* the bread book, and eleven years' worth of newspaper columns and magazine articles—were never really food writing in the strictest sense. In fact, several food page editors who wanted straight food writing despaired of me along the way. I wrote about world hunger, community gardens, family reunion picnics, vegetarian triathletes, and co-operative food buying. Without coming out and saying so—I didn't want to unsettle my readers by using words like *ashram* or *spiritual community*—I wrote out of the rich experience of the communal kitchen where I actually do my cooking now. I was always careful to include the obligatory two recipes at the end, but their connection with the column itself was rarely crystal clear.

Meanwhile—a meanwhile that included completing my doctoral work, marrying, and having a son—I was pursuing a line of inquiry that had tremendous personal meaning. Over and over, I found myself writing about women, extraordinary women of all kinds. Frances Moore Lappé was one, and Liv Ullman was another, particularly in regard to her work for UNICEF. But there were others less widely known. There was of course my friend Laurel, and my own grandmother. There was Jane Addams, founder of the Women's International League for Peace and Freedom, who had written with passionate eloquence, inspired by Tolstoy, about the meaning of bread labor. And more recently there was Dorothy Day, co-founder with Peter Maurin of the Catholic Worker movement, and Marian Wright Edelman, creator of the Children's Defense Fund. There were many more, and of course there was "Granny," my teacher's teacher, toward whom I would be more and more deeply drawn over the years.

Looking back, it is clear to me now that in celebrating these and other women, I have been constructing my own personal version of heroism and that I have done so out of a genuine hunger—one you could legitimately call, with Mrs. Fisher, "wild and insistent." One of my all-time favorite Wonderful Women is someone I saw for only a couple of minutes in a film called *Gandhi's India*. Her name was Asha Devi. She had known Gandhi when she was a young girl, and at the time the film was made—sometime in the mid-seventies—she was director of a boarding school run along Gandhian lines. The commentator asked her, "Do you think Gandhi used to drive people past their limitations as human beings?"

Asha Devi smiled a broad and nearly toothless smile, shook her head gently, and said with enormous sweetness, "We have no limitations as human beings."

I hope with all my heart that Asha Devi is right. When I look out across the world that my son is growing up into, I am staggered by its darkness and its turbulence. As I watch the breakdown of every "fix" imaginable—technological, political, economic, military—I am more and more inclined to believe that the only real wild card in human affairs may well be the human spirit itself, and that if we are to survive in a world worth living in, we will need to find our way into the depths where Gandhi walked.

A strong connective thread runs through the lives of all the women I mentioned above. All of them, to one degree or another, really did set aside personal comfort in pursuit of larger goals. Even if to only a modest extent, they came to feel the suffering of others as their own, and, in working to relieve it, they experienced a mysterious enlargement, often even a kind of exaltation, regardless of the disappointments or chronic exhaustion the work itself entailed.

As I pursued that bright thread, the logic of my obsession has led me back through time to the women who are the subject of this book, women who experienced that enlargement and exaltation to a degree we can scarcely imagine, and whose very names were a source of strength and hope for the times in which they lived: Clare of Assisi, Francis's foremost disciple and the first woman in history to write a "rule" for a monastic community; Mechthild of Magdeburg, whose poetic gifts allowed her to transmute intense personal suffering into mystical prose and verse of timeless power and beauty; Julian of Norwich, recluse with the human touch, who drew upon extraordinary visionary experiences to construct teachings on sin and forgiveness and on the motherhood of God that are as fresh and freeing today as they must have been to those whom she counseled; Catherine of Siena, impassioned spiritual teacher and tireless political activist; Catherine of Genoa, married, aristocratic, a hospital administrator whose mystical utterances may have inspired John of the Cross; Teresa of Avila, reformer of the Carmelite Order, whose writings on meditation are unsurpassed in the entire Catholic tradition; finally, coming almost into the present, Thérèse of Lisieux, the Normandy schoolgirl whose "Little Way" has virtually redefined the spiritual life for numberless Catholics of our time and has inspired a good number of non-Catholics as well.

I did not make the connection easily. Even though I cherished excerpts from the writings of Mechthild, of Julian, of Thérèse, the overall tenor of their lives was daunting. The terrible austerity—the single-mindedness with which they turned their backs on ordinary satisfactions—frightened me, seemed at times fanatic. Still, I kept coming back, reading a little more, finding here and there intriguing evidence that within their own very different contexts, these women might have been grappling with some of the same personal issues that my contemporaries are, and often even with the same imagery.

Teresa of Avila, with her warmth and irresistible humor and her extraordinary giftedness as a writer, was the first breakthrough. As I began to see the whole mystical endeavor from her point of view, the lives of other women mystics came into clearer focus. Or rather, it was as if I had been trying to learn a foreign language and found in her the perfect informant, one who "spoke mysticism" so clearly that even the regional dialects became comprehensible.

I began to see, too, helped by the brilliant outpouring of recent medieval scholarship, that those wild excesses, the plain *weirdness* that crops up in these lives, are really the equivalent of regional usages. No one needs to believe now that the strange eating practices that flourished throughout the Middle Ages, for example, are intrinsic to the mystical venture. Rather, they appear now to have arisen, quite understandably, too, out of the culture itself, that is, out of the stressed interface between the culture and the developing mystic. As a rule, the greater understanding we have of the times and places in which our subjects lived, the less likely we will be to make superficial, inaccurate assessments. Without denying the validity of the impulse toward "mortification," for instance (and we will look at this practice later, in context), we can with the help of historians like Caroline Walker Bynum "lift off" the layer of eccentricity that impedes our full appreciation of these women and their achievement.

I HAVE been tempted throughout this project to range beyond the Western mystical tradition and include figures from other religious and cultural traditions. Several considerations persuaded me not to. One is that my own scholarly training was in the literature of medieval Europe. I love the poems of India's Meera, for example, but I don't know Hindi, and in other ways, too, the cultural divide is so considerable that I could not do her full justice. The omissions I regret are not only of non-Western mystics. Saint Elizabeth of Hungary, for instance, is a favorite of mine, but our only sources of information about her life are a body of legends and a canonization procedure. We have nothing from her own hand.

I would so love to bring to light some of the unknown holy women from all over the world whose stature goes all but unrecognized because they did not happen to write or have literate secretaries. I imagine a book that would celebrate women mystics from Sufism and Buddhism, Native American spirituality and more—a book written in partnership with writers knowledgeable in these other traditions—one that would content itself with the paucity of information available on each, reasoning that even the small, bright scrap can find its way into a quilt if it is particularly beautiful or significant in its own right.

Writing that kind of book would have given me the chance to demonstrate the essential homogeneity of figures who were, in cultural terms, extremely diverse. In the book I have written instead, however, I have been delighted to discover the astonishing diversity of a group of mystics operating within the same religious tradition and roughly similar cultures. The temperaments, orientations, and "styles" of the seven I have looked at here are quite different, a most reassuring fact: if there is no one kind of personality best suited for the inward journey, none of us need write herself off![3]

One of the more exciting developments to come out of the field of women's studies in recent years is the recognition that the methods and perspectives of the traditional biographer of men's lives have only limited use to those who write about women. In particular, Carolyn Heilbrun in *Writing a Woman's Life* brings astute scholarship, warmth, wit, and a powerful feminist vision to many of the issues I have struggled with in this undertaking—the difficulties we have, for example, even *seeing* the life of an exceptional woman clearly because we need new narratives, new scripts in order to understand them. Indeed, Heilbrun wrote her book for motives that were close to my heart. She writes:

> Feminist criticism, scholarship, and theory have gone further in the last two decades than I, even in my most intense time of hope, could have envisioned. Yet I find myself today profoundly worried about the dissemination of these important new ideas to the general body of women, conscious or unconscious of the need to retell and re-encounter their lives. . . . We are in danger of refining the theory and scholarship at the expense of the lives of the women who need to experience the fruits of research.
>
> For this reason, I have chosen to write of women's lives, rather than of the texts I have been trained to analyze and enjoy. I risk a great danger: that I shall bore the theorists and fail to engage the rest, thus losing both audiences.[4]

It was heartening to know that Heilbrun had felt, as I had, a certain anxiety about her undertaking and the razor's edge it placed her on. Like Heilbrun, I have been disturbed to observe that the wealth of accumulated scholarship that brings Clare, Julian, and others much closer in spirit to contemporary women than we believed them to be has been largely inaccessible to readers outside the scholarly world. But she was most helpful of all when she challenged the whole basis of what I was doing—not in a formal way, but casually, almost in passing.

Pondering the conventional notion that "men can be men only if women are unambiguously women," Heilbrun asks what it means, from that perspective, to be "unambiguously a woman," and she replies, "It means to put a man at the center of one's life and to allow to occur only

what honors his prime position." One understands that the biogra
pher who holds to this version of womanhood will be as appreciative
of a Virginia Woolf or a Jane Addams as a cocker spaniel would of an
Impressionist painting.

So far, so good. But then Heilbrun adds, "Occasionally women
have put God or Christ in the place of a man; the results are the same:
one's own desires and quests are always secondary."

Sometimes fighting words are just what you need. As I read those
last lines, I knew that whatever else I wanted to accomplish with this
book, I wanted to refute the notion that women like Clare of Assisi or
Teresa of Avila did nothing more than replicate on a spiritual plane the
banalities of the conventional narrative for women.

One can understand how interpreting the mystical writing of
women fell into the error of assuming that a woman's yearning for the
divine is merely a misidentified yearning for a man. It is true that the language *available* to women like Mechthild or Teresa—the language they
had inherited from their own religious tradition—treated God as a father, a king, or, on good days, a lover. But when you look closely at how
Mechthild, for example, actually uses the language of courtly love, you
find she stretches and bends it to suit her purpose, subverting it all the
while she employs it.

In other words, recognizing that the mystical experience is inherently beyond words, mystical writers understand that the verbal constructs they use to convey it are approximations. The romantic construct
is a favorite one, for sound psychological reasons: falling in love is one
of the pivotal events in anyone's life. But it is not the only one, and mystics don't pretend it is. Some of us are more comfortable thinking of ourselves as students, or stewards, of God, than as lovers, while others
worship God as father or mother or even as their own child. Hinduism
is more explicit than Christianity about the range of possibilities, but
all of the relationships I have specified have also been celebrated by
Christian mystics.

What is *not* often celebrated explicitly in Christian mystical writings—and this is why there is almost always a verbal construct, a
metaphor, or an approximation, all of them the source of both richness
and confusion — is the experience of a formless god, one who is not so

much a being as a *state* of being. Unlike Hinduism, which acknowledges many paths to the same ultimate goal, some of which involve personal devotion to a divine incarnation, Christianity is by definition "christo-centric." The image and historic fact of Christ is the focal point of the orthodox Christian's devotional life.

And yet, the picture is not entirely clear, for certainly the culmination of the mystical life as many Christian mystics have described it is the so-called unitive state, during which the seeker feels herself wholly united with God. Helpless to describe this state, mystics reach for metaphors: a drop of wine blends into water, the wax of one candle melts into that of another, starlight is subsumed in the light of the rising sun, and boldly, Catherine of Genoa cries out, "My *me* is God!" The particular form in which she and other seers might have worshiped God up to that point—Christ as "the Beloved," God as the father, the "man at the center of our lives" that worries Heilbrun and others—would seem to have been provisional in a sense, supplanted finally by an experience of divinity that is without form, and therefore without gender, a divinity that is indistinguishable, as far as they can tell, from their own deepest sense of self.

To the outsider, it is hard to see that this "unitive state" differs significantly from the experience of "self-realization," the goal of the Eastern mystic, in which the self within and the self that underlies all of life are found to be one (a state compared, deliciously enough, in the *Upanishads*, to that of lovers: "As a man in the arms of his beloved is not aware of what is without and what is within . . . ")[5] For orthodox Catholics, however, as I understand, there *is* a difference. God must remain, in a certain and very important sense, "the other."

Nonetheless, it seems to me that as you read the lives and writings of women mystics, the conclusion is inescapable: each of them made a heroic quest that in its essential outlines resembles that of all seekers in all spiritual traditions. That quest was as much a search for their own identity—their "*me*"— as it was for the vision of a more-or-less anthropomorphic god. No matter how romantic their imagery might have been—and the lilies and ointments and erotic transports of the Song of Songs are rarely far away—they were making an arduous journey, solitary and often terrifying. They were making it, moreover, because they wanted to more than anything else in life. Their own "desires and quests," as Heilbrun would put it, were fused in this effort, made secondary to nothing and no one on earth. For women mystics living through the heresy-obsessed Middle Ages and afterward, in the heyday of the Inquisition, the use of orthodox language to describe their experience was a basic skill of survival. Nonetheless, as we will see, they managed to depict God as a being who likes to set aside his majesty and omnipotence now and then to enjoy the feminine side of himself. They describe Christ on occasion as "Our Mother." They say a great many remarkable things, only they say them carefully, and you have to read them carefully—their lives as well as their written works—to get the full import.

L AST spring my son brought home a packet of holographic baseball cards. If you hold one of these cards steady and look at it, you see Reggie Jackson with his bat on his shoulder. Tilt it just slightly, and he's starting to swing; a little more and the bat is flat out, about to connect.

Our perception of women mystics is a bit like those cards. At first glance, we see all that *language*. She's burning with love, can't eat, can't sleep; it's all too painfully familiar. Tilt the picture just a bit, though--really *read* her, that is, in a decent translation, with some sense of context— and look again. She's moving now, dancing in slow, stately circles, singing and striking a tambourine above her head, and she's surrounded by twelve other women who are also turning and singing, only they can hardly sing for laughing. The song is about fleas and how hard it is to keep them out of woolen habits.

Tilt it again, and the same woman is holding her own before a panel of black-robed inquisitors.

Again. It's the dead of night now, but that's her, in Seville, with two other sisters. She's sneaking into a vacant building. It's a hovel, really, but by dawn she will have established a new convent of reformed Carmelites there, and the whole town will be in an uproar.

Again, and she's in the kitchen, taking her turn as cook. She is easily the best cook in the community, but they're keeping a close eye on her, because last week she went into a rapture with a frying pan full of eggs in her hand, and dinner was spoiled. "God is not only found on your knees before the altar," Teresa used to tell her sisters, "but in the kitchen, among the pots and pans." Of course, no one had thought she'd meant it that literally!

These were real flesh-and-blood women, who understood hunger in all its guises. They knew the body's need, like Mechthild, who wrote in a poem of advice to abbesses: "Thou shalt also go to the kitchen to make sure that the needful provision is good; that neither thy meanness nor the cook's laziness may rob the Lord of sweet music in Choir" (*Flowing Light* 6. 1). But their own hunger was too great to be satisfied with anything short of everything, and they prayed, with Julian of Norwich: "God, of your goodness give me yourself, for you are enough for me, and I can ask for nothing which is less which can pay you full worship. And if I ask anything less, always I am in want; but only in you do I have everything" (*Showings, Long Text* 5).

Introduction

F OR reasons that are not altogether clear, thirteenth-century Europe represents the single greatest flowering of mysticism in the West. It was also a time nearly unique in Western history for the extent to which feminine voices were raised, tolerated, and even revered. On the face of things, this would not seem to be a startling coincidence, for women have typically been the custodians of spirituality. Whatever might have been happening—or not happening—at the level of institutional religion, women have gone on telling the sacred stories at bedtime, carrying out the timeless rituals of household worship, and seeing that the village priest gets fed. Of the Christian West I know this to be true, and of Hindu villages I'm told that it is from mother to daughter, by a kind of osmosis, that many of the essential religious practices and values of a people are transmitted. If a culture is experiencing a genuine "inward tug," it is therefore only natural that it should draw upon the experience of its feminine members: natural perhaps but, as history reminds us, far from inevitable.

The thirteenth century was turning inward, though, in ways that were especially propitious for women mystics. No one individual or event caused a major historical shift. But if we look for an individual whose thought and teachings truly embodied the changing spirit of those times, we would do well to look at Saint Bernard of Clairvaux, specifically at a series of sermons he gave sometime in the middle of the twelfth century in which he commented at length upon the Song of Songs.

Simplifying as we must, it is reasonable to say that up until this point in history, the God of Christians was imagined as a king or a judge, and the basic model of Christian experience reflected the feudal structure of life itself: Christ's followers were "warriors of God" in the great cosmic battle between good and evil. Bernard's teachings brought a new and powerfully attractive metaphor into play. Dwelling in turn upon each hauntingly beautiful line of the text ("Comfort me with apples, and stay me with flagons, for I am sick of love"), he moved beyond the traditional

1

interpretation, wherein the bridegroom was Christ and the bride the Church, and urged the monks under his direction to consider *themselves* the brides of Christ—to anoint and bejewel themselves inwardly and ready themselves in every way for the kiss of Christ—for the experience, that is, of mystical union with God.

Bernard's counsel swept like wildfire across the monastic orders of his time. Clearly, he had tapped into a deeply felt need and desire. From then onward, for men and women aspirants alike, the predominant metaphor for spiritual growth would be the sweet goings-on between lover and beloved. One can only imagine what it must have meant for male aspirants, struggling so long under a one-sidedly military model, to open themselves to the gentler, more tender, and devotional modes of "nuptial mysticism." For women, nuptial mysticism was an unprecedented validation of their own femininity. The motif of the young girl preparing to meet her lover is universal in secular folk culture. But up until this point it had no place within Christian spirituality, where in fact the image of Eve as the temptress would have countered it immediately. To receive this sudden new "permission" to indulge, even metaphorically, in one of life's oldest and most pleasurable rituals must have seemed a heady breakthrough.

Women felt increasingly emboldened now, despite powerful cultural conditioning to the contrary, to write and speak in their own voices. The very fact that they were writing from outside the establishment—a power structure that was solidly masculine—makes them all the more impressive and interesting to a modern audience. Departing from the impersonal, theological style of earlier mystical writers, they wrote in a newly personal, subjective voice. "They are not prophets," writes one scholarly admirer, "but passionate, often anguished minds. The beauty of their writing is bound up with their vulnerability."[1]

Femininity itself was coming to be perceived rather differently. The very qualities that had rendered women constitutionally unfit for service in a Church Militant seemed quite well suited indeed for the new model. One early commentator on the Beguines (the "order that was no order" that flourished throughout northern Europe during the thirteenth century and to which Mechthild of Magdeburg probably belonged) wrote, for example,

It seems to me that thus it is
A woman becomes good for God;
In the simplicity of her understanding
Her gentle heart, her frailer mind
Are kindled more quickly within her,
So that in her desire she understands better
The wisdom flowing from Heaven
Than does a hard man
Who is clumsy in these things.[2]

It's hardly an assessment that will warm the hearts of contemporary women, but as medieval depictions of women go, it's downright laudatory.

Scholars in the field appropriately caution us not to confuse a new valuation of "the feminine" with an enhanced appreciation of actual women or an improvement in the way they were treated. Still and all, the kinds of religious vocations open to women did multiply during the twelfth and thirteenth centuries. One important development was the rise of the preaching orders—the Franciscans, the Dominicans, the Augustinians—whose apostolic fervor ignited women as well as men. Existing convents were completely inadequate to the number of would-be entrants and often to the intensity of their spiritual practice as well. The friars did much to fill the gap between supply and demand, ministering to members of new communities, like the Poor Clares, but also to women who sought to lead Christlike lives outside the cloister, notably, the Beguines.

A recurring pattern emerges. Excluded by church law from active ministry in the church, women were more likely than men to spend long hours in contemplative prayer and to have the kind of visionary experiences that can result. Awed by their sanctity, humbled often, their confessors would assume responsibility for the correctness of their doctrinal understanding. Over the course of time, in dialogue with her confessor, a woman like Mechthild of Magdeburg or Julian of Norwich could absorb a considerable body of theological learning.

Medievalists often identify the mysticism of the thirteenth and fourteenth centuries as "feminine," a usage that has several meanings besides the recognition of the validity of the "receptive" mode, as opposed to the "active" mode, as reflected in the poem quoted above. On the most trivial level, it is sometimes observed that the visions of medieval women mystics more often feature detailed descriptions of the robes and jewels worn by the saints than do similar dream visions experienced by men. Scholars will also identify "affective piety"—the use of highly charged, emotional language and imagery to describe one's spiritual experience— as feminine, though this "mysticism of the heart" is also visible in the writings of certain male mystics, too, such as Henry Suso.

Contemporary readers are likely to see this particular designation as both familiar and suspect—as evidence not that women are inherently more emotional, but that most cultures tend to assign certain life responsibilities according to gender: "Let him earn the money," for example, "the serious money, anyway, and let her have the feelings." The resulting imbalance has of course hurt everyone concerned . . . but more of this later.

In recent years, even in this most stubbornly patriarchal society, it has come to be recognized that God is not universally regarded as masculine, that here and there throughout the world and back through time, God is and has been worshiped as the Divine Mother. Thanks to public television, archaeologists have been able to bring right into our living rooms evidence of cultures that gave full play to the feminine and defined gender relationships in terms of complementarity and partnership rather than competition and domination. They have placed before us magnificent images of the Mother from all over the world—mysterious, massive, voluptuous renderings of Isis, of Gaia, of "Mahamaya," the great weaver of illusions. We are beginning to grasp the reverence in which she was once held—she, and the forces she represents, like fertility, tenderness, wisdom, inclusiveness, and laughter. We are beginning to understand, too, I think, that even in the most repressively imbalanced patriarchy, one can find evidence that reverence for the Mother is continually trying to surface in consciousness and express itself in everyday life.

This reverence is highly visible in the writings of medieval women mystics. Aldobrandesca of Siena, for example, had this astonishing vision not long before she died: "She saw the Mother of God, dressed in the most glowing white linen and adorned with the most precious jewels, with a gold crown of marvelous beauty. And the Sunday after this, she saw her in a golden robe, having on her head a crown of twelve stars, with the moon beneath her feet, and a tablet in her hand, on which was written: 'Daughters, be obedient to the law of the Mother.'"[3]

It is not a tenderly inviting image. In fact, what intrigues us is its very grandeur and sternness. Part of what we will see in the writing of women mystics will be a breaking down of the traditional polarizing that makes a "magnificent" maternal figure seem contradictory to us.

The Virgin Mary was certainly a focal point for this kind of worship, but so, remarkably, was Jesus Christ. It was the mystics of the Middle Ages who discovered the maternality of Christ, and they discovered it as soon as they began to look hard at his humanity. Central to affective piety is devotion for the humanity of Christ. The suffering of Christ crucified became an object of fervent meditation, a spiritual practice that would have surprising results when carried out by women. It was certainly a meaningful devotional exercise for men, but for women it represented a kind of revolution in consciousness, for they brought to the exercise their own experience *as women*. To a male aspirant, for example, the bleeding, broken body of Christ would have carried with it, at least initially, associations of defeat in battle—of personal destruction. To women, though, who may not have given birth themselves but who would most certainly have seen sisters, mothers, and aunts in childbirth, the same image would carry deeply positive associations as well. Having witnessed firsthand the simultaneity of joy and suffering with which a child enters the world—having seen the precious reward that can come of blood shed and real agonies endured, they found paradoxical depths of meaning in the crucifixion that had eluded earlier Christian writers.

They also saw, meditating upon the humanity of Christ, that when God became man, he had regarded the multitudes as his children; he had healed them and fed them and cast out their demons, yearning over them "as a mother hen over her chicks." He had become woman, that is, as well as man. The very passivity with which he had yielded himself up into his enemies' hands served for medieval women as a kind of mirror of the social powerlessness that typically has been the lot of women. At the same time, it has been suggested that Christ's tacit affirmation of the sanctity of the feminine experience—his choosing to be both male and female—may have inspired women mystics to embrace the neglected assertive side of their own natures and come into their own as teachers, healers, and leaders.[4]

WHEN I was in my twenties, and thirties, too, for that matter, we did not like to talk much about "the feminine" or "the masculine." Too many of the people who enjoyed making that kind of distinction were doing it to justify gender inequality. Today, though, I think many of us feel that gender imbalance will persist until we begin to acknowledge and understand better the very different ways in which men and women tend to approach the task of living: differences that can shape the most fundamental issues, like the way we frame moral questions, and the most trivial, like how we entertain ourselves. Very few social scientists today see these as genetically predetermined differences, but even if they are *only* culturally conditioned, they have imprinted most of us at a fairly deep level. Many of us have come to feel that we can choose whether to let these differences go on dividing us into armed camps or learn instead to work with them—ultimately, even, to celebrate them, recognizing that each mode has its power, its authenticity, and even its *sanctity*.

To the cluster of meanings that medieval scholars tend to associate with "the feminine," therefore, I would like to add others that are only now being articulated, and by writers who are not medievalists at all. I am thinking in particular of the work of Carol Gilligan, author of *In a Different Voice;* Sara Ruddick, of *Maternal Thinking: Toward a Politics of Peace;* and Deborah Tannen, of *You Just Don't Understand.* These three and others have done ground-breaking work in identifying certain ways of thinking and acting as characteristically feminine. I say "characteristically" feminine, and not "essentially." I differ with critics of these writers who feel they may be proposing a dangerously essentialist reading of gender. Gilligan, a psychologist, has looked in particular at how women approach moral choices—how we assess them, and how we make them in contrast to the way men do—and at the inadequacy of traditional male-centered models for moral development when applied to women.[5] Building on Gilligan, Ruddick, who is a philosopher, set out to identify some of the ways of thinking that arise out of the "practice" of being a mother. Once she had done so, she showed how closely some of these cognitive styles parallel those of the practitioners of nonviolence. Were these ways of thinking to find a place in public policy, she suggests, a "politics of peace" would be at least conceivable. Tannen, a sociolinguist, has wittily and evenhandedly outlined the chief differences between masculine and feminine styles of conversation and has sketched out some of the far-reaching social and political consequences of those differences.

Maternal work, Ruddick recognizes, is open to men. Since it has rarely been undertaken by men, however, the store of knowledge that has accumulated in the collective experience of mothering is pretty much in the hands of women. Even if a woman is not biologically a mother, she is likely to have absorbed "a mother's way of thinking" somewhere along the line. To a considerable extent, therefore, feminine thinking can be understood in the light of maternal thinking. (Ruddick is on delicate footing here, obviously, but to my mind she does not at all slip over into the kind of old, stereotypical thinking that simply had no category for women whose gifts and strengths were not notably maternal.)

With apologies for oversimplifying Sara Ruddick's subtle and richly suggestive lines of reasoning, I shall outline some of the demands that she believes "maternal practice" imposes and the cognitive styles she believes arise out of the effort to meet those demands. It is remarkable to me, in considering how many ways the whole experience of mothering has changed, that I find these same patterns of thinking in the writings of women who lived and wrote four, five, and seven centuries earlier. Grasping these "ways of thinking" has been for me a critical step in unlocking the mysteries of their very different lives. As Ruddick argues,

1. Mothers are required to hold close and at the same time welcome change. The growing child needs a protective "holding," and yet even while she welcomes it, she is struggling to break free and assert a new identity. Mothers snuggle, therefore, and reassure; we reenact the family traditions tirelessly, telling the child in effect that her world is stable no matter what. And when she shrugs off the bedtime ritual one evening as if it had never mattered anyway, we know we must shrug it off, too, and move blithely with her into the next stage of life. The cognitive equivalent of this willingness, Ruddick suggests, is a "metaphysical attitude" that welcomes change and recognizes the limits of what we can control.

2. Maternal practice gives rise to a preference for concrete rather than abstract thinking. We deal always with a *particular* child after all, and not with children in general. Ruddick defines abstraction as "a clus-

ter of interrelated dispositions to simplify, generalize, and sharply define."[6] To think concretely, in contrast, is "to relish complexity, to tolerate ambiguity, to multiply options rather than accepting the terms of a problem." She observes that women have been said "to value open over closed structures, to eschew the clear-cut and unambiguous, to refuse sharp divisions between self and other or outer world and inner experience."[7]

It follows, then, that women will value "connected" ways of conversing. They try to have "an ear for the complexities and uncertainties of another's experience." It strikes Ruddick that this way of knowing might be related to the kind of entity a child is. "A child herself might be thought of as an 'open structure,' changing, growing, reinterpreting."[8]

"Women tend to know," Ruddick asserts late in her book, "in a way and to a degree that many men do not, both the history and the cost of human flesh." She cites Olive Schreiner's remark, "No woman who is a woman says of a human body, 'it is nothing.'"[9] For Ruddick, as for Schreiner, this awareness is a precious component of any politics of peace. If Ruddick is correct, it is no coincidence that at precisely the point in the history of Christianity when women were uniquely audible and visible, the humanity of Christ, particularly his bodily suffering, should have become so central to Christian worship.

3. Ruddick discusses "attentive love" as a discipline mothers teach themselves and one another to cultivate. Insofar as attention is involved, it is a cognitive capacity. Attentive love does not give place to self-serving fantasy; it stays focused upon the child as he or she really is. "It implies and rewards a faith that love will not be destroyed by knowledge, that to the loving eye the lovable will be revealed."[10] In this context, Ruddick gets very close to drawing parallels between maternal thinking and mystical perspectives.

4. Finally, Ruddick emphasizes that women tell stories to one another out of their daily experience, stories that are meant to strengthen these values in themselves and one another. Visionary writings, on the one hand, like Julian's or Mechthild's, and brilliant allegorical treatises like Teresa's, can be seen as just this—concrete, highly visual, and often quite intimate ways of presenting the spiritual teachings that a learned theologian might treat in a much more abstract manner.

The relevance of all this to current political events is not hard to find. In a world full of breaking up empires and emerging nations, respect for the "complexities and uncertainties of another's experience" is surely of the first importance. So are a strong sense of connectedness, tolerance for ambiguity, and the capacity to "hold on" while at the same time welcoming change. So, too, if we are to keep ourselves from destruction, is a reverence for human flesh itself—*all* human flesh: First World, Second, Third, and Fourth.

In explaining how maternal thinking can form the basis for a politics of peace, Ruddick demonstrates that the values that arise out of maternal practice are in fundamental opposition to those of a military-industrial complex and an academic world that are based upon abstract thinking. It has been fascinating for me to observe that within their own cultural context, over and against the established powers that dominated their own world, Mechthild and others drew upon their mystical experiences to plead for essentially the same values. Over the course of writing this book, I have found it immensely instructive to trace out these parallels and consider what might be their implications. Thanks to Sarah Ruddick *and* Clare of Assisi *and* Carol Gilligan *and* Catherine of Siena, those questions I could not even formulate in the late sixties—central questions having to do with my identity as a woman and my opposition to war, and a good deal more besides—are finding answers.

Finally, a word or two about vocabulary, always a vexed issue when one is writing about matters mystical. Exactly what do I mean when I call someone a mystic, and are mystics roughly the same as saints? I shall be brief and arbitrary. My own working definition requires that no one be called a mystic who has not made the experiential discovery that the source of all meaning—the God of truth, beauty, and love, if you will— is a living presence within herself or himself. They discover, as Catherine of Genoa did, that "My me is God!" Her "me" and everybody else's as well: "Even as you have done it unto the least of these," said Jesus, "you have done it unto me."

But suppose we are told that someone is a mystic: How do we decide to agree or disagree? It is the question that lies at the core of the *Bhagavad Gita*, known as "Mother Gita" to Mahatma Gandhi: "Tell me, Oh, Krishna, of the illumined man. How does he sit? How does he talk?

How does he move about?" Krishna replies with a series of practical criteria beginning as follows: "He lives in wisdom who sees himself in all, and all in him—whose love for the Lord of Love has consumed every selfish desire and sense-craving tormenting the heart." For Christians, the answer has been essentially the same. "By their fruits ye shall know them," said Jesus, and Paul added, "The fruit of the spirit is love, joy, peace, long-suffering, gentleness, goodness, faith, meekness, temperance" (Galatians 2:9, KJV).

The term *saint* is problematic: one becomes a saint of the Roman Catholic church only by being canonized, but that has never stopped Catholics from calling anyone a saint who they thought deserved the name. Since the word does not have a single precise meaning for me, I do not use it a great deal, though I find the cognate word *sanctity* to be nicely suggestive of the state of being I associate with mystics.

There are problems, too, where the vocabulary of prayer is concerned. The term *meditation*, as used by Catholic mystics, generally refers to a discursive form of prayer: one "considers" in detail the Passion of Christ, for example, rendering it as vividly as possible to the mind's eye, moving about from one element to another. The more intensely focused kind of mental activity that constitutes meditation for many of us today is closer to what Catholic mystics would have regarded as "mental prayer" or "interior prayer," which becomes in its most advanced stages, "contemplative prayer." Because this book is not really about various kinds of prayer or meditation, I have kept things simple by speaking for the most part of "prayer" plain and simple. I have assumed the reader realizes that while prayer can mean the vocal recitation of a *Pater Noster*, it refers in the case of most of our subjects to contemplative or "unitive" prayer.

Most problematic of all, perhaps, is the question, How does one speak of God? To refer to "Goddess" instead might feel more liberating to contemporary seekers, but it gives rise to the impression that Teresa, for example, envisioned the divine as a goddess. There is no evidence that she did. Even when Julian talks about Christ as Mother, she continues to refer to "her" as "him." The policy I finally settled upon is to restructure every sentence I could to at least minimize the use of gendered designations for the divine. I believe this is appropriate usage, because my intuition is that every one of these women did experience not just a being, finally, but a *state* of being, and one that transcends gender and all other human categories.

I REALIZE that one could not possibly do justice to all seven women in one book. Fools certainly do rush in. But I did not set out to do them justice anyway—I just wanted them all at the same party. I wanted to see them together, to eavesdrop as they talked with one another, and to try to learn what they had in common and how they differed. I wondered whether a composite might emerge, a discernible profile with a range of variations. I wanted above all to plant myself in their midst and see whether by sheer force of my admiration I might conjure them into my own life, not as role models or intercessors or even matron saints, but as fast friends and midwives of the spirit.

And they have become just that. They are certainly close by. I feel them brace and strengthen me as I struggle, not always even to make the right choices, but to see what my choices really are.

I've said "not as role models" with a certain vehemence. I have not been tempted to take the story of, say, Catherine of Siena's life and place it on the fabric of my own like a dress pattern and snip off everything that doesn't fit. I do not see these lives as precise templates for our own. Their relevance is subtler, and we must work out for ourselves what it is for each of us. There are, however, general areas where the lives of these women seem to speak with special force to contemporary seekers, and I would like to identify those.

There is, to begin with, the mystical premise itself, the positing of an inner world that is "more real" than the one around us, one that will receive us and strengthen us once we find our way into it. Women today are eager to find within ourselves a center of gravity, a remedy for the chronic needfulness that afflicts so many of us. The lives I have examined here testify that this kind of freedom is within reach. The joyous serenity of a Clare, a Julian, a Catherine, wells up out of the very rhythms of their writing and persuades us that they are speaking the truth.

There is emotional freedom, and courage as well, evident in all of these lives, not just physical bravery, though they possessed that in full measure, but also the capacity to endure the subtlest kinds of interior trials. Women today see so much in the world we want to resist and change, for our own sakes, and also for our daughters, nieces, and granddaughters. We know very well that far-reaching social and political reforms begin with individuals willing to change themselves, but we also know how hard it is to make those changes. Over and over in the lives of these women, perhaps most explicitly with Teresa and Thérèse, we come to see the incredible strength that comes of starting with "the littlest things."

I have found it consoling, as well as touching and amusing, to see that women like Catherine of Siena or Teresa of Avila or Thérèse of Lisieux had to struggle just as hard as women do today to balance the claims of family—the aging parents, the lonely sibling, the wayward niece—against the equally passionate claims of their own emerging selves and the absolute need for time and silence that these claims dictate. I say "consoling" not because their histories tell us what we should do, but because they dignify our own struggles, saying in effect, "Yes, it *is* hard, this sorting out of all the heart's yearnings, and we sympathize entirely!"

I have been grateful, too, for the persistence with which the theme of friendship keeps emerging in these stories. We see Catherine of Siena with her *bella brigata* ("delightful gang"), a circle of disciples held together whenever their teacher was absent by flurries of wonderfully affectionate letters peppered with nicknames like "Crazy Alessa" or "Fat Joan." We find Teresa pondering long and hard on what real friendship means, and Mechthild nursing wounds received from people she had thought to be her friends but who had turned upon her without warning. Again, what I come away with is not so much definitive, once-and-for-all instruction, but rather, simple acknowledgment that while there is indeed a vital place in any spiritual quest for friendship, it will not always be clear to us what that place is.

It is also encouraging to find that the sweetest friendships of all often lay between women and men—that in cultures where these friendships would have been otherwise impossible, so segregated were men from women, it *was* possible and even socially sanctioned when both parties were given over, body and soul, to the spiritual life.

Then there is the issue of community. How can we form institutions, or even temporary living situations, that will sustain and nourish spiritual growth? The reformed Carmelite convent, with its veils and grilles, might not match the needs of most of us, but what about the Beguinages? And even where the Carmelite convents are concerned, Teresa's teachings on love and humility within the community have obvious bearing on our own efforts to strengthen our families and communities.

Finally, a question that haunts the lives of most women that I know—and men—has to do with work. "Have I a calling?" we want to know. "Is there a particular piece of work I have been born and shaped by life to carry out, a bad business I am uniquely qualified to set straight?" "Career" is not the issue; in fact, our culture's obsession with career begins to look as detrimental to spirituality as drugs, alcohol, and compulsive gambling combined. Rather, it is vocation that concerns us, and here, once again, I find myself genuinely nourished by these mystics' lives. A kind of law emerges from the collective experience of Clare and the others, and I have come to trust it all the more for having seen it illustrated in contemporary figures such as Gandhi and Mother Teresa. The gist of it is that you do not have to go out looking for your calling, because it will be quite apparent to you once you have, in Gandhi's words, "gotten yourself out of the way." The very proximity of a task, placed where you all but trip over it, will make it indisputably yours and no one else's. The lives of those who bear witness to this unwritten law are characterized by a marvelous, enviable tranquillity.

Saint Clare of Assisi

(1195–1253)

What you hold, may you always hold. What you
do, may you always do and never abandon.
But with swift pace, light step, unswerving feet,
so that even your steps stir up no dust, may you
go forward securely, joyfully, and swiftly, on
the path of prudent happiness.

— Saint Clare of Assisi,
Early Documents 2.40

❦

I MAGINE, if you will, a woman of about forty, coiffed and veiled,
fine of feature, and thin as a willow. She is propped up in bed,
though maybe we should say "on pallet," lest we suggest even a trace of
comfort, and the spinning that normally occupies her is set to one side.
She is writing, deeply absorbed: "What you hold. . . ."

The year is 1235. Francis of Assisi has been dead for nine years. His
friend and foremost disciple, Clare, is abbess of the Poor Ladies at San
Damiano, and at least twenty-two other houses of the order look to her

for leadership. Her mother has joined her, as has her sister Agnes. The woman to whom she is writing is another Agnes who is particularly dear to her, though they have never met.

Agnes of Prague was a princess, daughter of the king of Bohemia. From her infancy she had been victimized by the elaborate system of political marriages that connected the royal families of medieval Europe. Betrothed as a baby to the son of the duke of Silesia, she had been packed off to the Silesian court to live until she and her intended were grown. She was just three when the young duke died and she was sent back to Prague. Off to Austria next, sometime in her early teens, slated now to marry the son of Emperor Frederick II. Her fiancé jilted her, though, and once again she was back in Prague. Her father would have avenged her with a full-scale war, but Agnes dissuaded him.

Fresh offers of marriage came in—one from England's royal court, another from Frederick II himself, whose wife had since died. At this point, though, Agnes had had enough, and to his credit, her father backed her up. With his blessing, she would forego marriage and undertake a life of charitable works. About this time she met a small band of Franciscans who had come to eastern Europe telling tales of wondrous goings-on in Assisi. They spoke of a beautiful young noblewoman who had renounced everything to follow God.

To the twenty-year-old princess, as to thousands of European women, the story of Clare and her Poor Ladies was a powerful catalyst. In 1232, Agnes built a hospice and then a convent for Poor Ladies with an adjoining residence for the Friars Minor who would be their spiritual guides. When construction was well under way, she wrote to Clare, and in 1234 Clare sent five members of her order to Prague. Along with seven young women from Prague's wealthiest families, they entered the new convent. Agnes herself was among them.

In a worldly sense, Agnes was perhaps Clare's greatest "catch." We have only the four letters Clare wrote her and none of the ones Agnes presumably wrote. The joy they convey and the utter confidence are supremely Franciscan, and so is the unconcealed affection. In the fourth and final letter, written just before her death, Clare writes: "If I have not written to you as often as your soul—and mine as well—desire and long for, do not wonder, or think that the fire of love for you glows with less delight in the heart of your mother. No, this is the difficulty: the lack of messengers and the obvious dangers of the roads" (*Early Documents* 47).

Until rather recently, Clare's story has always been told as an adjunct to that of Saint Francis. This is understandable enough, for Clare fits into that narrative with such exquisite rightness that if she had not turned up on cue, the chroniclers would surely have had to invent her. If they *had* invented her, they could not have improved on what she truly was—beautiful and courageous, as fair and serene as Francis was dark and lively, the contemplative fulcrum to his life of active preaching and teaching. From the minute she enters Francis's life, an irresistibly romantic subplot opens out.

Indeed, in some tellings, the subplot very nearly takes over, for as soon as Clare and Francis meet, the conventions of the courtly love tradition swing into play, if only on the subliminal level. The elements that make for romantic legend are all there in the story as it has come down to us. Clare's contemporaries swore she really was beautiful, that she was nobly born and widely esteemed for her kindness to the poor. Before her birth a mysterious voice was said to have told her mother she would bring a brilliant light into the world. The chroniclers loved to play with her name and called her "bright," "unsullied," "spotless," "gleaming." They spoke of Clare's radiance when she rose up from prayer and reported that even the place where she prayed would be lit up afterward. They marveled that despite her enclosed life, the light that was "Chiara" spread nonetheless throughout the world.

Francis himself, "God's troubadour," was at least as romantically appealing a character as Clare. Leader of the revels in Assisi before his conversion, a one-time knight-in-arms, he was a man with a past and, even after his conversion, a kind of spiritual outlaw. Clare's initiation into the spiritual life at Francis's hands, moreover, was easily as dramatic as any elopement. And if their liaison was never consummated in any worldly sense, all the better, for unconsummated love was a staple theme of the courtly love tradition.

To say of Francis and Clare that they were "in love" with each other in the ordinary sense is, I think, incorrect—inadequate—and I will try to explain why. But the courtly love elements in their story are not just a superficial overlay. They reflect accurately the enormous tension between earthly and spiritual love that pervaded the early Middle Ages—tension between men and women, for that matter, and between what we now call the "masculine" and "feminine" in every psyche. The "romance" of Clare and Francis represents in a sense the culmination of what was best in the courtly love tradition and a corrective to what was worst.

Contemporary readers, in any event, are restless with the limitations of the romantic lens. We are impatient with love stories that end at the beginning and heroines who fuzz out at the edges. We know there was a Clare who was more than a mere reflex of Francis—a spiritual teacher in her own right, who survived her beloved mentor by about twenty-seven years—and we would know more of her.

The church initiated a process of canonization for Clare immediately after her death. The record of these proceedings is our only source of information about Clare's early life and our most reliable source for her life as a whole. It contains firsthand testimony, given under oath, from members of her community, including two of her own sisters and several childhood friends, as well as a few citizens of the town. It tells us that her family was one of the wealthiest in Assisi and that the family tree had a generous scattering of knights. Clare herself is said to have been quiet as a girl, obedient and prayerful. One searches the text for some episode that might round out the picture—one fit of temper, one bout of greed—but medieval hagiographers typically portray women saints as having been virtuous from birth, in contrast to men saints, who usually undergo dramatic conversions. If Clare ever sassed her mother or struck a playmate, the fact was not admissible.

For an adolescent boy or girl to be drawn to the mysteries of religion certainly is not the rarest thing in the world. To be idealistic and impulsively generous at that age—to think it completely reasonable that another reality should exist that is a real improvement over the one we can see and touch and smell—these almost *define* a particular kind of teenager we have all known or even been. But to meet someone at that critical moment who can confirm those powerful intuitions—a man or woman who is on fire with God and says, "Yes, God is real, come and see for yourself"—that is rare and wonderful, and Clare met that man in Francis, son of Pietro di Bernardone.

She may have heard him preach in the Cathedral of San Rufino in 1210. Certainly by the spring of 1212, when she was eighteen, she had gone to him several times to receive spiritual instruction, accompanied always by a girl cousin. When she heard that her family was about to have her married, she asked Francis's advice, and he urged her to follow God instead. To what extent either of them understood him to mean she should follow Francis as well, we cannot say. Or rather, it is clear enough that Francis would be Clare's spiritual director, but what would become of her now probably was not clear at all, and it helps us get a feeling for just how courageous her next step was if we remember that Francis and his followers were still highly controversial. They had gone to Rome in 1210 to have their way of life ratified but had received only verbal approval from the pope. Scruffy street people, they must have seemed to many, whose self-imposed poverty and evangelical stance were surely irritants to the local establishment.

Clare chose Palm Sunday as the day for her withdrawal from worldly life. Palm Sunday, the Sunday before Easter, commemorates Christ's entry into Jerusalem on a donkey—an event that had fulfilled a prophecy that Jerusalem's king would come into the city on a donkey. Palms were strewn at his feet, and, accordingly, it became traditional to hand out palm fronds as a symbol of Christ's coming martyrdom.

In Clare's Assisi, Palm Sunday had devolved into a kind of coming-out party. The daughters of the town's best families would line up before the bishop in their finest gowns and receive their palm fronds from him while the congregation watched proudly.[1] On this particular Palm Sunday, Clare's turn came to go forward, but she did not rise. Was she put off by the empty theatricality of the ritual? Undoubtedly she was. But surely, too, in the light of her decision, the full symbolic significance of the palm frond might have overwhelmed her. Perhaps she slipped into a kind of rapture. It is public record, in any event, that the bishop saw her sitting with her family, immobile, and walked down to hand her the palm himself. In all likelihood, this was the same bishop who had wrapped his own cloak around Francis a few years earlier, the day Francis stood before him in the town square and divested himself of every last thread of his paternity. Small towns being what they are—Clare had already begun giving away her personal property—the bishop may well have guessed something was up now with another fiery-eyed young person in his charge. In any event, the two scenes are similar: the unfettered passion of a young person in love with Christ is recognized publicly by an official of the church—recognized, and supported, even when it defies a social order with which the church is deeply enmeshed.

That same night, Clare left her home—not through the front door, but through the house's only other exit, which had been barricaded with heavy wooden beams and an iron bar. Later commentators have observed that this door would normally have been used only for removal of the bodies of the deceased. The symbolic meaning, then, would have been clear enough, though it may have been that Clare just did not want to be seen or stopped.

With a friend—for the helpful cousin was on pilgrimage now—she walked to the small Saint Mary's Church in Portiuncula, a forest just outside of town where Francis and his followers had settled some years before. Accompanied by the whole brotherhood, Francis cut off Clare's long, gleaming hair and gave her the rough tunic that would identify her as his follower. But what was he to do with her? It appeared that initially he had no clear plan of action. Not that he was particularly troubled: God had sent him Clare, God would tell him in good time what he wanted of her. And Francis had had some glimmering of this development. The first task he had felt called by God to carry out was the restoration of San Damiano, a little church outside Assisi. While he was working on it, he had called out to passersby, "Come and help me build the monastery of San Damiano, because ladies will again dwell here who will glorify our heavenly Father . . . by their celebrated and holy manner of life."[2]

Even though Clare was established eventually at San Damiano, she could not go there directly. She had to be protected first from the wrath of her family. (From a modern point of view, we marvel that Francis himself seems to have had no fear of reprisal, nor does anyone else on his behalf.) The Benedictines had not long before won the right to provide sanctuary, so the nearby Benedictine church, San Paolo de Abbadesse, and its community of nuns, was a logical choice. Even so, Clare's relatives pursued her there and tried to make her leave. In another of those wordless, marvelously dramatic gestures that characterizes all the Franciscan literature, Clare seized the altar cloth and in the same instant pulled off her own veil. Shorn of the beautiful hair that had attracted rich suitors, her bare head conveyed the irrevocability of her decision. She was Christ's bride now, living under his protection, and life would be one of continuing sacrifice, patterned after his. The family accepted defeat and left, but they returned a few weeks later, even angrier, because now Clare's sister Agnes had slipped away to join her. This time they were rougher, but again they were foiled: one source claims Agnes's body became so heavy no one could carry her.

The new wine of Franciscan spirituality—its evangelical passion and its rejection of elaborate ritual, handsome buildings, and religious art—was fundamentally incompatible with the beautiful old ways of a Benedictine house. Clare and Agnes quite probably were restless there, and their hostesses could not have been desperately eager to keep them around: two incursions of their menfolk were surely two too many, and there was still one more sister at home! Francis did not move them into San Damiano right away, though. He might have wanted Assisi to calm down a bit first, and he undoubtedly needed time to prepare the tiny church for its new occupants. Buying time, he moved the sisters temporarily into another community of women. Soon afterward, though, once he and the brothers had made the necessary renovations at San Damiano, he brought them there, and other women of the region gathered around them swiftly. Clare would remain there for the rest of her life. Agnes would leave only to help establish a convent of Poor Ladies near Florence, returning shortly before Clare's death.[3] Their younger sister Beatrice did indeed join them in 1229 and their mother, Ortulana, at an unknown date.

Her biographers have suggested that Clare had hoped to join the friars in their itinerant life—a kind of Maid Marian with a vocation. Nothing in the contemporary sources, though, supports this reading of the story. We must be cautious about projecting modern attitudes into a cultural setting so different from our own. Over and over we will see that the enclosure of a convent represented genuine freedom to women like Clare, Teresa, and Thérèse—women whose lives were so seriously constrained by time and place.

Here she was, then, a girl of just eighteen—barely a bride, and already a mother, for the women who came to San Damiano all viewed her as such regardless of their own ages. Three years would pass before she would actually agree to direct them, and then only at Francis's prayers and insistence. ("He almost forced her," says one Sister Pacifica.)

To pass out food from a well-provisioned town house is one thing. To accept responsibility for several dozen women when you have renounced every earthly possession is fundamentally another. Clare saw that she was to regard herself as mother to the other women. But out of what stores was she to nourish her daughters and cover them and keep them well—nourish not their bodies only, but their spirits, too? Nothing short of God's infinite grace would do all of this, and it seems to me that Clare set out to make herself a living conduit for divine grace. With that passion for the literal and the concrete that is so Franciscan, she emptied herself absolutely. She had already sold her possessions and given the proceeds to the poor—the first payment Christ asked of all followers—but there must be more she could let go of. Her logic was that of the ascetic in every religious tradition, and so was her recklessness. She would ferret out all personal desires, including the ones we think of not as desires but as simple, human needs, like warm blankets at night, food, and enough sleep.

Because this is the first time we are encountering the phenomenon of asceticism, it would be well to pause for a moment and consider its place in the mystical traditions.

Without endorsing the more extreme expressions of the ascetic impulse, we need to understand the motive that underlies it. Meister Eckhart would state it in simple enough terms a hundred or so years later when he announced that there are three obstacles to God-realization: multiplicity, temporality, and corporeality. Our difficulty is not so much with the concepts themselves, but with the hold they have over us: the belief that we are many, and not one; that we are at the mercy of time (and therefore death); and that our very being is physical—that we *are* our bodies.

The interesting thing is that in a sense the first two illusions flow out of the third. If I firmly believe I am my body, then it follows that you are yours too, and that we are separate from each other and all others. If I am my body, then certainly when time brings an end to this body, I vanish, too. For the budding mystic, then, who has glimpsed the possibility that we are in truth one, eternal, and infinite, it becomes imperative to break once and for all the nexus that seems to connect soul and body. Hence the impetuous, headlong rush to oppose the body's dominion over spirit, even to the point of endangering physical existence. (We will be returning to this theme, which is particularly vexing to modern readers, in subsequent chapters.)

And indeed, through excessive fasting Clare did put herself in jeopardy during those early years. For decades of her life she was too weakened to walk. At the canonization process, her sister reported that Francis repeatedly had to intervene: the object of what is called "mortification," he would probably have told her, was not death in the literal sense, but death to the created world—mastery of the ultimate balancing act whereby one lives "in the world, but not of it."

Clare never advised others to live as extremely as she did. She thanked God for her vocation and urged her sisters to do so as well, but she fully recognized that it was not everyone's, that it would not have been possible to live as the Poor Ladies did if they had not been called to it and if God had not given them the grace to live it out. Clare's life of poverty was not a grim, calculated handing over but rather a joyous, easy, impatient flinging aside: lovers don't feel the cold, lovers don't care what they eat—and Clare was a lover, running full tilt toward her Beloved, "with swift pace, light step, unswerving feet, so that even your steps stir up no dust" (*Early Documents* 2.40).

The motif is perennial in mystical writings: the journey is arduous, and you must travel light if you would reach the goal. And yet, there is manna in the wilderness. In her third letter to Agnes of Prague, Clare reveals, by way of encouragement, what has nourished her in her own austerities. She speaks of "the hidden sweetness that God Himself has reserved from the beginning for those who love Him." Clare's "secret" was simply that she was a genuine contemplative. Not that she tells us much of her inner life. She offers no scheme of the stages of spiritual development. But then, neither did Francis. Both of them taught more by who they were than by what they said or wrote. Clare did set down her understanding of contemplative prayer, however. Once again, it was in a letter to Agnes of Prague:

> Place your mind before the mirror of eternity!
> Place your soul in the brilliance of glory!
> Place your heart in the figure of the divine substance!
> And transform your entire being into the image
> of the Godhead Itself through contemplation.

> (*Early Documents* 44)

She would expand upon this "formula of prayer" in her fourth and final letter to Agnes where the vision of Christ is "the brilliance of eternal light and the mirror without blemish" (*Early Documents* 48). Agnes is invited to gaze upon that mirror every day, "and continually study your face within it." She is to adorn herself before that mirror with "the flowers and garments" of all the virtues, for they are there, in Christ's life—humility, charity, poverty. In other words, when we look as closely at the image of Christ as the depth of our prayer will permit us, we will be looking also at our own real selves. The purpose of contemplative prayer, then, is to draw as close as we can to God incarnate so that ultimately we can discover our own unity with God—not to *make* ourselves one with God, though we may feel along the way as if we are doing that, but to discover we have never been anything else.[4]

Just how this is supposed to take place Clare does not tell us, but I think there is an implicit clue. We cannot "place" our minds, our souls, or our hearts anywhere if they are absorbed somewhere else. Out of Clare's passion for poverty there had arisen the perfect detachment that allowed her to direct her attention, her devotion, her love, at will, wherever she chose. Christian contemplatives have always taught that poverty "of the spirit" leads to unitive prayer, prayer so undistracted and so deep that all barriers between oneself and God vanish. By undertaking spiritual disciplines, you free yourself from all attachments and all preoccupations, creating a kind of inner vacuum that God cannot help but fill. The fourteenth-century Rhineland mystic John Tauler wrote, "When we thus clear the ground and make our soul ready, without doubt God must fill up the void." To Clare, though, holy poverty had to begin with actual physical poverty: having nothing—having no *things.* No room here for the rationalizing impulse that says, "What's a warm cloak or two so long as I have my mind fixed on God?" For her, holy poverty was an expression of her union with God, not just a means for reaching it. If your mind is truly fixed on God, she seems to be saying, you won't need a warm cloak, because God's love will surround and embrace you. Indeed, what impressed others was not so much the deprivation of her daily life, though they do mention it, but the joy. "She was never upset," said one sister. "Never disturbed," said another, "always rejoicing in the Lord" (*Early Documents* 51).

Furthermore, Clare appears to have been able to absorb herself so deeply in prayer that she went beyond ordinary levels of consciousness. On Good Friday one year, she experienced something of what Francis had at La Verna.[5] For nearly twenty-four hours she was insensate—lost in union with Christ crucified. Sister Filippa persuaded her to revive and eat only by reminding her that Francis had ordered her never to let a day pass without taking bread.

The deficit Clare carved out of her own creaturely needs did not work as an advantage only to her. It became an unfathomably vast fund out of which she could give: give food, for she is credited with more than one "feeding miracle"; give health, for she is said to have healed a remarkable variety of ailments of body, mind, and soul; give safety and bestow peace, for she is believed to have protected her convent from invading mercenary troops on one occasion and Assisi itself from an attacking army on another. It was written of her, "This clear spring of the Spoleto Valley furnished a new fountain of living water."

Once Clare had glimpsed the mysterious wealth and power concealed in the practice of holy poverty, it became the central work of her life to see that the right to live *sine proprio*, with nothing of one's own, would be assured to her Poor Sisters forever. Francis himself had of course been called "Il Poverello," "the little poor man," and one of his first acts as a spiritual teacher had been to tell his erstwhile drinking companions that he had married a beautiful woman—one whose identity he revealed as "Lady Poverty" only after he had teased them into a frenzy of curiosity. All of his followers, in turn, embraced the ideal of poverty. But it was Clare who lived out that teaching radically and unequivocally in the face of powerful opposition from church authorities. There is in her brave and uncompromising stance, maintained over the course of thirty years, something of the proud, pure tenacity of the "Domina," or "Donna," the great lady of the courtly love tradition. In the deepest sense, the wealthy young girl really did become Francis's cherished "Lady Poverty."

To understand what was so radical about Clare's version of apostolic poverty, we need to realize that while the individual religious would have possessed nothing, the convents of the time were typically supported by large landholdings. They had *corporate* incomes, permitting the monasteries to perform what are called "the corporal acts of mercy," which include sheltering the traveler, feeding the hungry, curing the sick, and so forth. Hence the large orchards, guest houses, vineyards, breweries, bakeries, and herb gardens for which the great Benedictine monasteries were famous.

The sisterhood at San Damiano, though, held no property at all beyond a piece of land big enough to grow a small garden and to preserve the privacy of the house. The sisters lived on whatever alms found their way to the convent (unlike the friars, they were enclosed and could not go out and beg for alms) and on the work of their own hands, trusting divine providence and the generosity of surrounding lay people to provide a subsistence.

Members of the church hierarchy were of course uncomfortable with a version of holy poverty that went beyond even that of the Friars Minor. They may have felt a little embarrassed at their own relative ease, but certainly, too, they felt responsible for the Poor Ladies. Wouldn't Clare accept an endowment? Couldn't she see the wisdom of having just a little something to fall back on? She refused, over and over, and the implications of her refusal are interesting. For one, the cardinals and the pope were *not* responsible for the Poor Ladies; God was, and God could be trusted. Clare trusted the local people, too, to be God's instruments. She seems to have been sure they would bear the burden of the sisters' needs, whatever the weather, whatever the harvest. The people of Assisi would know that through its prayers Clare's community was earning its keep.

Clare would further irritate church authorities with her insistence on the right to a special ongoing relationship with the Friars Minor themselves. In her rule, she quoted the promise Francis had made to her and her sisters in his will: "I resolve and promise for myself and for my brothers to always have that same loving care and solicitude for you as I have for them." That solicitude had expressed itself in two ways: the brothers obtained alms for the sisters and gave them spiritual instruction. In time, after Francis's death, many of the friars wanted to be released from part of this obligation. They were itinerants, after all, not inclined to settling down near a convent. Besides, ministering to women asked of them a level of chaste self-control to which some of them probably did not feel equal. Francis himself had warned them of the dangers of being around women, and he had always said that no one should visit the sisters who *wanted* to; only the genuinely reluctant should preach to them. After Francis's death, Pope Gregory IX went so far as to try to curtail the friars' visitations. Clare declared in response that if the brothers were not going to give the sisters the spiritual sustenance Francis had enjoined them to give, the sisters would not accept bread from them either. In the face of a virtual hunger strike, Gregory mitigated the prohibition.

To understand why Clare clung so obstinately to the connections she believed Francis had forged between his first two orders, I find it helpful to look as closely as we can at the relationship between Clare and Francis themselves.

Only eight years passed between Clare's installation at San Damiano and Saint Francis's death in 1226. Of meetings between Clare and Francis during these years, we are told extremely little. Indeed, it seems there was very little to tell. The story of how Francis brought the Poor Ladies a lamb he had trained to genuflect has the ring of truth to it. But that's the whole story, no details, no dates, just a charming allusion. Francis's visits to San Damiano appear to have been so rare that they aroused a measure of indignation in some quarters. His chief biographer, Thomas of Celano, writing while Clare was still alive, gives us the saint's reply to charges by his own friars that he was neglecting the Poor Ladies. "Do not believe, dearest brothers, that I do not love them perfectly. . . . But I must give you an example. . . . I do not want anyone to offer himself of his own accord to visit them" (*Early Documents* 270).

In the *Little Flowers of Saint Francis,* a beautiful story is told. (One would wish it were confirmed elsewhere, for *The Little Flowers* was published a good hundred years after Francis's death, which makes it one of our least reliable sources.) The story concerns a rare occasion when the brothers persuaded Francis to honor the yearnings of his faithful disciple Clare and dine with her. Francis decided she would be particularly pleased if the meal were served at Saint Mary of the Portiuncula, where she had been professed. She came, with one or two sisters, and the meal was served on the ground in typically Franciscan simplicity. The food was never touched, though, because no sooner did the party sit down than they were all thrown into an exalted state, where they remained for some time. When they did return to normal consciousness, they had no

appetite left for earthly food. Meanwhile, a crowd of peasants came rush-
ing to the monastery. From far away, they had seen a bright, fiery glow as
if the entire monastery were in flames.

I suspect that the story is apocryphal, compounded in part from a
better documented episode I'll relate in a moment, in part from the association of that particular place, Saint Mary of the Portiuncula, with the
torches that were supposed to have lit up Clare's ordination, and in part
from the imagery of fire and light and brightness that always hovered
around Clare's name.

There is a deeper truth to the story, though, and it has to do directly
with that fiery glow. For the "romance" of Clare and Francis has always
exuded a warmth and a brightness that cannot be accounted for by the
actual events. I believe the source of that fire is partly our own awareness that in their relationship the ardor of human sexuality was perfectly,
beautifully sublimated—not suppressed or denied, but transformed, as
the mystics have always insisted it can be, into a nearly boundless love for
everyone around them. Whether we ourselves ever come within reach
of such a transformation—whether or not we even want to—something
in us rejoices at thinking it possible. The purity of Clare and Francis's
friendship has been a source of tremendous inspiration to their followers, because the atmosphere that surrounds their memory is not one of
desiccated, grim self-denial, but of merriment and outright joy.

Thomas of Celano records another occasion when Francis agreed,
after being asked repeatedly, to preach the word of God to his daughters
when he was near San Damiano. An extraordinary scene ensued. Francis
raised his eyes to heaven and began to pray. Afterward he had ashes
brought to him and made a circle with them around himself on the pave-
ment, then sprinkled the rest of them on his head. Everyone waited for
him to begin preaching, "but the blessed father remained standing in the
circle of silence." To everyone's amazement, in place of a sermon, he
then recited the *Miserere mei, deus* (Psalm 51, KJV): "Have mercy on me,
oh God, according to thy lovingkindness." Immediately upon finishing
it, he left. The sisters wept copiously, and Thomas concludes that by his
actions, Francis had preached a "symbolic sermon" that taught them "to
regard themselves as ashes, and that there was nothing in his heart concerning them but what was fitting this consideration" (*Early Documents*
270–71).

Thomas of Celano was partially correct: Francis was reminding the Poor Sisters that he was not affected by their being women because he knew all flesh to be transient. But I believe there is more.

It is such a stark little episode. It feels almost brutal, in a way, for we can empathize readily with how thrilled the sisters must have been to have had Francis among them. With his unexpected, prolonged silence and his enigmatic formation of the circle of ashes, he must have seemed a kind of conjurer. Unquestionably, the attention of everyone present would have been absolutely riveted upon him by the time he did recite the psalm, and I suggest that this was his real motive. In their eagerness for a sermon from him, I suspect they triggered the same response in Francis that one of his own young friars did on another occasion. Members of the brotherhood were expected to travel light; as Jesus and the apostles carried no books with them, neither would the friars. One young man balked, however. He wanted to keep a book of psalms. Francis begged him to understand—first he would want a psalter, then a breviary (an abbreviated form of the Divine Office), and so on. Finally, exasperated, Francis reached down into a nearby fireplace for a handful of ashes and smeared them all over the young man's tonsured head, saying repeatedly, "*I* am your breviary."[6]

So profound and complete was Francis's renunciation—of every conceivable human consolation—that he had, in effect, in the words of Mahatma Gandhi, "made himself zero." He had become a kind of keyhole through which he knew those who loved him, or even saw him clearly, could see God. It seems to have been his calling, then, to draw attention to his life—through his eloquence, his sense of theater, and sometimes simply his charm—so that those who knew him might meet God. For an individual of his profound and genuine humility, the necessity to do this must have constituted its own kind of martyrdom, but he did recognize it as a necessity.

Why the ashes? Symbolic always of humility, they are the other half of the paradox: Yes, I am your teacher; you do well to open your heart to me. But at the same time, I am nothing, a blank space you must look through, for like you, and like everything that lives and dies, I am ashes.

I have wondered whether this sermon that was not quite a sermon is perhaps the germ of the story about the dinner party that was never really a dinner. What unites the two is the image of Francis as showman, as *jongleur,* he who turns things topsy-turvy and makes a hash of all conventions. "You want a dinner party? Fine, but it will be my kind of party," and so forth. In any event, Clare herself will reenact the drama at a later date for her own purposes.

We do know that Clare and Francis were in touch, for we know he regulated her enthusiasm for bodily penance. We know, too, that on at least one occasion he sent a friar to her to be cured. Brother Stephen was mentally ill, and Francis asked that Clare make the sign of the cross over him. She did, and after he slept a little, he went away cured. Clare's sisters related this episode during the process of her canonization, and one of them also testified that Francis had once sent five women to Clare to be admitted to the monastery. She looked them over and said she would take four, but that the fifth would not persevere. The woman was accepted anyway, because of "pressure," and indeed she did not last half a year.

One loves these episodes. They constitute a kind of *billet doux* between the two friends or even a playful test of Clare's powers. You can almost imagine Francis sending off the five applicants with a twinkle. "Will she catch the counterfeit?" But in fact, he did trust her prophetic gift implicitly. Troubled one day as to whether he should continue preaching or give himself entirely to prayer (one senses here the weariness he must have sometimes experienced), Francis sent a friar to Clare to ask her to pray for guidance on his behalf. It is characteristic of his humility that he would not presume to make the decision on his own. She did as he asked and sent him word afterward that it was God's will he should continue to preach as Christ's herald.[7]

When Francis was known to be dying, Clare herself was so ill she feared she might precede him in death. He wrote to her, urging her not to despair, for she and her sisters would see him once again "and take great consolation." Soon afterward he died, but to fulfill his promise, the brothers carried his body to San Damiano. The iron grille was removed, and for an hour Francis's body was held before the window while the sisters gazed their fill.

Considering what a hold this love story has over the Western imagination, the historic record is slender. But two more episodes, neither of them involving any actual meeting or conversation between Clare and Francis, suggest to me that the real appeal of their story may be on the unconscious level anyway—may have to do, that is, with human needs that are deeper than the merely romantic.

The first concerns the circumstances under which Francis wrote his magnificent *Canticle of the Creatures*. The year was 1225, and he was staying at San Damiano, recuperating in a hut outside the convent walls from one of the last preaching tours he would undertake. He was ill and nearly blind, and his brotherhood was in complete turmoil. These were among Francis's darkest hours, and his return to San Damiano is completely understandable, for his spiritual life had begun there. Thanks to Clare, too, San Damiano was the one place where his teachings were being followed without compromise—the one place where he *could* rest. Everywhere else his own brothers were embroiled in bitter conflict over the interpretation of his rule. The canticle itself, a love poem to all creation, seems to have burst forth as a kind of paean against the despair that threatened to overtake Francis.

> Praised be You, my Lord, with all Your creatures,
> especially Sir Brother Sun,
> Who is the day and through whom You give us light.
> And he is beautiful and radiant with great splendor;
> and bears a likeness of You, Most High One.
>
> (*Early Documents* 248)

The lines are all the more poignant for knowing how little sunlight Francis's ruined eyes could bear by this time. These lines are followed by what is surely a graceful tribute to Clare and her sisters: "Sister Moon and the stars, in heaven You formed them clear and precious and beautiful." What we realize in reading the canticle is that not only were earth, air, fire, water, sun, moon, and stars fully alive for Francis, they were gendered, too. In his vision of things "the masculine" had its place (Brother Fire is "playful and robust and strong"), and so did "the feminine" (Sister Mother Earth "sustains and governs us, and brings forth fruits, flowers, and herbs"). Implicitly, the song instructs us to love and serve one another— brother and sister, mother and father. It is a joyous celebration of complementarity, and of diversity, too.

In contemporary psychological terms, Francis apparently integrated completely the masculine and feminine sides of his own personality. Clare confided to one of her sisters a dream or vision she had that strengthens that impression, implying that ordinary notions of gender came finally to be irrelevant to both her and Francis. Not long before his death, Francis dreamed he was a mother hen struggling to bring her chicks under her protective wings. The image is drawn from Christ's own comparison of himself to a mother hen (Matthew 23:37). Here is Clare's way of telling us much the same thing about Francis:

> Lady Clare related how once, in a vision, it seemed to her she brought a bowl of hot water to Saint Francis along with a towel for drying his hands. She was climbing a very high stairway, but was going very quickly, almost as though she were going on level ground. When she reached Saint Francis, the saint bared his breast and said to the Lady Clare, "Come, take and drink." After she had sucked from it, the saint admonished her to imbibe once again. After she did so, what she had tasted was so sweet and de-lightful she in no way could describe it.
>
> After she had imbibed, that nipple or opening of the breast from which the milk came remained between the lips of blessed Clare. After she took what remained in her mouth in her hands, it seemed to her it was gold so clear and bright that everything was seen in it as in a mirror.
>
> (*Early Documents* 144)

It is remarkable to see how some of Clare's favorite motifs come to-gether in this dream, specifically, themes she had used in her letters to Agnes of Prague. She walks quickly ("with swift pace and light step," *Early Documents* 40), and the indescribable sweetness she tastes recalls the "hidden sweetness" that she had told Agnes God holds in reserve for his lovers (*Early Documents* 44). The image of the mirror recurs, and we remember that Christ was for Clare, as for many medieval mystics, the "mirror of eternity" (*Early Documents* 44). And by one of the marvelous "one-ings" that characterize medieval dream visions, the sweetness as-sociated with devotional worship actually becomes the brilliance and clarity of perfect understanding. For the wholehearted follower of Francis ("I am your breviary!") love was—is—the source of all knowledge. Was Francis, then—source of that "gold so clear and bright"—Clare's "Brother Sun"? It is hard to think otherwise.

Between the two friends, moreover, the barrier of gender had altogether fallen away. "Our beloved Father" (Clare's way of referring to Francis) had become for Clare her beloved mother as well. We recognize easily the feminine qualities of Francis, but by the same token we observe that Clare, granitelike in her resolve, could behave in ways her culture regarded as masculine. She too, of course, had become "Mother" not only to her own spiritual daughters but to the brothers too, particularly after Francis's death. The "Legend" of Clare cites the prophecy of Isaiah, saying that in her it was fulfilled; "Many are the children of the barren one, more than of her who has a husband."

I mentioned much earlier that elements of the courtly love tradition have a way of slipping in when the story of Clare and Francis is told. But, in truth, their story is fundamentally at odds with that tradition. The favorite motif of courtly love poets is love suspended eternally, love that never descends into the compromises, makeshifts, and imperfections of earthly, lived-out love. In contrast, we encounter in the story of Clare and Francis a version of romantic love that retains the idealism of the chivalric mode—its restraint and purity, its poetry and beauty—but that moves courageously out into life, fecund and joyous, supremely productive down through time.

Clare could not have had any real illusions about how difficult it would be for other men and women to achieve the kind of miracle she and Francis had in their own lives. If Francis had his doubts, she probably had hers. But she insisted nonetheless, to the end of her days, that the sisters and the brothers were meant to be connected in the ways Francis had spelled out. One might conclude she was acting out of simple obedience. More probably, it seems to me, she herself saw in that connection a precious opportunity for mutual instruction—saw that even aside from the social, economic, and sexual arrangements that bind men and women together in conventional life, we truly and deeply need one another. For surely if the "masculine" and "feminine" poles within ourselves are to be integrated in the ways we say we want them to be, it cannot hurt to have living situations within which *actual* men can cherish and respect *actual* women and be cherished and respected by them in turn.

A recurrent theme runs through the writings of women mystics. It has to do with the experience of breaking through the almost universal proscription against women speaking outside of the personal context. The woman who becomes a mystic reaches a point, often early in life, when she finds her own voice and she feels, "There. Now I've *got* to speak up." The hagiographers often exhibit a certain conflictedness on this point. The traditional model of the "good woman" requires docility, obedience to parent and spouse, and silence. And yet the young girl bound for sainthood almost invariably breaks that mold. She leaves the parental home. She refuses to marry, or she insists upon a celibate union. She utters prophecy, will speak forth her visions.

Clare is an excellent case in point, for she did indeed rebel against filial bonds; in fact, by insisting upon the privilege of poverty, she rebelled against church authority, too. Within her community, the sisters who survived her report that she never hesitated to say what needed to be said. Still, she apparently spoke very little and inspired her sisters mainly through the power of her presence and her example. She undertook writing her own rule only when it was clear she would not be able to continue teaching in this manner much longer and had to put what she could into words. With the writing of her rule, then, she broke her silence and found her public voice.

Clare was the first woman in the West to write a rule for monastics. The document gives a world of insight into the kind of leader she must have been. Its tone is assured and joyous, and its vision of community bears out beautifully everything that writers like Carol Gilligan and Sara Ruddick have told us about how we women tend to organize ourselves when left to our own devices. To grasp the full originality, liberality, and great good sense of Clare's rule, though, we must compare it to those it replaced.

Clare had come to San Damiano in the fall of 1212. Just three years later, the Fourth Lateran Council [8] met and forbade by law—in opposition to that genuine friend of the Franciscans, Pope Innocent III—the establishment of new religious orders. Only the approved and time-tested religious rules were to be followed. The Poor Ladies were thus in an anomalous position. Despite their having received a papal privilege allowing them to live in intense poverty, the council did not approve their way of life.

It was in keeping with this new legislation, then, that in 1219 Cardinal Hugolino, appointed as their protector, gave the Poor Ladies a detailed rule based on the Rule of Saint Benedict. Drawn up originally by Saint Benedict of Nursia during the early part of the sixth century to regulate the lives of his own monks, the Benedictine rule drew heavily upon earlier rules. "Excessive austerities are excluded, and the whole is marked by a spirit of prudent leniency."[9] Under this rule, monks took vows of stability of place, obedience, and "monastic virtue," but, as mentioned above, no particular vow of poverty. The chief task was performance of the divine office.

Omitted from Hugolino's rule were Clare's two deepest concerns: absolute poverty and the link with the brethren that Francis had promised the Poor Ladies. Later, Pope Innocent IV ruled that the sisters did not have to follow Hugolino's rule, and later still, in 1247, he offered them a rule of his own composing. This one at least omitted mention of Saint Benedict, but it was still far from satisfactory to Clare and her sisters. Clare began to write her own rule three years before her death in 1253, when she was about fifty-five years old. She had lived at San Damiano for thirty-seven years, and her rule resonates with the experience accumulated during those years. She is supremely confident of every word she writes. She knows this pattern of life can work, because she has watched it work, not only within her own convent, which had the unique advantage of her presence, but in sister communities scattered all across the region.

Hugolino's rule began by advising that women who would be received into the order should be told "the hard and austere realities" of that life. Clare, who would never have characterized San Damiano's life as primarily "hard" or "austere," says only, "Let the tenor of our life be thoroughly explained to her." Clare does not use the Latin word *monache* or *nun*, moreover, but rather *sorore*, or sister, and that informality extends into the procedure she prescribes for admission of a new member into the community. She provides no formula for profession, and she omits much of the prescriptive fussiness of Hugolino's and Innocent's language. Instead, she opens simply, "If, by divine inspiration, anyone should come to us desiring to accept this life, the Abbess is required to seek the consent of all the sisters" (*Early Documents* 62).

The reference to divine inspiration is extremely important, because underlying everything she will say about her sisters hereafter is the

understanding that the same Holy Spirit that had brought them together would most likely continue to work in and through them. Clare
asked that the abbess call her sisters together at least once a week and
consult with them, "for the Lord frequently reveals what is best to the
least among us."

Innocent's rule splits a great many hairs regarding the circumstances under which a sister might be permitted to leave the enclosure.
Clare, though she takes enclosure very seriously, says simply that a sister
will only go out "for a useful, reasonable, evident and approved purpose." Implicit is the assumption that those concerned will have the good
sense to recognize such a purpose. Similarly, after enjoining silence
under most circumstances, she specifies, "Nevertheless, they can communicate always and everywhere, briefly and in a low tone of voice,
whatever is necessary." Again, good sense is anticipated. A lovely sense of
the "spirit of the thing" rolls through the rule, continually lifting the
reader's gaze, imparting a bright vision and a strikingly feminine confidence that "we can work it out as we go along."

Pope Innocent busied himself a good deal about exactly what
everyone should wear: cover this, cover that, and "Let them not dare to
appear in any other way before outsiders." He specifies that every sister
should be issued at least two tunics and a hair shirt. Clare, for all her
vaunted austerities, makes no provision for hair shirts. Instead of pre-
scribing a wardrobe, she simply exhorts her sisters "to always wear cheap
garments out of love of the most holy and beloved Child Who was
wrapped in such poor little swaddling clothes and laid in a manger and
of His most holy Mother" (*Early Documents* 64).

Of critical importance throughout the rule is the word *discretio,* or
discernment. The whole community would elect eight sisters "from the
more discerning ones" whose counsel the abbess "should be always
bound to use in those matters which our form of life requires." Thanks
to this second tier of authority, the abbess' own position would be less
powerful but also less demanding.

Firm as she is on questions of enclosure and purity, Clare omits
Innocent's stipulations that an overhead light be kept burning all night in
the dormitory, that everyone sleep in separate beds, and that the abbess'
bed be placed where she could see everybody in the room. The abbess
was not a watchdog, but "the servant of all the sisters." Again and again,

in testifying at the process of her canonization, her sisters recalled her going about at night covering them against the cold and washing their bedding when they were ill. Indeed, when the serving sisters[10] returned from their trips to town, Clare would wash their feet and kiss them too; one serving sister tried to pull her foot away, abashed, and kicked Clare by accident. Clare smiled and kissed the sole of the offending foot.

Once you have absorbed the sweetness and tenderness of Clare's rule, the aridity of Innocent's is almost shocking. He makes the sisters sound like prisoners one minute and wanton temptresses the next. He writes about grilles and double locks and the fine points of fasting and what kind of woman should be portress. He seems obsessed with maintaining a strong line of authority. Clare's, in contrast, emanates joy and gratitude for the vocation itself and deep respect for those who shared it with her. Her whole organizational style rejects the more hierarchical mode described often today as "pyramid structure" and anticipates the "web" structure—more egalitarian and interconnected—favored by many women in business and the professions today.

Clare's teachings on what should happen when two sisters quarrel typify her high expectations and the beauty of the way of life she had inaugurated. She asks that the sister who has been the cause of the trouble (who will presumably admit her error) should prostrate herself humbly and ask pardon. The other must generously comply, remembering the words of the Lord, "If you do not forgive from the heart, neither will your heavenly Father forgive you" (*Early Documents* 72).

The abbess herself was the key to making it all work. She must be "kind and available so that they may safely reveal their needs, and confidently have recourse to her at any hour" (*Early Documents* 58–59). Indeed, she must be so familiar with her daughters that "they can speak and act with her as ladies do with their servant" (Early Documents 73). Should a problem arise between two sisters, then "humbly and charitably" the abbess should correct the wrongdoer. One of Clare's sisters recalled, "If Lady Clare ever saw any of the sisters suffering some temptation or trial, she called her secretly and consoled her with tears, and sometimes threw herself at her feet." In times of illness, particularly, the sisters must feel free to confide their needs. "For if a mother loves and nourishes her child according to the flesh, should not a sister love and nourish her sister according to the Spirit even more lovingly?" (*Early Documents* 71).

Apostolic poverty is the keynote of the Poor Ladies' Rule. Once more, I would emphasize that Clare did not merely accept poverty as a precondition of sanctity; like Francis, she embraced it with a lover's passion, joyously. It had opened two areas of experience to her, the first of which was unitive prayer. The second door that Clare knew poverty could open—poverty that was chosen, we must specify, and experienced within community—was to perfect charity, "the unity of mutual love that is the bond of perfection" (*Early Documents* 74).

Out of Clare's description of voluntary poverty there arises an enthralling picture of human relationships as they could be. For once the community has placed its trust in God to meet its essential needs, then whatever comes in is *by definition* enough: it is up to the abbess and the community as a whole to determine whose needs for what commodity are most critical at a given moment.

Viewed as an economic policy, this is a dramatic departure from most we are familiar with, for instead of striving to increase the goods coming through the system, it strives to perfect the means of distribution by developing within the members of the group an intensely close attunement to one another and, by the same process, a sturdy faith in one another. Gradually, in such a climate, trust arises, along with the tacit recognition that the supportive environment you have helped create will be there for you, too.[11]

For the Middle Ages, the death of a saint was an enormously important event. When a Bernard of Clairvaux or a Francis of Assisi was passing over, the border between heaven and earth was believed to lie open and you could see a lot if you kept your eyes open. Clare's last days certainly followed the pattern. As if wanting to alert her sisters, she said, "Precious in the sight of the Lord is the death of his holy ones." Indeed, one sister saw the Virgin Mary with all her attendants come and place a kind of veil over Clare, and another saw in the host given to Clare a small, beautiful boy. Best of all, listening closely just a few days before her death, several of them heard her murmur, "Go calmly in peace, for you will have a good escort, because He Who created you has sent you the Holy Spirit and has always guarded you as a mother does her child who loves her" (*Last Document* 143).

Asked to whom she was speaking, she astonished those around, saying, "I am speaking to my soul." The sisters present knew they had heard something extraordinary and must have felt responsible to record it, for one of them said to another, "You have a good memory; remember well what the Lady says." Clare overheard them, though, and her words suggest she was already well into the transition between life and death. There is a playfulness in her gentle rebuke that is characteristically Franciscan: "You will only remember these things I now say as long as He Who made me say them permits you." But just before she died, she seemed to recall for them what she had said, for she gave them a special blessing that included these words: "Always be lovers of your souls and those of all your sisters" (*Last Documents* 79).

On August 9, 1253, Clare received from the papal court her own rule with the seal of Pope Innocent IV affixed, signifying his full approval. She is said to have touched and kissed it many times over. The next day, she died.

It remains to consider the miracles Clare is said to have performed. Whatever private reservations one might have about miracles, their regular occurrence in the lives of mystics does underscore the central, mysterious principle of a life like Clare's: when a human being empties herself of personal desires, she can become "a clear stream of God's bounty." Clare is supposed to have multiplied loaves, filled jars with olive oil, cured several of life-threatening diseases. Her miracles against violence, though, are probably of special interest to those of us who are living today, under the constant threat of violence from one quarter or another. If we look at these two episodes superficially, they tell us little. But if we remind ourselves that violence arises out of forces deep in human consciousness and that Clare walked around in those depths every day, the details of these stories light up with meaning. Both incidents are well attested in the Process of Canonization.

As background, it needs to be said that intermittently, during most of Clare's life, her home region of Umbria was a war zone. Between wars, the countryside was threatened continually by bands of soldiers-for-hire who were temporarily out of work. It was common for warring noblemen to hire soldiers from the Holy Land as mercenaries—"Saracens"—and then release them to shift for themselves. One day a number of these fierce soldiers had scaled the convent walls and were already inside the enclosure. Clare had herself carried to the entrance of the refectory (for long periods of time she was too weakened by fasting and illness to walk) and asked that the sacred pyx—the small box containing the eucharist— be brought. "Throwing herself prostrate on the ground in prayer, she begged with tears, saying among other things, 'Lord, look upon these servants of yours, *because I cannot protect them*' " (*Early Documents* 157). Clare told her daughters then that she would be a hostage for them, that no harm would come to them as long as they obeyed God's command- ments. And indeed, the men departed without giving harm.

On the second occasion, Clare is believed to have averted a deadly attack on Assisi itself. The army of one Vitale d'Aversa was camped out- side the city walls, sworn to level the town at daybreak unless it was handed over. The prayers of Clare, the abbess, had driven away so many of Assisi's ills—leprosy and epilepsy, and even a rock up the nose (it fell out when she made the sign of the cross over the little boy in question, and I find this perhaps my favorite of all her miracles). Could she drive away war itself? Clare called her sisters together and said, "We have re- ceived many benefits from this city and I know we should pray that God will protect it" (*Last Documents* 157). She directed them to come in the morning for some time with her. "The Lady made them bring her some ashes," one sister recalled, just as Francis had on the day years ago when he had come to speak at San Damiano. Clare removed her own veil and placed a quantity of ashes on her head, "as if she had been newly ton- sured," then did the same for each of her sisters. She directed them then to go to the chapel to pray. This was all. But the army left the next morn- ing, and Assisi was henceforth unchallenged.

In effect, these two legends tell us the same story twice. In the first, all Clare really did to invoke God's protective strength was declare that she herself could do nothing. In the second episode, she did not even say it but merely acted it out in a brief but deeply resonant ritual. Both times, then, she simply stood back.

It was a contemporary of Clare's, Mechthild of Magdeburg, who said, "That prayer is powerful that a person makes with all her might." "With completely unified desires," we might paraphrase, and this was Clare. Attending to nothing but God, she opened wide her arms in a ges- ture that was at the same time a fierce, joyous, unconditional letting go and an embrace. Clare's whole life was about letting go, and it strikes me that in these episodes, she was reaffirming that central motif and instructing all who would pray with power: look to your letting go.

I have dwelled at greater length on Saint Francis of Assisi than readers might have expected, considering my stated intention to treat Clare's life "in its own right." This has proven necessary for reasons I hope are by now clear. One reason that may not be obvious is that Francis was by vocation a spiritual teacher. He was given no choice but to "find his voice" and use it, publicly and eloquently. Several of the women we will be looking at felt they had received similar callings that they had to obey, and I hope that my description of Francis as a kind of "divine keyhole" can help make sense of the willingness of a Catherine of Siena or a Teresa of Avila to break with cultural norms and allow herself not only to speak and write but to be a spiritual focal point also, however reluctantly, for her devoted followers.

Clare's life, in contrast, was very much hidden, and perhaps it was this that drew me to her in the first place. For most of us lead hidden lives—enclosed lives, one could argue—enclosed not by convent walls, but by a thousand intractable givens. When we wonder, with her biographers, whether Clare wished she could be out in the world with the friars, preaching God's word and sleeping where night found her, we could well be giving voice to the unrest of our own pent-up spirits. But Clare's life challenges our very understanding of freedom, suggesting that it has less to do with mobility than we usually assume. If she frightens us with her extremes—her long fasts appear to have damaged her health so much that she spent some thirty years of her life an invalid, and I cannot think that was a good idea—we need to recognize that she had been seized by the beauty and power of what the church calls a charism, a gift, that is, of the Holy Spirit. It is said that if you hold any one of these entirely, you hold all the others too. Holy poverty was Clare's own track into sanctity, and in her passion to live it out, she could no more have restrained herself than Einstein could haveconfined himself to making clocks.

And yet for all those ashes, and all that fasting, she rejoiced in life itself and the people and the world around her, just as Francis had. In her rule, there is a section concerning how the serving sisters ought to behave when they are obliged to go outside the convent. Clare gives all the appropriate cautions—though she is, as usual, far briefer and far less censorious than was Innocent in his rule. But what she actually said to the serving sisters as they left the convent we learn from the Process of Canonization. Nothing about dangerous strangers and nothing about keeping one's eyes to the ground. Rather, on the contrary, "She reminded them to praise God when they saw beautiful trees, flowers, and bushes; and likewise, always to praise Him for and in all things when they saw all people and creatures" (*Early Documents* 169).

Mechthild of Magdeburg

(1210?–1297?)

Wouldst thou know my meaning?
Lie down in the Fire
See and taste the Flowing
Godhead through thy being;
Feel the Holy Spirit
Moving and compelling
Thee within the Flowing
Fire and Light of God.

— Mechthild of Magdeburg,
The Flowing Light of the Godhead 6.29

✦

THANKS to her contemporaries, we can picture Saint Clare quite
easily. In one light-filled tableau after another, the events of
her quiet life pass before the mind's eye like frescoes by Giotto. Of
Mechthild, though, we struggle in vain to compose any image at all.
She was only "Mechthild," not "Saint Mechthild" or even "Blessed
Mechthild," and she had no official biographer. We know almost nothing about her except what she tells us in her own book, and that is only
enough to let us sketch the roughest outlines of her life. What she *has*

given us, and it is to my mind an even greater treasure than a conventional biography might have been, is a voice, authentic and idiosyncratic, incomparably passionate and lyrical. Most of what we know of Clare's life is from the outside; Mechthild takes us *inside* unitive consciousness—the state of being where all divisions are healed and all dualities transcended—and lets us glimpse its terrors as well as its consolations, conveying these in powerful and unexpected imagery.

Mechthild was a woman who had absolutely no use for abstractions ("Lie down in the fire. . . . See and taste. . . . Feel the Holy Spirit . . . . ") Asking herself at one point why she continued to write despite fierce censure, she said, "I cannot nor do I wish to write, except that I see it with the eyes of my soul, and I hear it with the ears of my eternal spirit and feel in all the members of my body: the power of the Holy Spirit" (*Flowing Light* 4.13). She writes of the act of prayer: "It drives the hungry soul up into the fullness of God, and draws the great God down into the little soul" (5.13).

Describing the soul's relationship with God, she marvels at "the powerful penetration of all things and the special intimacy which ever exists between God and each individual soul," concluding that it is "a thing so delicate that had I the wisdom of all men and the voice of an angel, I could not describe it" (3.1). The paradox enchants her: God is everywhere and surely, therefore, impersonal; and yet in relation to the individual soul, God is entirely intimate and surely, therefore, personal.

"Our redeemer has become our bridegroom!" Mechthild exults. Others had said as much, but in a relatively formal, allegorical mode. When Mechthild writes of the soul's romance with God, she is no allegorist: in the depths of her being, she has found a lover who is fully, deliciously responsive. "Thou art my resting-place," God tells her, "my love, my secret peace, my deepest longing, my highest honour. Thou art a delight of my Godhead, a comfort of my manhood, a cooling stream for my ardour"(1.19). God is there, Mechthild insists, for every one of us, not in a general, impersonal sense, but *there*—so exquisitely right for you it's as if you'd made him up. He "whispers with His love in the narrow confines of the soul" (2.23). Her language is almost shockingly erotic at times; for Mechthild, the sweet goings-on between God and the soul are the reality—all-consuming and exquisitely fulfilling—of which human sexuality is only a pale shadow.

Perhaps we need to emphasize this. The astonishing concreteness of Mechthild's imagery—its unembarrassed physicality—is somewhat deceptive if she is read casually. One might think she was celebrating the senses, the body, and even sexuality in and of themselves. In a way, she is, but readers of her time would have understood unequivocally that she conjures up the pleasurable experiences of the physical realm as presentiments, or intimations, of an awakening into supreme joy—joy that is interior and immaterial and unending. Rather than distinguish sharply between the physical and spiritual realms, then, and reject the physical, she joins them in a natural continuity and progression. We are led inward by way of everything in this life: everything in this life, therefore, has its own sanctity. This is an attitude that has deep roots in the Christian mystical tradition, taking lyrical form in works like Francis's "Canticle of the Creatures."[1]

It is indeed plain "Mechthild." The sanctity of this thirteenth-century German mystic would seem to be as great and evident as that of some far less colorful people who made the final cut for canonization, and I fret. How could they have passed her over? This is silly, I'm not a Catholic. Why should I care? Still, it rankles, much as when a dear friend fails her orals, though you know she knew the reading list. Did "they" have it in for her?

Mechthild had contemporary friends, too, who felt she had been underrated. One was Gertrude of Hackeborn, abbess of the renowned Benedictine convent at Helfta who took Mechthild in during her last years when she was ill, nearly blind, and had run into serious difficulties with "them" back in Magdeburg. After Mechthild died, Gertrude asked God to send signs to silence her critics. Alas, though, no signs appeared—no recorded miracles and no canonization process either, though Gertrude's own sister would become Saint Mechthild, as would another Helfta nun, Gertrude the Great.

Nor was Mechthild canonized in the secular sense: her book was not drawn into the "canon" of treasured mystical writings. Worse, soon after she began to write, certain individuals warned her that she should not: that her book, in fact, should be burned. God consoled her, promising that her book would not be burned. God did not promise that it would always be in print, or that it would be featured prominently in anthologies of the great European mystics, and indeed, it has not been. *The*

Flowing Light of the Godhead passed into oblivion soon after the end of the fourteenth century and would not reappear until 1860. Not until 1953 were Mechthild's writings translated into English.[2]

One grieves at Mechthild's long neglect by both the church and the scholarly world, but it is not incomprehensible. For Mechthild's mode of discourse is extremely feminine: she wrote in that "different voice," whose inflections are only now being fully grasped. Informality, earthiness, warmth of feeling, a preference for open-ended literary form—these qualities have traditionally baffled and disconcerted men of letters. It is all the more heartening, then, to read the commendation one Heinrich of Nordlingen gave the book in 1345 when he sent it to his friends and fellow seekers Margaret and Christina Ebner: "To me, this book, in delightful and vigorous German, is the most moving love-poem I have ever read in our tongue. Read it eagerly with the inner perception of your hearts"(*Flowing Light* 1.23).

On the balance, it may be just as well that Mechthild has remained so long in the shadows. We can lament how little we know about her, but, on the other hand, we don't have to sift through pious legends or official biographies. The rough places in her personality have not been smoothed over for public consumption. Mechthild's very anonymity has helped preserve her for us in all her peculiarities, and that is a blessing, for her peculiarities suit us, I think, in many ways. We turn to her life, now, or what we can construe of it, and then, to that *voice.*

Mechthild's story is painfully different from Clare's. Uprooted by choice from her home and family, exiled later from her adopted home at Magdeburg, betrayed and abandoned (we are not told the circumstances) by trusted spiritual companions, barred at least once from taking communion—her inner life, too, was marked by long periods of deep loneliness and grief.

Her date of birth has been placed somewhere around 1210. Or maybe 1207 or perhaps even 1217. Her family was wealthy enough to have educated her to some degree. She did not learn Latin, though, and we can be everlastingly grateful she didn't, because she wrote instead in a rich, colorful German dialect that is as far as it possibly could be from the formality and abstractness of Latin. She is, in fact, the first European mystic known to have written in the vernacular.

Mechthild's use of metaphors drawn from courtly life led earlier commentators to speculate that she might have come from noble stock. Now that more is known about the spirituality of her time and place, it is clear that the language of courtly love, developed during the preceding century, was the favorite metaphor of an entire movement. The question of her social background remains, therefore, open. When Mechthild was just twelve, she received her first "greeting from God," a visitation so powerful she felt she would never be able to commit a serious sin again. Thirty-one years later, when she began to write, she said this experience had been repeated every day since. She described it as follows: "The true greeting of God, which comes from the heavenly flood out of the spring of the flowing Trinity, has such power that it takes all strength from the body and lays the soul bare to itself. Thus it sees itself as one of the blessed and receives in itself divine glory" (1.2).

Mechthild was probably twenty-three when she felt compelled to leave her family and friends—"to whom I was most dear"—and travel "to a town [Magdeburg] where I had no friends save one only." She feared that because of this one person "my renunciation of the world and my love of God might be interfered with." But in fact "God never left me."

It is reasonable to ask why she did not enter a convent, but we don't have to look far for our answer. The convents of her day were few in number, crowded, and set up to accommodate the nobility in a great many ways that had nothing to do with a life of prayer. Assuming Mechthild did have the requisite social standing—and dowry—and assuming she had located a convent that had room for her, she still probably would not have found an atmosphere particularly conducive to serious spiritual endeavors. Under pressure, convents were known to accept small children, illegitimate offspring, even political prisoners. They were refuges for well-to-do women who for any number of reasons were not marriageable and really had no place else to go.

Our imaginings of the Middle Ages are so dominated by the feudal castle on the one hand and the convent and monastery on the other, that other social structures do not come readily to mind. But in fact the thirteenth century was a period of dramatic transition. Towns, built around marketplaces and often cathedrals, were increasingly more important centers of human interaction than were the feudal estates. Nor were monasteries any longer the unchallenged stronghold of either spiritual authority or learning. In the religious sphere, the new itinerant preaching orders—the Dominicans, the Franciscans, and the Augustinians—were winning followers all over Europe. Since these friars lived on alms, they gravitated to the towns, where citizens were prosperous enough to support them. There they often became deeply involved in the rich, tumultuous intellectual life of the great universities, where Aristotelian science and metaphysics were being assimilated into Christian doctrine. The draw went both ways: a good many scholars became Franciscan or Dominican friars, because doing so allowed them to pursue their theological studies without having to pursue secular positions as well.

Magdeburg itself did not boast a university, but it was a good-sized town—seat of an archbishopric—and its Dominican friars had certainly attended the universities. Heinrich Halle, who would eventually compile Mechthild's writings, and who was also probably her confessor, had been a student of Albert the Great, under whom Thomas Aquinas, too, had studied. In contrast to the backwater village where Mechthild had lived, Magdeburg was a lively center of religious ardor and intellectual inquiry; a powerful magnet, surely, to a young woman as gifted in spirit and intellect as Mechthild. On the other hand, it must have taken considerable courage for her to leave the comfort and safety of her family home. At some point after arriving in Magdeburg—it could have been years afterward or within the first weeks—this remarkable young woman affiliated herself with one of the most extraordinary movements in European history, the Beguines.

When contemporary women learn about the Beguines, our hearts beat a little faster. Suddenly, in the allegedly monolithic structure of medieval Europe, there is a rift—an anomaly—incredibly enough, a women's movement. The exact nature of the movement and its origins continue to be debated by medieval scholars. In the past, some historians gave priority to socioeconomic factors, almost to the exclusion of religious impulses, but today the genuinely spiritual nature of the movement, this "order that was not an order," is virtually unquestioned.

The first Beguines probably lived in the vicinity of Liège, in what is now Belgium, around the year 1210, the year that Francis first preached in the cathedral in Assisi. Soon, though, Beguine communities sprang up in

Germany and France as well. Adherents led strict religious lives, lauded by contemporary chroniclers, but they never adopted a rule. Some lived with their families, while others formed communal households. They looked to no saintly founder, and they asked no authorization from Rome. They never organized, and they sought no patrons. The spontaneity of the movement and its supremely open structure are all but breathtaking.

Of Mechthild's own circumstances, we know little. But we know enough of the Beguine pattern of life to have a rough idea how she lived. Perhaps she joined a household of other Beguines. Doing so would not have required that she take permanent vows, but that she simply state her intention to follow Christ in a life of chastity and poverty.[3] Had she wished to marry at a later date, she could have done so freely. She would not have been enclosed and would probably have gone out each day to work, for the Beguines earned their keep in a variety of ways. Some wove, some embroidered church vestments, many of them worked among the sick and poor. Long after the Beguines themselves had all but disappeared, the homes for the elderly and the hospitals they had founded remained.

Part of Mechthild's day would have been given over to personal prayers, meetings with her community, and corporate worship. Both the Franciscan and Dominican friars provided spiritual direction for the Beguines, and in some areas the Cistercians did too. Mechthild herself looked primarily to the Dominicans, and from them she appears to have absorbed some of the controversial "new-old" doctrines that place her mystical writings among the most innovative of the period. The names of these orders sound so venerable to the modern ear that we forget that when Mechthild arrived in Magdeburg, the Franciscans had been at work for no more than twenty years, the Dominicans even fewer. The friars really were the new faces in town, and not altogether welcomed by the church establishment—the "cathedral clergy" in particular—though their work did have papal sanction.

Some suspicion of heresy hovered around the Beguines. One etymology for their name suggests that it is a corrupt use of the word *Albigensian,* referring to one of the most notorious heresies of the age. In 1310, the French mystic Margaret Porete, who may have been a Beguine, would be burned at the stake for the supposedly heretical nature of her

Mirror of Simple Souls. Perhaps Mechthild had her own brush with the defenders of orthodoxy. Certainly around the fringes of this, as of so many of the new spiritual movements, there must have been doctrinal irregularities. But historian R. W. Southern adduces other motives for the virtual shutdown of the Beguines that took place in the fourteenth century. He cites the complaint of one Bishop Bruno of Olmutz, in East Germany, who wrote to the pope in 1273 that Beguines were using their liberty to escape "the yoke of obedience to their priest" and "the coercion of marital bonds." The bishop concluded unpleasantly, "I would have them marry, or thrust into an approved order."[4] In 1312, the Council of Vienne decreed that "their way of life is to be permanently forbidden." Again, the note of insulted masculine authority is struck: "Since these women promise no obedience to anyone, and do not renounce their property or profess an approved Rule, they are certainly not 'religious,' though they wear a habit and are associated with such religious orders as they find congenial."[5]

To the credit of the deliberating body, the document does close with a paragraph that seems almost to reverse that sentiment. Feelings were apparently divided, and that division was reflected in the unevenness with which churchmen actually enforced the decree. By this time though, the major impetus of the movement had spent itself, and gradually over the ensuing years the Beguines declined in number and visibility. At the height of the movement, however, its adherents numbered in the thousands, and the Beguinage was much more than a household. Early in the fourteenth century, the Great Beguinage at Ghent was surrounded with walls and moats. Inside were two churches, eighteen convents, over a hundred houses, a brewery, and an infirmary. So much we can construe, then, of Mechthild's daily life: work, prayer, and the companionable support of like-minded women.

Mechthild apparently concealed her spiritual experiences until 1250, when their sheer intensity made her feel she could no longer keep silent. Her confessor urged her to go ahead and write about them: "He said I should go forth joyfully; God Who had called me would take good care of me" (4.2). She probably just wrote on loose sheets and eventually handed them over to the Dominican Heinrich Halle, the same confessor, most likely, who had urged her to write. He might have been a bit shaken by what she actually wrote, because she says at one point, "Master

Heinrich! [this could also have been directed at her brother Heinrich, a Dominican friar himself], you are surprised at the masculine way in which this book is written? I wonder why that surprises you?" (5.12). She defends herself vigorously: the apostles, after all, so weak at the outset, had become strong and fearless once they had received the Holy Ghost.

Halle organized the loose sheets into book form, and they began to circulate, winning admirers but creating enemies, too. Small wonder, considering passages like the following: "God calls the cathedral clergy goats because their flesh stinks of impurity with regard to eternal truth . . . " (6.3). The church itself she regards as a maiden whose skin is "filthy, for she is unclean and unchaste" (5.34).

At one point Mechthild's soul cries out to God that no one will read the offices before her or celebrate the mass. God assures her, though, that "I am in thee and thou in Me, we could not be closer, for we two are fused in one, poured into one mould, thus, unwearied shall we remain forever" (3.5). And, indeed, whatever charges of heresy might have been leveled at her, they did not stick, because in 1270, Mechthild was welcomed at the Benedictine convent at Helfta (near Eisleben in Saxony). The convent had been founded, typically enough, by and for daughters of the nobility, but it was in other ways decidedly atypical. Under the direction of Abbess Gertrude of Hackeborn, Helfta had become a vibrant center of learning and spirituality. Novices were instructed in the seven liberal arts and theology, with special emphasis on the works of Saint Bernard of Clairvaux, and older nuns busied themselves with translating and copying books for the convent library.

Settling in at Helfta must have been a tremendous relief for Mechthild. She was about sixty-three by now, seriously ill, and nearly blind. Feeling useless and burdensome, she asked God why she was being kept in the world. "Thou shalt enlighten and teach," God replied, "and shalt stay here in great honour" (7.8). The seventh and final book of *The Flowing Light* was dictated at Helfta after she had gone blind. Sown throughout are pieces that reflect her gratitude and appreciation of the community. She may have repaid her debt to Helfta more amply than she imagined, for the most celebrated works from the convent are the autobiographical writings of Gertrude the Great and those dictated to Gertrude by Mechthild of Hackeborn, and neither book was written until after Mechthild of Magdeburg had come to live with them. Mechthild had struggled at length before she had consented to write in her own voice, having to battle, first, the feelings of presumptuousness all mystics encounter when they try to translate their experiences into words and, second, the knowledge that as a woman she would be opening herself to criticism for writing at all, about anything whatever. It has been suggested that her decision to write and accept the consequences inspired the two younger visionaries to break their own silences.[6]

Somewhere around 1282, Mechthild died (unless it was in 1285, as one scholar believes, or 1297, as others maintain). All her life she had had recurring anxieties over whether she would "make a good death." Shortly before her end, though, she received divine reassurance: "It shall be thus: I will draw My breath and thy soul shall come to Me as a needle to a magnet" (5.32).

Unburdened by the weight of theological studies, a "learned" language, or elaborate stylistic constraints, Mechthild wrote directly and uninhibitedly out of her own experience. It is tempting to wonder whether the growing individualism and the relatively liberated atmosphere of the towns where the Beguines lived and worked helped to nourish the freedom of expression that is so characteristic of their writings. Mechthild is unexcelled in conveying the heights of mystical union, but passages like the following suggest the down-to-earth practicality of these working women who were contemplatives as well:

What hinders spiritual people most of all from full perfection is that they pay so little heed to small sins. . . . When I refrain from a smile which would hurt no one, or cherish some sourness in my heart, or feel impatient at my own pain, my soul becomes so dark . . . that I must . . . humbly make confession. . . . Then only does grace come again to my soul and I creep back like a beaten dog to the kitchen. (5.33)

If I am truly to show forth the goodness of God, then I am obliged to speak of myself. But that hinders me now truly no more than it hinders a hot oven to fill it with cold dough. (3.15)

If Mechthild herself had not affixed the title *The Flowing Light* to her work, a contemporary translator could be forgiven for calling it

"Jottings of a Beguine" or perhaps "A Mystic's Notebook," for the work as a whole lacks the architectural unity of the more systematic spiritual treatises of the time. It moves along with the free-form spontaneity of a journal, the kind of journal into which one might copy lines from a particularly good letter written that morning or a snatch of poetry or a list of aphorisms or even a list of gripes; Mechthild includes all of these.

The overall coherence of the work derives not so much from formal qualities as from a consistency in preoccupation of the kind that knits together a collection of lyric poetry. That is, an image or theme will be evoked, but only barely, after which it might be dropped for a few pages or a few books, only to reappear much later, full-blown and rich in meaning. Mechthild begins by saying, "All who want to study this book should read it nine times," and indeed, each fresh reading is rewarded on the literary as well as the spiritual level, for new symmetries and correspondences reveal themselves, and gradually, through repeated exposure, one comes to see what Mechthild's central concerns really were. Among those concerns none is more prominent than divine grace, and for Mechthild, the essential quality of God's grace is fluidity. All of her favorite images are of things that flow: water, milk, wine, blood, tears, honey, molten gold, and, by a visionary leap, light. Scripture and liturgy had already endowed all these substances with rich symbolic meaning. Mechthild draws upon that wealth of traditional associations, but by giving so much prominence to liquids of one kind or another—evoking each one over and over, and even turning them *into* one another in the transformative medium of her poetry—she endows them with a significance that is altogether original with her and exceedingly powerful.

By things that flow, we are cleansed, healed, nourished, and consoled, and by things that flow, the void between the human and the divine is closed: "We two are fused, poured into one mold (3.5). And again, "God's love flows from God to man without effort, as a bird glides through the air without moving its wings" (2.3).

Connection, or connectedness, is a key concept in the writings of so-called "difference feminists" (Carol Gilligan, Sara Ruddick, and the four authors of *Women's Ways of Knowing*, for example). Gilligan and her colleagues tell us, for example, that women look at moral dilemmas in terms of the "connectedness" of the individuals involved as opposed to contractual agreements into which they might have entered or abstract schemes of "rights." The very practice of mothering tends to strengthen connected ways of knowing, suggests Ruddick, who also sees in mothers of developing children the tendency to allow one category of experience to melt rather readily into another: "Neither the child nor, therefore, the mother understanding her can sharply distinguish reality from fantasy, body from mind, self from other."[7] Furthermore, according to Mary Field Belenky and her co-authors, women tend to learn most easily in educational settings that foster connected as opposed to separate modes of knowing.[8] In addition, historian Caroline Walker Bynum observes that "women's symbols express contradiction and opposition less than synthesis and paradox."[9]

It has seemed to me that Mechthild's images of flow are a supremely apt poetic translation of connectedness—that they allow her to communicate her own exceedingly "connective" version of spirituality, which contrasted sharply with the very hierarchical, stratified model presented by the official church. "Feminine" as opposed to "masculine"? Provided we recognize that neither term refers to inborn or "essential" qualities, why not? It is certainly interesting to note how many of the liquids Mechthild celebrates are associated by tradition with the mother of Christ: tears, milk, blood, and even wine (for it was at her instance that Christ had turned water into wine at Capernaum).[10] Insofar as God's love is something that flows, the way to receive that love is to yield to it and open oneself to it, and it was a commonplace in the Middle Ages that women were by nature more receptive. (Recall, for instance, the poem quoted in my introduction: ". . . in her desire she understands better / The wisdom flowing from Heaven / Than does a hard man / Who is clumsy in these things." Clare's chroniclers loved to describe her as a vase filled with precious ointments, Catherine of Siena's described Catherine as one who "contained" all of Christendom.) In Mechthild's fullest defense of herself as a seer, she says that when she asked God why he had chosen her as his scribe, he had answered: "The flood of My holy Spirit flows by nature into the valley" (2.26).

Just as God's grace takes many forms, so, Mechthild believes, does our desire for God. She describes the longing for mystical union now as hunger, now as thirst, now as pain to be assuaged or a fever to be cooled, and of course as sexual yearning. But even as these desires are evoked, they will blur or flow into one another. A scholar who has analyzed

Mechthild's use of liquidity images points out that she uses the verbs *suck* and *kiss* almost indiscriminately.[11] The infant Jesus suckles "at the breast he has so often kissed." The soul in mystical union with God "begins to taste [*sugen*] his sweetness . . . and the power of the Holy Trinity flows through soul and body" like mother's milk (6.1). Elsewhere, the soul is depicted as soaring up without effort and finding itself in Holy Trinity "as a child finds itself under its mother's cloak and lays its head on her breast" (7.27). There is an incredible tenderness in all this, as well as a polymorphous sensuality. The pleasurable bonding that takes place between a nursing mother and her child[12] is equated tacitly with the physical delight that joins a lover with her beloved, and both are subsumed in the mutual longing that unites God with the soul: all forms of desire really are the desire for God. The source of God's love is Holy Trinity, and those mysterious headwaters are as central a symbol for Mechthild as the *minne-flut* itself, the divine "flood of love" that constituted for her the "true greeting of God." On almost every page she speaks of the Trinity—never as a theological construct or abstraction, but always as a fecund, living, *moving* reality, one that is imprinted, moreover, deep in the human soul.

Divine grace, then, in all its metaphorical forms; human desire, in all its expressions; and Holy Trinity, the wellspring of all creation: these are the themes that pervade Mechthild's poetic and spiritual world. Keeping them in view, we can begin to explore that world in earnest.

Late in life, Mechthild grieved that her old age brought forth "no shining works." The quality of her writing did fall off somewhat over time. Though her later books contain some wonderful passages we honor her achievement best by selecting for close reading a passage from the very first book, a "shining work," to be sure. One set of pieces, in Book 1 (numbers 38 through 44) seems more integrally connected than any other series in the entire work. The pieces occur after a heady dialogue, a kind of graceful sparring match written very much in the manner of the courtly love poets. God speaks, delighted in his new love: "Look how she who has wounded Me has risen!"[13] She comes, he marvels,

> . . . racing like a hunted deer
> to the spring which is Myself.
> She comes soaring like an eagle

> Swinging herself from the depths
> Up into the heights.

God is once again the spring, the *minne-flut* or "torrent of love" that pours out of the Trinity, and the soul is a thirsty deer. He sees that his beloved is carrying something and asks what it is. She keeps him in suspense, though, playful and riddlesome as the conventions of courtly love would have her be: "Lord! I bring Thee my treasure."

> It is greater than the mountains,
> Wider than the world,
> Deeper than the sea,
> Higher than the clouds,
> More glorious than the sun,
> More manifold than the stars,
> It outweighs the whole earth!

God replies, in a form of gallantry transposed, once again, from the language of the court. He flatters her, not by praising her lips or eyes, but by perceiving in her a reflection of the Holy Trinity:

> O thou! image of My Divine Godhead,
> Ennobled by My humanity,
> Adorned by My Holy Spirit,
> What is thy treasure called?

Her answer comes, but with it another question:

> Lord! it is called my heart's desire!
> I have withdrawn it from the world,
> Denied it to myself and all creatures,
> Now I can bear it no longer.
> Where, O Lord, shall I lay it?

That desire should have weight and substance is an astonishing proposition. That it is our greatest wealth, even more. But this is what mystics have always told us: desire is the human being's most precious resource, and when we spend it heedlessly, we lose forever what it would otherwise purchase—nothing less than union with our own truest self. God's reply is immediate and, once again, framed in the language of the Trinity:

> Thy heart's desire shalt thou lay nowhere
> But in mine own Divine Heart
> And on My human breast.
> There alone wilt thou find comfort
> And be embraced by My Spirit. (1.43)

Before she can enter this embrace, though, she must overcome not only "the love of the world, temptation of the devil, pride of the body," but also "the need of remorse, the pain of penitence, the labour of confession . . . and annihilation of self will which drags so many souls back that they never come to know real love." Remarkably, the very disciplines we undertake as spiritual aspirants can themselves become obstructions in the latter stages of spiritual development. "The height of soul is reached in love," Mechthild will explain later, "therefore those who would storm the heights by fierce inhuman effort deceive themselves sorely and bear within themselves grim hearts, for they have not the virtue of holy humility which alone can lead the soul to God" (2.1).

A period of preparation ensues—a kind of forest interval very much in the courtly love mode—and the soul awaits her tryst with the Beloved, which will take place in "the shade of a brook, the resting place of love, where thou may cool thyself." She sends her handmaidens away. Allegorically, they represent the senses, but they also embody prudence and a conventional religiosity that Mechthild rejects scornfully. Dismissed, they fly into a panic and try to dissuade their mistress: "Lady, to refresh you, the tears of the love of Holy Mary Magdalene should suffice for you." She refuses. Instead, she insists, "I would drink of the unmingled wine." This is of course the very blood of Christ. It inebriates unto ecstasy, "beyond human sense."

Desperately, the handmaidens offer every imaginable alternative they can to the dangerous course their mistress is embarking upon. But despite her thirst, the soul rejects every drink they offer, even Mary's milk:

That is a childish joy,
to suckle and rock, a Babe.
I am a full-grown Bride
I must to my lover's side!

The culmination of all religious life, Mechthild insists, is mystical union. Her companions plead, "If you go there, then we will be blinded, for the divinity is fiery and hot. . . . Who can remain there for even one hour?" But Mechthild is ready with her reply:

Fish cannot drown in water,
Birds cannot sink in air,
Gold cannot perish
In the refiner's fire.
This has God given to all creatures,
To foster and seek their own nature,
How then can I withstand mine?

"Fish gotta swim, birds gotta fly." At moments like these, Mechthild brings to mind some of the best blues singers. "I must to God," she insists now and asks, "Do you think that fire must utterly slay my soul? No! Love can both fiercely scorch, and tenderly love and console." The soul goes now, in secret, to the innermost chamber of love. But her trials are not over, for God says, "Stay, Lady Soul!" She wonders what is left to give, and he tells her. "Thy *self* must go," the last trace, that is, of "me" and "mine." She protests: "Lord, what will become of me?" God reassures her that she can shed not only fear and shame, but all outward virtues too. All that will be left of her then will be her longing and desire, and that is all he wants. He will fill them both with his generosity, the "flood" of his love. She obliges at once, and stands before him:

Lord, now am I a naked soul
And thou a God most Glorious!
Our two-fold intercourse is Love Eternal
Which can never die.

Utter stillness falls now, "welcome to both," and the love is consummated. "What shall now befall her," the soul alone will know. The passage ends with a beautiful, enigmatic coda:

> When two lovers come secretly together,
> They must often part, without parting.

At each stage in this beautiful sequence, it seems that the level of intimacy between the lover and beloved cannot be exceeded, but every time, over and over, it is. By degrees, the soul is drawn into a more and more mysterious and all-consuming unity with God. Mechthild has drawn upon dazzling poetic gifts to convey a doctrine that was central to much of medieval mysticism, *epectasis,* the teaching that the depth of God is never exhausted. And yet that haunting coda pitches us headlong into the other half of Mechthild's experience as a mystic. She sees that the fire of God not only consoles, but it scorches, too. By the same token, the unmingled wine—wine uncut by water—becomes a symbol double-edged in both meaning and effect. As wine, it induces a divine inebriation and a joyous oblivion, but to anyone of Mechthild's time, place, and faith, wine was Christ's blood, too, symbol of unutterable suffering inflicted upon body and soul alike. No wonder the senses shrank back in horror.

In Book 3, Mechthild returns to this theme in a poem of tremendous power. A drinking song in the classic tradition, it has all the mingled humor and grief and love longing of any lyric Billie Holiday ever sang:

> Wouldst thou come with me to the wine cellar?
> That will cost thee much;
> Even hadst thou a thousand marks
> It were all spent in one hour!
> If thou wouldst drink the unmingled wine
> Thou must ever spend more than thou hast,
> and the host will never fill thy glass to the brim!
> Thou wilt become poor and naked,
> Despised of all who would rather see themselves
> In the dust, than squander their all in the wine cellar.

> This also thou must suffer,
> That thy friends look askance at thee
> Who go with thee to the Inn.
> How greatly they will scorn thee
> When they cannot dare such costs
> But must have water mixed with wine. (3.3)

"Nobody loves you when you're down and out." But observe, too, the defiance and the confidence of the last few lines. You can almost feel Mechthild's delight, as an artist, at hitting upon such a vivid and serio-comic metaphor for one of the most terrifying of the mystical path: while most of us are content with mere glimpses of truth, the real lovers of God, who want the entire vision, can hold back nothing. "If thou wouldst have all that mine is," God will say to Mechthild, "thou must give me all that thine is." Saint Francis conveys his own understanding of the price of mystical union in his prayer to experience both the love Christ felt for all creatures and the suffering he experienced on the cross.

What, then, was the exact nature of the suffering Mechthild endured? She cites the pain of leaving friends and loved ones, and she speaks of having undergone severe bodily penances that undermined her health. She laments a painful illness contracted soon after she arrived at Helfta, and we know she went progressively blind during the same period. In consequence of making her spiritual experiences public, and of lambasting the local clergy, she was censured and even excluded from holy rites.

When we consider these latter kinds of suffering, however, those that caused Mechthild to describe herself as a "post or target at which people throw stones" (6.38), it is important that we place them in an appropriate frame of reference. That is, the essential teaching of medieval mysticism was *Imitatio Christi*, perfect imitation of Christ in all things. Clare's devotion to poverty and Francis's to obedience were special applications of that principle. In a sense, Mechthild embraced exile and abasement in the same spirit and with the same single-minded determination that Clare did poverty. When she was very young, Mechthild asked God that she be "reviled through no fault of her own." This can sound a bit pathological, in a way that Clare's vocation does not. But it sounds perfectly reasonable when we remember Christ's own instruction in the Beatitudes: "Blessed are ye when men shall revile you and say all manner of evil against you falsely, for my sake" (Matthew 5:11, KJV). Mechthild would speak the truth as she had experienced it, whatever the cost, and the cost really was high. She records a conversation with the Lord: "Thou didst show me more than six years ago that spiritual people would treat me with contempt. That they do diligently and often, with anger." The Lord answers out of his own experience: Yes, his own Father had given him knowledge, too, then suffering and ignominy, but at the last, honor and reward. The same would happen to her.

"I have suffered much," she tells us in a particularly poignant and revealing passage, "because I could not bring good will to good works. That made me unstable and powerless, and as no one ventured to advise me, I did not dare to go against my nature. For since the time when God let me fall from the heights of bliss down to my own discretion, I was so bewildered I could find no end of things . . . no foothold"(6.19). She compares herself then to a mad dog. With that phrase "unstable and powerless" (and doesn't it have a modern ring?) I think we are getting closer to the essence of Mechthild's suffering. Submitting to the power of Love, she has lost her sovereignty. Interestingly, her Beloved has also: "You are the downfall," God had said to the human soul, "and failure of my power."

We *fall* in love, after all; the joy of the experience is always undercut by the fear of loss, and the love songs of every culture betray this fear. The lyrics may be joyous ("I've found you, and you love me, and I'm so happy I could turn inside out"), but the subtext is written firmly between the lines ("Oh, but what if you should *stop* loving me?"). Love makes us vulnerable—"woundable," quite literally.

Mechthild dramatizes her insistence that love and suffering are inseparable in a long dialogue between the Bride and her Beloved (2.25). There is something of Emily Dickinson in the whimsy and the longing of these lines.

> I seek thee with all my might,
> Had I the power of a giant
> Thou wert quickly lost
> If I came upon Thy footprints.
> Ah! Love! Run not so far ahead

> But rest a little lovingly
> That I may catch thee up.

God replies, explaining his elusiveness at some length. He tells her, "I must needs order My gifts to thee, else couldst thou not bear them in thy poor body." Before she can receive him entirely, she must in a mysterious sense enlarge herself over time. She declares her anguish in still more vivid terms, but again he insists that her sufferings will be recompensed. "If thou hast the weights, I have the gold." Again, though, she holds him accountable and cries out, in language that reminds one of a soliloquy by Hamlet or King Lear:

> Should my flesh fall from me, my blood evaporate,
> My limbs shrivel, cramp torture every vein,
> My heart dissolve in loving you,
> My soul burn as the roar of a hungry lion
> —How shall it be with me then?
> Where wilt Thou be then? Beloved, tell me!

The last lines ring out almost like a scream, and God replies, acknowledging her plight.

> Then art thou like a new-wed bride
> Whose lover has left her sleeping
> —He to whom she has given herself in all trust;
> She cannot suffer that he should part from her
> Even one hour.

God insists that the separation is not real, though, and adds, "If thou but hide thy grief, The power of love will grow in thee!" The forgetting of self that must take place, the emptying of all personal desires, cannot happen all at once. We only let go by degrees—as little, in any one round of the upward spiral, as we are absolutely sure we have to! On the path to God, light gives way to darkness, and darkness to light, at intervals. A measure of integration takes place, and we enjoy a moment of peace and joy, but the longing sets in again, and we must again exert the terrible effort.

I think we could be forgiven for thinking the relationship Mechthild depicts here is decidedly asymmetrical—one that today's feminists might see as uncomfortably "power-down"—and not genuinely romantic after all. The archetype of the wanton bridegroom coming and going as he will is not enormously appealing to contemporary women, even if the mystical theology parses out to our satisfaction. And indeed, I think it does not really work for Mechthild either, because in presenting this motif, she tinkers with it so that ultimately it conveys an extraordinary degree of parity and reciprocity between God and the soul. We can look at that relationship in a moment, when we have finished tracing out Mechthild's insistent and baffling pursuit of a kind of "rock bottom"—a state of being absolutely stripped of consolation and even expectation.

When Mechthild describes the ultimate stages of isolation and abandonment, she makes it quite clear that she herself chose to experience them. And yet that choosing amounted really to an acquiescing, not to the expressed will of another, but to forces deep within herself. Things that flow are prominent in her imagery, but so are things that draw. "Like a needle to a magnet" she will be drawn to God at her end, but that feeling of being drawn inexorably toward one's destiny and truest self are expressed throughout her writings. She will speak of an "inward tug" and "the rippling tide of love which flows secretly from God into the soul and draws it mightily back into its Source" (6.22).

Irresistibly, as we have seen, she was drawn to a position of exile and repudiation. But exile from ordinary human companionship was not enough. The "inward tug" that would draw her in time to God drew her first into the darkest depths of abandonment, where even God was only a recollection. The progression, the "pilgrim's progress," is markedly like that of the *Divine Comedy.*[14]

In the last books of Dante's *Inferno,* the pilgrim Dante has traveled to the icy floor of hell itself. There he learns that if he is to reach purgatory, and then paradise, he must approach Lucifer, seize the very hairs on his flanks, and grapple hand over hand downward and thence out. To his amazement, as he climbs, the downward journey begins to point upward. Gravity shifts, and he emerges into the fresh air and sunlight of purgatory mountain.

Mechthild describes the ultimate stages of her own downward travels in two places. The first is in Book 4, and it begins as follows: "When this wonder and this consolation had continued for eight years, God wished to comfort me more mightily, far above my deserts." Mechthild refuses, saying that even the lowly place she occupies at present (the human state) is beyond her merit. At that moment, "the soul fell down below the ill-fated souls who had forfeited their reward, and it seemed good to her so." The Lord follows her there and asks how long she would stay. She asks Him to let her sink further still, whereupon "soul and body came into such gross darkness that I lost light and consciousness and knew no more of God's intimacy." Love itself vanishes. The soul calls upon her allies—Constancy, then Faith, and then each member of the Trinity—for encouragement.

We observed earlier that as Mechthild unfolds the story of her flight to God, new levels of intimacy between God and the soul keep opening out; just so, now, the soul keeps breaking through to new depths of abandonment. Forsakenness comes and surrounds her, and when, to her joy, she finds that her faith is unbroken, we begin to guess her motive for this otherwise inscrutable impulse. She makes it explicit later in the same book. "Souls that are completely surrounded and penetrated by God become stronger with temptation" (4.16). She is tempering the steel of her own will. God offers to cut short her journey into darkness, using language—once again trinitarian—that is fully as passionate as any she has used toward him: "Grant me that I may cool the glow of My Godhead, the desire of My humanity and the delight of My holy spirit in thee." The soul gives the mystic's ultimate answer, "Yea, Lord, but only if that is well for Thee alone—and not for me!"

To the question Mechthild had posed earlier, "Should cramp torture every vein . . . How shall it be then?" she now offers her own answer. Pain has reached its highest power in her: "Such great darkness that sweat and cramp racked her body." And yet, "Ah! Lord! even in the depths of unmixed humility, I cannot sink utterly away from thee. In pride I so easily lost Thee—but now the more deeply I sink the more sweetly I drink of Thee!"

By humility, Mechthild does not mean self-deprecation or what we might today call low self-esteem. She is speaking, rather, of the profound sense of "Thou and I" and the essential difference between the two that the mystic is insisting upon when she speaks of genuine self-knowledge. In Book 5, she describes how one reenters ordinary consciousness after the experience of perfect union. The soul begins to sink and cool, like steam precipitating into water, dropping down into such profound humility that it lands in the lowest place God has in his power.

> When the soul . . . has come to the Mount . . . then it does as pilgrims do who have eagerly climbed a summit. They descend with care lest they fall over a precipice. So it is with the soul. Irradiated by the fire of its long love, overpowered by the embrace of the Holy Trinity, it begins to sink, and to cool—As the sun from its highest zenith sinks down into the night, thus also, God knows, is it with the soul and with the body. (5.4)

Of humility, she remarks further, "It produces much sweet wonder. It chases the soul up into the heavens and draws it down again into the depths."

What Mechthild gives us here is a kind of variant reading of the alternating joy and abandonment that so many mystics undergo, prompting some to speak of "dark nights" of the soul. Love draws us toward God, but the nearer we get to the divine magnificence, the more aware we are of our own relative insignificance. "I was swept up to Thee by Thy Beauty," Augustine grieved, "and torn away from Thee by my own weight" (*Confessions* 7.17). That sinking back into oneself—a kind of embarrassment at one's own presumption—feels to the aspirant like abandonment. And yet, we have already learned that God's grace flows inevitably into the low places, into the waiting souls of the most humble. The soul's movement is like that of a yo-yo; the very force of the downward drop precipitates an equally strong thrust back toward God. "When it has thus climbed to the highest to which it may attain while still companioned by the body and has sunk to the lowest depths it can find, then it is full-grown in virtue and in holiness. But it must yet be adorned with suffering in patient waiting."

The soul is now imperturbable; "Thy going and coming, O Love, are equally welcome to the well-ordered soul" (5.30). What she enjoys above all else is "that in poverty, contempt, misery, days of sorrow, spiritual poverty most of all . . . one can and will rejoice in praising God from the heart" (5.25).[15]

I have drawn a comparison between Mechthild's journey and Dante's, but the need one can feel to enter the part of oneself where all the deepest fears lie and to "experience the worst," at least vicariously, is something many of us have felt at one time or another. One contemporary writer, describing the deterioration of his own eyesight from severe impairment to "deep blindness," speaks of reaching a point within himself finally where he felt he had "touched the rock," that point beyond which he knew there could be no deeper darkness and after touching which a process of healing and integration could begin to take place. The metaphor, if we can even call it that, seems extremely apt, for Mechthild, too, seems to have "touched the rock" of her own absolute faith in God and, simultaneously, in herself. Not, I would surmise, that this touching of the rock is something that takes place only once for any human being.[16]

O F the heavenly things God has shown me," wrote Mechthild, "I can speak but a little word: not more than a honey-bee can carry away on its foot from an over-flowing jar" (3.1). I feel very much that way myself with regard to Mechthild's writings. She was the supreme poet-mystic of her time. Her voices are as varied as a good cabaret singer's: from an exquisitely lyrical passage, all light and piercing sweetness, she can drop into pure, gravelly voiced blues:

> Ever longing in the soul,
> Ever suffering in the body,
> Ever pain in the senses . . .
> Those who have given themselves utterly to God
> Know well what I mean. (7.63)

The content of her teachings is just as rich and varied as the form in which she conveys them. Every time I think I have succeeded in throwing a net of explication out across her writings, I look again and see that their richness and power is spilling out on all sides. Hopeless to capture it all.

What I would like to do in the remainder of this essay is to identify elements in her writing that reflect some of the ways of thinking currently regarded by many of us as feminine. For, like Clare, Mechthild allows us to speculate that whenever women have been free to speak their minds, by whatever historical accident, they do so in that "different voice" and make a particular *kind* of assertion, whatever their context: a preference for concrete and contextual thinking instead abstract analysis, for example, and for modes of relationship that are connective rather than hierarchical, an insistence that a place be given in the scheme of things to flesh itself—to our "embodiedness."

In depicting the relationship between God and the human soul as being connective and dynamic—as opposed to the hierarchic and static model that had dominated earlier thinking and worship—Mechthild echoed several mystics of her time. But she may be unique in her belief in an astonishing reciprocity—one that she herself experienced—between God and the soul. Her book opens, for instance, with the soul's rather strange tribute to love: "Love, thou didst wrestle long years with the Holy Trinity till the overflow fell once and for all in Mary's lap!" We learn the meaning of this image in Book 3, in a mythopoetic account of creation, where we find out that the whole thing was Love's idea—Love in its primordial form, as Holy Spirit. God, we learn, had to be talked into it!

"Everything was enclosed in God just as in a cell without lock or door. The lower part of the cell is a bottomless prison below every abyss. The upper part is a height above all other heights. The circumference of the cell is inconceivable. God had not yet become the Creator" (6.31).

Unhappy with this situation, the Holy Spirit "put a plan gently before the Father and struck the Holy Trinity asunder[!] and said, 'Lord and Father . . . We will no longer be unfruitful! We will have a creative Kingdom. . . . For that alone is Joy which . . . we share with others in Thy presence.'" The plan is accepted, and God the Father gets right into the spirit of things: "I will make myself a Bride who shall greet Me with her mouth and wound Me with her glance. Then first will love begin." The very suggestion that the Trinity was unstable enough to be "struck asunder" startles us, as does the notion that God himself, the all-powerful Father/King/Judge, might have *chosen* to subject himself to Love's power. There is probably a theological basis for this account of creation, but surely it has never been rendered with such a fine sense of theater.

For Mechthild, reality was not held in place by a set of irrevocable and unalterable laws. Love, which is interchangeable with Holy Spirit, can turn everything upside down whenever she chooses, and Love acts upon God, for the most part, through the human soul. While the motif of "frozen" and incommunicative masculinity that is thawed and humanized by the warmth of an ardent young woman is a staple of romantic literature from Jane Eyre on out, we are taken aback to find it in the writing of a medieval mystic. Again and again, it is visible in Mechthild's dialogues between God and the soul. In one passage, God says of the soul: "It flows right through My Three Persons and moves and charms and makes for love" (5.25). And later, "Before the world was I longed for thee; I long for thee and thou for Me. When two burning desires come together then is love perfected!" (7.16).

So "head over heels" in love is the first person of the Trinity that the soul is able to intercede repeatedly on behalf of other souls, persuading God, in several cases, to throw out the book and set aside the laws he himself has established. Some of the most extraordinary passages in Mechthild's writings are those that describe her encounters with souls in purgatory and in hell, and her subsequent negotiations with God. One is reminded at times of Dante but also, disconcertingly, of a staple theme in a certain kind of historical novel: the beautiful young woman from the north who marries a plantation owner and ultimately gets him to free his slaves.

In one instance, Mechthild goes boldly to God and asks him to let her be a ransom for the prisoners of hell. God allows her to lead him down into hell, to a vile pool of pitch and dirt where the souls "stewed and roasted together" in an unspeakable kind of bouillabaisse. After God explains all that Mechthild is seeing, she lies down at his feet and asks mercy for them. God obliges. "Thou didst well to bring me here. I will not be unmindful of them." He takes them to a flowery hillside and waits on them like a servant and companion. Their sentence has been cut short, but how long must they wait here now? "As long as seems good to us." Note the final pronoun.

Again Mechthild recalls, "I, poor wretch, was so bold in my prayer as to lift corrupt Christianity in the arms of my soul and hold it up in lamentation. Our Lord said, 'Let be! 'Tis too heavy for thee!'" God lets her have her will, though. She carries Christianity to his feet, and the two gaze upon her in grief and shame. She is a "poor maid . . . half blind in her understanding and crippled in her hands, which do no good works . . . lame in the feet of her desire for she thinks seldom and idly of me . . . unhealthy in her skin, unclean and impure." God tells Mechthild he will wash the maiden clean in his own blood, and that her very book is part of the way he will do this, for "My heart's blood . . . is written in this book" (5.34).

In still another of these episodes, rescued sinners emerge before God and the human spirit, "blackened, burned, dirty, bleeding, reeking." What to do with them? God says that the human spirit can bathe them in tears of love. A great basin appears, into which the wretched souls plunge and are "bathed in Love bright as the sun" (2.8). Much, much later, Mechthild explains to us exactly how such a basin is filled:

> Great is the overflow of Divine Love which is never still but ever
> ceaselessly and tirelessly pours forth, so that our little vessel is
> filled to the brim and overflows. If we do not choke the channel
> with self-will, God's gifts continue to flow and overflow, Lord!
> Thou art full, and fillest us also with Thy gifts. Thou art great and
> we are small, how then shall we become like Thee? (7.55)

Our tears of love pour *through* our eyes, but they come from God.

What we have in these dramatic vignettes is a kind of allegory of a traditional Christian theme, one of the Christian mysteries, in a sense: the relationship between God's justice and God's mercy. Typically, of course, it is Christ who represents or embodies God's mercy. But in a dream-vision Mechthild described near the very end of her book, all of humanity is marching toward God, each at his or her own pace, and along the way two figures appear. One is God's Righteousness, and the other his traveling companion, a maiden. She has entered the world through Christ.

> Compassion is her name; All who seek and call upon her stead-
> fastly conquer the sorrow of their hearts. She is very perfect. She
> has taken my righteousness from me. Where trouble comes to
> man and he flees to her in remorse, she lays her gentle hand on
> what is crooked, while I stand by powerless and dumb and cannot
> withstand her . . . *She has taken much power away from me.* She
> loves me and I love her. (italics mine)

This is one of those texts where a dream-vision becomes almost mythic in its suggestive power: "the feminine" has affected "the mascu-line," reshaping the whole structure of salvation, and everyone is the happier for it. We begin to see how it is that Jesus took on an increasingly feminine aspect during the thirteenth and fourteenth centuries.

ONE finds throughout traditional mystical writings a tendency to revile the body as a brutish obstacle to achieving union with God.
Contemporary women strongly resist this kind of language, and rightly,
I think, for we sense in its cruelty the origin, or at least foreshadowing,
of the hostility toward the feminine body that is so evident in contemporary culture. (While it is true that medieval mystics were not repudiating feminine flesh alone, but all human flesh, women were much more
heavily identified with the body for many reasons, including the fact that
woman was believed quite literally to "give flesh" to the infant during
pregnancy.)[17] One would hope that perhaps women mystics were less
likely than their male counterparts to be dismissive or contemptuous of
the body: we would like to think that Sara Ruddick's observations hold
true even here—her attribution to women, that is, of a strong sense of the
"histories of flesh," the marvelous *value* of every man, woman, and child,
even as physical beings.

Mechthild was certainly speaking in the spirit of her age when she
wrote lines like the following: "When I came to the spiritual life and took
leave of the world I looked at my body—it was heavily armed against my
poor soul with . . . the full powers of nature. I saw it was my enemy . . . "
(4.2). Overall, though, she is considerably gentler than the norm in this
regard, and even a little humorous. She will speak of the body as the
Bride's packhorse, with a note of affection, just as Saint Francis had
called the body "Brother Ass." But more typically she characterizes the
body as a dim-witted or timorous retainer. (One thinks, in fact, of Juliet's
nurse, dithering on endlessly and comically about her lady, yet proving
utterly incapable, finally, of understanding the depth of Juliet's love for
Romeo, so that at last Juliet had to cut her out of her confidence and
carry on alone.) On one occasion, the soul has slipped away from the
body to receive a "greeting the body may not know," and the body com-
plains afterward: "Where have you been? I can bear this no more!" The
soul replies much as a headstrong young Juliet would have, "Silence! You
are a fool! I will be with my Love even if you never recover!" (1.2).

On the other hand, Mechthild later describes the faithful soul
"leading the senses after it as a man with sight might lead one who was
blind" (1.26). The paradox—the assertion that the senses are blind—is
arresting, and so is the implicit kindness. It is telling, too, that on the occasion when she rejected the counsel of the senses and sent away her

handmaidens so that she could seek full mystical union, she comforted them: "Be not troubled! You still will teach me. When I return I will need your teaching, for the earth is full of snares." The body and senses are useful and worthy, as servants and sometime counselors, as long as their limitations are understood. And they will be rewarded, for she writes of love, "It wanders through the senses and storms with all virtues on the soul . . . melts through the soul into the senses, that the body also may have its share, for it is drawn into all things" (5.4).

Finally, there is Mechthild's tender farewell to the body, given at the very end of her book:

> Ah! Beloved prison in which I have been bound, I thank thee for all in which thou hast followed me. Though I have often been troubled by thee, yet didst thou often come to my aid. All thy need will yet be taken from thee at the last Day. Therefore we will lament no more, but will be filled with gladness for all that God has done to us both. Now let us only stand fast in sweet hope!

Whatever harsh words ascetics might have had for the recalcitrant body, God had nonetheless honored human flesh by assuming it, and it followed that *all* human flesh deserves our reverence. The great heretics of Mechthild's time were the Cathars, who taught a kind of gnostic repudiation of everything fleshly. Late in her book, perhaps as an explicit rejection of that heresy, Mechthild speaks of what she understands to be the greatest sin of all:

> I have heard of a certain sin. I thank God that I do not know of it for it seems to me of all sins the worst, for it is the height of unbelief. . . . I thank Jesus Christ the living Son of God that it never entered my heart. , , , They would fain be so holy as to draw themselves up into the eternal Godhead and pass by the eternal holy humanity of our Lord Jesus Christ. (7.47)

Mechthild's passionate devotion to Christ's humanity blossomed quite naturally into a rich appreciation of his mother. Mary is first introduced in Book 1, not simply as the historic Mary but as the spiritual mother of all humanity—the Mother of Sorrows, near equivalent, symbolically,

of Christ himself. In fact, Mechthild's imagery almost conflates the two figures.[18] (Observe that Mary is speaking in the first paragraph, while there-
after it is Mechthild herself):

> . . . I suckled the prophets and sages, before God was born. Later
> on, during my childhood, I suckled Jesus, and during my youth I
> suckled God's Bride, holy Christianity, at the cross, and I became
> emaciated and miserable at the thought that the sword which in-
> flicts physical pain should cut Jesus spiritually in my soul.
>
> There they were both opened, his wounds and her breasts. The
> wounds poured out and the breasts flowed, so that the soul quick-
> ened and was even cured. As he poured the bright red wine into
> her red mouth, she was born out of the open wounds and quick-
> ened; she was childlike and very young. In order to recuperate
> completely after her death and her birth, she needed the Mother
> of God as mother and nurse. God, it was and is right. God was her
> rightful father and she His rightful bride, and she is like Him in all
> her sufferings. (1.22, trans. Galvani)

Mary and Christianity are each identified as God's bride. Both
Mary and Jesus suckle the child that is Christianity, she with her breasts
and he with his wounds, but when Jesus pours the wine that is his blood
into the child's mouth, "she" has become the soul. Is the *she* of that final
sentence Mary, Holy Church, or the individual soul? I would guess that
it is all of them. Subsequently, in any event, Mechthild addresses Mary.

> Lady, at your age you suckled the Holy Apostles with your mater-
> nal teachings and your fervent prayers . . . you are suckling to this
> day martyrs with great faith . . . maidens with your chastity, wid-
> ows with constancy, fools with kindness, sinners with intercession.
>
> Lady, now you must suckle us, for your breasts are still so full
> that you cannot suppress it. If you no longer wished to suckle, the
> milk would cause you much pain. . . . (1.22, trans. Galvani)

If Mechthild has not bothered to keep her *dramatis personae* separate,
it may well be because for her, ultimately, they are not separate. We are all
acting out the same drama, in a sense, and that is the eternal one at the very
heart of life. We struggle endlessly to learn what life means and what we are

here for, and yet the answer etched out in the life of Christ and discovered by everyone who follows him is relatively simple: we are here to give and cleanse and nourish, and to the extent that we do, we will be fed and sustained in turn. Whether one is God, Mary, Christ, or any ordinary human being, the nourishment that we offer another—the wine and blood and tears, the milk and water and honey— all of this richness flows directly and solely out of whatever depths we have carved out within ourselves.

> Even though we are as a small vessel, yet Thou hast filled it. . . .
> We alas! are so small that a little word of God or of Holy Scripture
> so utterly fills us that we can hold no more. Then we empty this
> gift into the large vessel which is God. How can we do this? We
> must pour out what we have received with holy desire on sinners,
> that they may be cleansed. But now the vessel is full again! . . .
> Again we pour it out, on the needs of poor souls who suffer in
> Purgatory. . . . God loved us from the beginning; He has laboured
> for us from the beginning and has suffered greatly for us. If we
> would be like Him we must give it all back to him. (7.55)

The imagery here is clarified if we recall the basin mentioned above, full of tears, in which, Mechthild has learned, she and people like her could bathe sinners. What prompts us to shed those tears, it was explained, is our love for God, which is elicited in turn by our receiving the Word of God. Weeping those tears of love, then, is merely our "passing on" the river of grace that has been pouring into our own hearts. Implicit is the understanding, once again, that opening oneself to God's love means opening oneself to suffering as well, both personal and vicarious. The volume of the vessel has much to do with the volume of sorrow one has accepted, but that very acceptance comes of a deliberate openness of heart and mind:

> Nay! Sister! Before all things thou must have breadth of under-
> standing, then only canst thou attain a willing heart and an open
> soul into which grace may flow. If without advice thou make thy
> need too narrow, then thou wilt never be ready for the height of
> holy desire, nor the breadth of Divine perception nor the depth of
> the flowing sweetness of God. (5.11)

One sees a distinction drawn often today between two different "ways of knowing": the "separate," and, by contrast, the "connective" ways.[19] The first, which involves "mastery" of a subject, is the mode that traditional educational systems celebrate, and it is believed to be rather more congenial to men than to women. The second, seen as more typically feminine, has more to do with intuition rather than logical deduction. It entails a kind of patient regard, an opening of oneself toward the subject and a postponement, as long as possible, of "closure."

On the face of things, we might be tempted to see connective knowing as more inherently "mystical," and, again, on the face of things, we can see in the mystic Mechthild an extraordinarily connective mode of knowing. But in marveling at the richness of her imagery of flow and connectedness, we need to recognize that she experienced a transcendent God as well as an immanent God, and she celebrated both. When she writes of "the powerful penetration of all things and the special intimacy that ever exists between God and the human soul," she is certainly writing in a connective mode. But she could write just as thrillingly of a transcendent God. Of her vision of the court of heaven, she said, "Above the Throne of God is nothing but God, God, God, immense, great God" (3.11). The transcendence we impute to God appears to answer a human need as real as the need for connectedness. This world of becoming, throughout which God apparently spread divine being, and in which our own fleshly being takes part, is subject to change and decay. If God would be God, we require him or her to be transcendent too—to be one as well as many—pure being, outside time and limited to no bodily form. Upward the soul struggles toward God, then downward it plunges into humility. Up once again, and then down, over and over. Mechthild knew the immanent and the transcendent and celebrated both in a continuous, ecstatic dance.[20]

And yet she remains, in our mind's eye, a lonely figure, battered by time and circumstance, compelled to speak in her own authentic voice no matter what the cost. She could not have suppressed that voice if she had tried: "Fish gotta swim, birds gotta fly." At one point God offered her a simple exchange: "Give me all that thine is, and I will give you all that mine is," and she agreed to the terms. She never regretted it, but she never pretended it had been easy. In her very last days, she wrote of her soul, endearing her everlastingly to those of us who are "of a certain age":

Alas! now in my old age . . . it no longer has youth to help it to bear the fiery love of God. It is also impatient, for little ills afflict it much which in youth it hardly noticed. . . . Seven years ago a troubled old soul lamented these weaknesses to our Lord. (7.3)

God's reply is marvelous, addressing her once again as the human reflection of the Trinity, but in the homeliest language imaginable. Now she is God's *hausfrau:* "Thy childhood was a companion of My Holy Spirit; thy youth was a bride of My humanity, in thine old age thou art a humble housewife of My Godhead."

Because we know so little of Mechthild's life, and because her writings are so complex as to require a more "literary" mode of interpretation than those of our other subjects, I was briefly tempted to omit her from this inquiry, despite my enormous affection for her. No sooner had I considered doing so, however, than I realized that Mechthild, whose writings very nearly didn't come down to us at all, is the voice for all the women mystics who remain silent—silenced, in many cases. A tremendous poignancy pervades her story.

Mechthild had bad days, and since she was never in the running for sainthood, no one ever rubbed out the things she wrote on those days. Thanks to her we know that mystics do not always live happily ever after and that human frailty does not vanish just because one has experienced "the true greeting of God." With Mechthild I think we can see clearly the enormous courage it requires to follow the law of one's own being. Her extraordinary poetic gifts allowed her to make relatively concrete and comprehensible some of the more recondite truths of the mystical experience. Late in life she composed a perfect memorial to herself.

> See there within the flesh
> Like a bright wick, englazed
> The soul God's finger lit
> To give her liberty,
> And joy and power and love,
> To make her crystal, like
> As maybe, to Himself. (7.1)

Julian of Norwich

(1342–1416?)

For I saw no wrath except on man's side, and He forgives that in us.

> —Julian of Norwich,
> Long Text of *Showings* 48

This fair lovely word "mother" is so sweet and so kind in itself that it cannot truly be said of anyone or to anyone except of him and to him who is the true Mother of life and of all things. To the property of motherhood belong nature, love, wisdom and knowledge, and this is God.

> —Julian of Norwich,
> Long Text of *Showings* 60

WHEN we look at the life and work of Julian of Norwich, what comes into focus is the issue of the relationship between the mystic—any mystic—and her received religion. From early childhood, a Mechthild or a Clare absorbs the basic teachings of her faith through both Scripture and oral transmission: a rich and often bewildering mix of story, precept, history, lyric poetry, and prophetic vision. Eventually, when she has experienced firsthand the truth that is at the core of her religion, she in turn draws upon that mélange to frame and describe her own experience. Even as she is using the language of her own tradition, though, she alters it. Irreverently, she corrects its excesses; reverently, she breathes new life into old doctrines.

Because they open out and illuminate the spiritual traditions they inherit, mystics are our greatest liberators, and Julian of Norwich is among the foremost of these. Her teachings are as exhilarating as any I can think of, and they are cast in a prose that does them full justice: simple and clear, devoid of affectation, yet hauntingly musical throughout. Chaucer's exact contemporary, Julian was the first woman to write a book in English. She gave it no title; it has come down to us as *A Book of Showings to the Anchoress Julian of Norwich.*

Julian wrote only that one book, but to the intense satisfaction of the scholarly world, she wrote it twice. She wrote it once soon after undergoing a series of mystical experiences, "showings," in the vocabulary of her time, that occurred over slightly more than twenty-four hours in May 1373. She wrote it again some twenty years later, and this time it came out about two and a half times as long. For twenty years after the showings, she received continuous "inward instruction" on their meaning. "Freely and often" God would bring the whole revelation, from beginning to end, before the "eyes of her understanding," initiating her little by little into its full depth of meaning. Over time Julian realized that her initial report had been little more than a bare outline. Accordingly, she made a great many small emendations in the Short Text and inserted large blocks of new material throughout, particularly in the latter half of her narrative.[1]

Taken together, the changes Julian made record a fundamental transformation in the author's own perception of herself. Over the two decades following her revelations, the astonished visionary evolved gradually into a confident, fully established spiritual teacher. In the Short Text, she wrote, "God forbid that you should say or assume that I am a teacher, for that is not and never was my intention; for I am a woman, ignorant, weak and frail" (Short Text 6). Twenty years later, she removed this disclaimer, for by then she had accepted her role as spiritual counselor, knowing full well by that time that whatever she might accomplish in that role was not her own doing anyway, but God's.

All of the material Julian added seems intended to move the reader away from the sort of unexamined conventional religious beliefs that can impede genuine spiritual growth. At regular intervals, indeed, one prominent Catholic writer or another feels compelled to step forward and insist that Julian's teachings really are orthodox. Their sensitivity on this point is understandable, because her teachings on sin and forgiveness and on the motherhood of God, which have won her such a wide following in recent years, do not look like what most of us imagine "mainstream" Catholic doctrine to be. I will make these particular teachings the focal point of this essay because they really do have extraordinary appeal for modern seekers. First, though, we would know all that we can of Julian herself. Once again, we must content ourselves with stray bits of biographical data and a good measure of historical reconstruction. Once again, what we have is not so much the record of life as it is a voice, and Julian's is every bit as distinctive and powerful as Mechthild's.

Between Julian of Norwich and contemporary readers, however, two formidable barriers interpose themselves. One is her religious vocation. For she was a recluse, an anchoress, whose calling entailed a more drastic withdrawal from ordinary life than even the cloistered nuns of her time had undertaken. Many of us are willing to read books like Anne Morrow Lindbergh's *Gift from the Sea* and Annie Dillard's *Pilgrim at Tinker Creek* and grant that three weeks by the sea or a summer in the woods can be enormously therapeutic. But the prospect of being walled up for life, voluntarily, is a different thing altogether. Can we really open ourselves fully to the teachings of someone who has made that choice?

Second, and this is a much more complex issue, Julian was above all else a visionary. She founded no order, she set up no hospital or school, she launched no reform movement. She simply *saw*, and, realizing that what she had seen was not intended for her alone, she reported it back to the rest of us. She did so with such detachment and coolheadedness that she has won extravagant praise from scholars and theologians who have little good to say for women visionaries in general.

Visionary writing, particularly by women, has waited a long time to receive the informed and sympathetic reading it deserves. Its emotional intensity, imaginative flights, and erotic imagery have alienated more than a few male medieval scholars, for whom these qualities can seem as symptomatic of hysteria or irrationality as they are of sanctity. A thinly veiled misogyny haunts much of this kind of scholarship. On the other hand, none of us is altogether free of skepticism where visionary writings are concerned, and there is no reason why we should be. Suppose, after all, that a friend or relative claimed to have had "showings." Under what circumstances might you listen—with interest, even, let alone credulity? You might accept that she has "seen" something outside ordinary sensory experience, though you would probably feel better about the whole business if she said she had dreamed it. You might "believe" her in the sense of accepting that for *her* the thing she has seen has weight and meaning. But what might persuade you that it had weight or meaning for you as well? If we are going to spend time in the presence of a Julian— or a Catherine of Siena, as we will see shortly—it behooves us to weigh thoughtfully our feelings about visions and people who claim to have had them.

It has helped me a good deal first to identify these two sources of difficulty, and then to address them by learning all I could about Julian's own world. Medieval historians and literary scholars have pulled together a considerable body of information about the anchoritic life and about the city of Norwich. They have also given us a perspective on visionary activity itself and what it would have meant in Julian's time and place. With their help, then, let us reconstruct Julian's life as best we can.

Julian states in both texts of the *Showings* that in May 1373, when she received her revelations, she was thirty-and-a-half years old. This would place her birth date somewhere around December 1342. Historical evidence indicates she was still alive in 1416 and that she lived in a cell adjoining the parish church of Saint Julian in Conisford at Norwich, "opposite the house of the Augustinian Friars." Beyond this, we know virtually nothing of her life—not even her name, for she probably took the name Julian from the church where she was enclosed.

The word *anchoress* is a cognate of a Greek verb that means "to retire." In early Christianity, anchorites withdrew to the desert for the sake of undistracted prayer and meditation. By Julian's time, though, the withdrawal of anchorites and anchoresses was not as extreme. They remained in towns or villages, enclosed, typically, in cells built right up against the walls of churches.[2] The ceremony of enclosure (one, at least, that has survived), was for all practical purposes a kind of burial. Extreme unction was given, and the anchorite was literally sealed in, obliged under threat of excommunication to remain there until death. Through a window or "squint," she could watch and hear the church service;

through another that opened out to the world, she could give spiritual counsel, and that she was expected to do.

The purpose of anchoritic enclosure was not heroic asceticism, however, but rather a complete openness to God in prayer. Julian's way of life would have been rigorous, therefore, but not impossibly austere. Rules written for anchoresses during the early Middle Ages indicate that Julian would have had at least one fair-sized room, possibly several, with her own oratory. The window that opened out for those who sought her advice might have opened onto a parlor, sheltered from the weather. She would have had a maid to cook and clean for her—one bequest that mentions Julian by name mentions her maid Alice as well—and probably a cat to catch mice. Her diet would have been simple but not meager by the standard of the day. The terms of enclosure often included permission to walk in the church courtyard or even an adjoining garden. Julian would have been expected to recite the full office each day, beginning well before dawn, but she would have been encouraged to dress warmly enough to do this in reasonable comfort.

We might still shudder at the whole idea of such radical enclosure, but we must bear in mind, too, that the gifted artist in any medium requires a measure of silence and privacy, and the man or woman with a bent for contemplative prayer—a genius for inwardness itself—is no exception. The crowded, noisy interior of most households of the time would have made serious meditation impossible. An ordinary medieval convent, however austere and constrained it might look to you and me, might not have been much better. Julian's anchorhold was the condition that allowed her to go as deeply inward as she could, free of external distractions. It was, quite simply and necessarily, a room of her own—a privilege rarely available to women of any time or place, but one for which they have regularly been willing to pay as high a price as Julian did.

Norwich itself, moreover, was nobody's sleepy village in the countryside. It was a noisy, lively seaport through which most of England's European textile trade passed (England's southern ports were unusable at the time because of piracy). Its population was greater than any town's in England outside of London. Saint Julian's was one of about a hundred churches the townspeople had become prosperous enough to build.

All the mendicant preaching orders had establishments in Norwich. Through them, and through members of a nearby Benedictine

abbey, Julian could easily have gained access to the most important theological ideas of her time. She may even have been a Benedictine nun before becoming an anchorite; we have no idea when she entered her
anchorhold and what her status was before that time. Even as an anchorite, she might have borrowed books from the Augustinians across
the street. Interestingly, too, Norwich was the one town in England
where a community of Beguines had established itself; Julian could easily have been associated with them as well.

The roadway that carried goods out of Norwich went right past the
Church of Saint Julian. From her cell Julian probably heard the wagons
rumbling by—and a good deal more. Historian Barbara Tuchman called
the fourteenth century a "calamitous time," for it was a period of almost
unparalleled human distress. Bubonic plague swept through Norwich for
the first time in January 1349 when Julian was just six, but it would recur
over and over during her lifetime. At the height of an outbreak, carts
would pass through the streets at night and collect the dead, removing
them to mass graves outside the city. Cattle diseases combined with dis-
astrously bad harvests to bring about famine and, subsequently, violent
social unrest. The Hundred Years' War between France and England had
broken out in 1337, and in 1377 the Great Schism commenced—the terrible time of "two churches" with two popes, each regarding the other
as the Antichrist. During the last decades of the century, disgusted by the
worldly excesses of England's churchmen, John Wycliffe and his followers, called Lollards, rose up in protest. In consequence, they were declared heretics and put to death, burned, many of them, at the Lollards'
Pit, not far from Julian's cell.

Filling in the picture around Julian is useful in many ways. It forces
us to revise our most simplistic conceptions of her lifestyle. It helps us
recognize that her ideas did not develop in a cultural vacuum: that the
full spectrum of theological doctrines was available to her. As we place
Julian in context, we are reminded, too, that the full extent of human suffering was continuously visible to her, rendering all the more impressive
the joyous optimism that permeates her teachings.

I love knowing she had a maidservant and probably a cat. I would
like to think she was among the anchoresses who had to be cautioned
against spending time teaching the little girls of the neighborhood to
read. And like every medieval scholar I know, I love to imagine the visit

that Margery Kempe paid Julian in 1413. We know about this only because Margery herself wrote about it. In retrospect it looks like something of a summit meeting, because Julian is the first woman known to have written in English, and Margery is the first individual of either sex to write her memoirs in English. Margery was a garrulous and essentially likable figure, a perpetual pilgrim whom someone has playfully designated a "paramystic" (not fully qualified perhaps but, like a paramedic, better in a pinch than no mystic at all). Margery consulted Julian about her spiritual difficulties because she was said to be "expert in such things and good counsel could give." The advice she says Julian gave her is very much in keeping with what Julian has said elsewhere. We smile at the probable contrast: Margery in her perpetual dither and Julian—for we can't imagine her otherwise—perfectly serene. "And all shall be well, and every kind of thing shall be well."

Even when we have put all of this together, though, the blank space in the middle remains, for of the actual events of Julian's personal life we still know next to nothing. All we really know about Julian is what she said about God, and how we receive that—whether we give it more than passing intellectual approbation—seems to depend rather heavily on what we think about visions and visionaries in general.

Some of Julian's most ardent admirers are so uncomfortable with visionary writing that they tend to downplay the fact that Julian was a visionary at all. One maintains that "Julian's importance as a mystic is due not so much to her experience of extraordinary phenomena—including her visions of May, 1373—as to her theological position."[3] Are we then to regard the visions, with their wealth of imagery, as a mere jumping-off point for the more respectable act of discursive thinking? On the contrary. What draws us so powerfully to the *Showings,* and what persuades us that they are authentic, is not just Julian's theology, but the force and the beauty with which she communicated it, and these arose out of Julian's direct, unmediated encounter with God—out of her *visions,* that is.[4]

The difficulties most of us have with visionary literature are related to how we construe reality in the first place, and that is to a considerable extent culturally determined. Examining the perceptual differences between us and our counterparts in the Middle Ages, historian Carolly Erickson characterizes our own perception of the universe as "controlled, atomistic and one-dimensional," in contrast to the "chaotic, holistic and multi-dimensional reality" within which men and women of Julian's time lived.[5] Most of humankind, she reminds us—nearly all those who lived in times past, and a great many living even now, outside industrialized society—have subscribed to that richer, multidimensional world. Inherently "more real" than everyday reality, this noncorporeal world has always been thought to surround and sustain it and to percolate up into it at regular intervals, visible and audible for those who are attuned to its presence. Erickson writes,

> Our lexicon associates visions with mysticism, irrationality, occultism, impracticality and madness. From our point of view the visionary is a person who sees what isn't there; his visions separate him from reality. In the middle ages, visions defined reality. . . .[6]
>
> Medieval men and women blended the evidence of their senses with firm convictions about the presence and power of unseen creation. Their concept of the real embraced much that we would now call imaginary; planes of truth we perceive as distinct and clashing they saw as concurrent parts of a harmonious whole.
>
> To accommodate this understanding they engaged in a continuous vigil with the visible world, believing that from time to time it yielded evidence of the more powerful realm of the invisible. This vigil was continuously rewarded by messages, warnings, clarifications and revelations communicated to the visionary imagination. Most important, it was encouraged by the enduring belief that spiritual understanding was linked to visual acuity—that man's perception of God would ultimately come through the purification of his sight.[7]

Julian is full of wonder as the showings unfold before her, but she is calm and trustful, too. To a modern reader, her self-possession seems remarkable. Erickson's reading of the period makes it less so, for Erickson observes that when you live in a culture that accepts the authenticity of visions, you know roughly how to behave when the ground trembles and the room starts to glow. Julian maintains that her revelations are fully equivalent to Scripture as a source of truth. Indeed, so confident is she that her experiences do not depart or conflict with Scripture in any way that she invites others to regard them in the same light.

The Long Text is certainly the more comprehensive of Julian's two texts, but it is useful to read the Short Text first as a kind of fast-paced synopsis of the much longer and more complex later work.[8] The Short Text begins abruptly, in the first person, "I desired . . . " and recounts the whole experience in just twenty-five short chapters, making no attempt to catalog its elements. At first Julian believed the showings were a form of final temptation, a kind of trial before a death she thought imminent. As the hours passed, she realized she was not going to die immediately after all and that the experience must have wider meaning. It was not at all clear to her, however, what that meaning might be. She made relatively little effort to interpret what happened and in fact omitted certain details that she would include later, because at the time they made no sense to her.

This preliminary account, then, concerns itself with the illumination of a single soul and the subsequent testing of that soul's capacity to cling to divine truth, even against the powers of hell (an ordeal that takes place in the final revelation, complete with the stench of sulfurous smoke). The entire adventure takes place within a little more than twenty-four hours and leaves the protagonist triumphantly and permanently united with Christ.

Because the Short Text implies that all of us can expect our faith to be tested as Julian's was, in a single, dramatic, once-and for-all instance, it is of limited use as spiritual counsel. When Julian wrote the Long Text, an experienced counselor now, she set out to correct this impression in a host of ways, suggesting instead that the real challenge of the spiritual life lies in the way we meet with the daily, uneventful bitterness of existence apart from God. This time she distanced herself from the narrative a little, beginning now with an impersonal catalog of sixteen distinct showings and slipping only gradually into the first-person mode. Now she treated the revelations even more emphatically as Scripture—a God-given allegory, meant for all Christians, whose surface had to be scanned over and over before its full significance would yield itself. Julian's "detachment" from what she had written down—the words of the Short Text were to her as sacred as any Gospel, and she was merely its exegete—amounts to a brilliant way around the barriers that might otherwise have kept her from writing.

Since Julian tells us in the Long Text that there were sixteen revelations in all, the reader anticipates there will be sixteen actual visions—things seen. But the imagery of a particular showing is not always mentioned in the catalog, and many of the showings consist entirely of what we might think of as insights or pieces of understanding, accompanied by no image at all. For Julian, though, these less concrete showings are as distinctly "showings" as are the more highly pictorial revelations. By listing them as showings, Julian insists that she has experienced them firsthand. She has felt them—one remembers Mechthild—in her very bones. Indeed, she will sometimes say that in addition to "seeings," she has "touchings," by which she means forms of understanding that are not merely cerebral at all.

Julian begins her account of the revelations by describing her request for "three graces by the gift of God." She herself, that is, by God's grace, had initiated the whole process. The first grace she requested was "recollection of the Passion." She wanted to experience not Christ's own suffering (she seems to feel that would have been presumptuous), but the vicarious suffering of those who witnessed his. She wanted, second, to experience an illness so severe that she and everyone around her would think her to be dying. She even suggested a time: it should occur when she was thirty, Christ's age at the time of the crucifixion. She hoped that by enduring all the pains and terrors of death, she would live "more to His glory" afterward. The third desire was for three wounds: "The wound of contrition, the wound of compassion and the wound of longing with my will for God."

A story that begins with three wishes is off to a familiar enough start, and indeed, the sheer wondrousness of what transpires partakes of the order of magic. The first wish granted is for severe illness. Julian's description of the ordeal is riveting. Her curate administers last rites and sets a cross before her eyes. Gradually her sight fails so that she can see nothing clearly but the crucifix. She documents the experience carefully, recalling, "My greatest pain was my shortness of breath and the ebbing of my life." Then "suddenly"—a word she uses over and over—the pain vanishes and she feels herself to be quite sound. She remembers now to ask for her first grace, recollection of Christ's passion.

Blood begins to flow copiously from under the crown on Christ's head. This is the first incursion of that noncorporeal world, and Julian's description, startlingly concrete and curiously matter-of-fact, does indeed suggest that this is a "more real" world than any with which we are familiar. The language has a somewhat hallucinogenic quality. Notice, too, in how many ways it conveys abundance, much as Mechthild did with her "flood tide" of God's love:

> The great drops of blood fell from beneath the crown like pellets, looking as if they came from the veins, and as they issued they were a brownish red, for the blood was very thick, and as they spread they turned bright red. And as they reached the brows they vanished; and even so the bleeding continued until I had seen and understood many things. Nevertheless, the beauty and the vivacity persisted . . . The copiousness resembles the drops of water which fall from the eaves of a house after a great shower of rain, falling so thick that no human ingenuity can count them. And in their roundness as they spread over the forehead they were like a herring's scales. . . . This vision was living and vivid and hideous and fearful and sweet and lovely. . . .
>
> (Long Text 7)

Since this showing is presumably God's response to Julian's request for deeper feeling of Christ's sorrows, we are braced for expressions of grief or torment on Julian's part. But in fact her tone is exuberant.

The blood goes on flowing throughout a complex series of teachings that together comprise the first showing. The vision of the bleeding Christ functions as a kind of transitional zone from normal waking consciousness to a more inward state and a different kind of seeing, a "seeing" that is more like understanding. At several points the seer seems to "bob up" to a state of mind close to normal waking consciousness, but upon seeing the bleeding crucifix, she drops down again into the realm where the showings impart themselves.

Julian places special importance on this first showing, claiming that in it all the others were "founded and connected." It contains a series of teachings. Those accompanied by images Julian calls "bodily sights." Others, more abstract, she calls "spiritual sights." She also offers illustrative images that are of her own coining. This, for example, is one of several that prefigures her celebrated teaching on the motherhood of God:

> I saw that he is to us everything which is good and comforting for our help. He is our clothing, who wraps and enfolds us for love, embraces us and shelters us, surrounds us for his love, which is so tender that he may never desert us.

She follows this with a "bodily sight" that would surely delight the astronauts of our own time:

> And in this he showed me something small, no bigger than a hazelnut, lying in the palm of my hand, . . . as round as a ball. I looked at it with the eye of my understanding and thought: What can this be? I was amazed that it could last, for I thought that because of its littleness it would suddenly have fallen into nothing. And I was answered in my understanding: It lasts and always will, because God loves it; and thus everything has being through the love of God.
>
> (Long Text 5)

Julian wants us to see, as she did, how incidental the created world is, compared to its creator. (She has second thoughts about the way she has stated things, so she comes back in a few pages to make sure she does not sound unappreciative of the created universe. In language that recalls that of Saint Francis, she explains: "I know well that heaven and earth and all creation are great, generous, and beautiful and good. But the reason why it seemed to my eyes so little was because I saw it in the presence of him who is the Creator.") She celebrates the generosity of creation in a passage whose exceedingly down-to-earth meaning has only recently been recognized:

> A man walks upright, and the food in his body is shut in as if in a well-made purse. When the time of his necessity comes, the purse is opened and then shut again, in most seemly fashion. And it is God who does this, as it is shown when he says that he comes down to us in our humblest needs.
>
> (Long Text 6)

She is describing here nothing more exalted than a bowel movement, and God's own generosity in devising a system so "seemly."

I SPOKE earlier about how the mystic often has to reconcile her own experience of divine truth with the content of her received faith; but in fact I cannot think of another mystic who was pressed in this regard as much as Julian. She was pressed, but she pressed in turn, asking over and over for clearer understanding. She is the ideal student, the one whose rejection of facile answers forces the teacher to a level of clarity that more passive students will never elicit. She is absolutely confident that God wants us to ask. "Truly of his great goodness he wishes that we desire to know" (Long Text 44). Repeatedly, too, she remarks how "courteously" he gives her the space and time to take it all in.

Julian really did need "space and time," because she had fudged a bit when she insisted in the Short Text, "I never understood anything from it [the revelations] which bewilders me or keeps me from the true doctrine of Holy Church" (Short Text 6). Much later, she admitted that she *had* felt there to be a troubling discrepancy (or at least an apparent one, for she hurried to blame her own faulty perception).

Sin was the problem: Holy Church seemed to say one thing, the God of her revelations another. The teachings of the church had given Julian to understand that we are sinners before a justly wrathful God, and that many of us are such inveterate and irredeemable sinners that we will be condemned to eternal sorrow. They had led her to understand also that God is omnipotent and omniscient. The question that apparently elicited the thirteenth revelation was simply this: How could it be that "the great prescient wisdom of God" had not prevented sin?

Jesus first answers her question in words that T. S. Eliot has immortalized: "Sin is necessary, but all will be well, and all will be well, and every kind of thing will be well." The phrases are beautiful, but they do not constitute the answer Julian is looking for. Unsatisfied, she talks at length with God. Sometimes he speaks to her, often he simply "forms words in my understanding," and sometimes Julian just "sees." Repeatedly, though, she says she is still baffled. The full discussion takes up about thirty-five chapters out of the Long Text's total of eighty-six (none of the other fifteen showings extends over more than a couple of chapters). The reading of sin and forgiveness that finally emerges from this strenuous interchange challenges everything most of us think we know about Christian theology. It is pure, unadulterated compassion, from beginning to end. Here are its essential features:

1. "Sin" has no ultimate reality. We see it only by the pain that results from it. By "sin" is meant "all which is not good" including, of course, Christ's own suffering. It does not arise out of wickedness but out of the fact that we are "changeable in this life." We fall into sin out of naïveté and ignorance. Our mistakes bring us to self-knowledge, though, and to a humble seeking of God. It is in this sense, then, that "sin is necessary" (the beautiful Middle English word is *behovely*). In the fullness of time, sin "will be no shame, but honour," for just as every sin has a grievous consequence here on earth, each will have a commensurate "bliss" in the afterlife. The more we sin, the more we suffer and the more we learn. Life is a school. (Julian cautions her readers not to conclude from this teaching that they should go out and sin deliberately so as to reap more glory.)

2. There is no wrath in God. There is wrath only in us, and God forgives us for this. God does not blame us for our sins. As for hell and purgatory, Julian wanted some sight, but "I saw nothing." Indeed, "No more cruel hell was revealed to me than sin."

3. There is "hidden in God an exalted and wonderful mystery." At the end of time, it will make all things well. Its exact nature is hidden from us, but just as the Trinity had the power to create the world in the first place, it will have the power to set right the contradictions that baffle us so. When we are in sorrow, we should remember that miracles have always taken place in the most difficult times; by analogy, at the end of time, this miracle, too, can be counted upon.

Julian knows she must hold tight to the teachings of both Holy Church and her own revelations, but it is not easy. It is an article of faith, she points out, that "many creatures will be damned." How does that square with "everything shall be well"? God reminds her, "What is impossible to you is not impossible to me." (This is not really as lame as it sounds: by definition God is omnipotent. If everything we see is created from nothing, why can we not anticipate a satisfactory finale as well?) Gradually the idea of that great eschatological mystery becomes more and more attractive to Julian and more plausible. Still, she is not completely persuaded. Struggling to accommodate the traditional scheme of sin and forgiveness to her new understanding that in fact there is no blame, she comes close to suggesting— ingeniously—that even if the crime-and-punishment scheme is not literally true, it is provisionally useful:

> When we see ourselves so foul, then we believe that God may be angry with us because of our sin. Then we are moved by the Holy Spirit through contrition to prayer, and we desire with all our might an amendment of ourselves to appease God's anger, until the time that we find rest of soul and ease of conscience. And then we hope that God has forgiven us our sin; and this is true.
>
> (Long Text 40)

We have misread our plight: our mistakes have so "befouled" us that we conclude God must be angry at us. Contrite, wanting to win back God's love, we amend our lives. Softening our own will through prayer and contrition and transforming our own anger into love, we open ourselves to God, who in truth has never left us in the first place. Our analysis was incorrect, but the strategy works anyway.

In the fourteenth showing, which concerns prayer, God tells Julian, "I am the ground of your beseeching." When we are moved to pray, it is because God is prompting us. Reasoning that her own desire to make sense of sin and forgiveness is, in effect, a prayer, she regards this teaching as divine encouragement to persist. Accordingly, she lays out her dilemma still again. The "higher judgment" of her revelations says one thing, while the "lower judgment" of Holy Church (and that is indeed how she identifies them) says another. How can they be reconciled? "I could have no patience because of great fear and perplexity." She recalls, "I cried within me with all my might, beseeching God for help."

Words have failed her, including even the special potency of "words formed in my understanding." Julian is asking for an altogether different kind of answer. What she receives, and what eventually does resolve her dilemma, is not a verbal formula at all, but an image, or rather a symbolic configuration—a kind of tableau—vivid, compelling, and, initially, inscrutable.[9] The parable of the servant and the master supples her answer.[10] She sketches it out first in its bare-bones outline and then begins to elaborate, filling in details and interpreting them as she goes along, laying on colors until the story fairly glows, like the windows of a medieval cathedral. No summary can possibly do it justice. She begins:

> The lord sits in state, in rest and in peace. The servant stands before his lord, respectfully, ready to do his lord's will. The lord looks on his servant very lovingly and sweetly and mildly. He sends him to a certain place to do his will. Not only does the servant go, but he dashes off and runs at great speed, loving to do his lord's will. *And soon he falls into a dell and is greatly injured:* and then he groans and moans and tosses about and writhes, but he cannot rise or help himself in any way. And of all this, *the greatest hurt which I saw him in was lack of consolation,* for he could not turn his face to look on his loving lord.
>
> (Long Text 51)

I have italicized what seems to me to be the core of the parable, the elements Julian herself emphasizes. She has already been taught, and told her readers, that we sin not out of wickedness but out of naïveté and ignorance. Here she equates that ignorance with a fall we take because like children, we are running headlong, fully believing we are doing God's will—eager, in contemporary language, to "do the right thing" but running so fast we do not see the ditch. Julian sees what acute pain the servant has fallen into and looks carefully "to know if I could detect any fault in him." She cannot, though, and neither does the lord. The lord speaks, asking whether it would not be ungracious for him to reward the servant for the injuries he has undergone, and the logic we fought before (why should sins be rewarded?) seems more acceptable.

At this instant, "An inward spiritual revelation of the lord's meaning descended into my soul, in which I saw that this must necessarily be the case." She sees that the servant deserves a far greater reward than he would have if he had not fallen; she "sees" in the special sense that the word has come to mean in her narrative.

Julian had sensed all along that the parable held the answers to her anguished questions. But those answers emerged only after her inner voice told her to read the vision like an allegory, interpreting the color of the garments, where the lord was sitting, the demeanor of the servant.

"The colour of the clothing was azure blue . . . and within him there was a secure place of refuge, long and broad, all full of endless heavenliness. . . . The amplitude, billowing splendidly all about him, signifies that he has enclosed within himself all heavens and all endless joy and bliss" (Long Text 51).

Julian begins her interpretive task by noting the background. It is vague and spacious, and its expansiveness contrasts sharply with the feeling of constriction—of being "cornered"—that had overwhelmed her just before she related the parable. The figure of the lord merges imperceptibly with that spacious background and with his own garments. God is not an entity, Julian suggests, God is heaven itself—pure freedom.

As Julian continues to explicate her dream-vision, she discovers that the fallen servant is Adam—all of us, by extension—and his garment, a dirty white tunic, worn and ragged, symbolizes humanity itself "with all the harm and weakness which follow."[11] But the servant is Christ as well. The torn and dirty white tunic is his flesh, "ready to go to rags and to tear" as Christ's had been (Julian had said of Christ's flesh earlier: "It was torn in pieces like a cloth, and sagged down" [Long Text 17]). The servant's fall, also, has meaning on two levels: Adam fell "from life to death" and then into hell. To rescue Adam, Christ too fell "into the maiden's womb," taking on humanity for all of us.

All of this allegorizing can seem laborious or heavy-handed to modern readers. But as Julian interprets the parable point by point, I think we begin to understand the thrilling power of the doctrine of atonement at a deeper level than a mere verbal statement could convey. In the course of her commentary, Julian identifies herself initially with the servant—as Adam, or Everyman—but then observes that the servant is merging in turn with Christ. In the climax of the parable, Christ returns to God the Father. So, by implication, does the reader, and the tremendous "one-ing" is completed.[12]

We have been prepared for this teaching in many small ways, among them the observation that "in our Lord's intention we are now on his cross with him in his pains, and in our sufferings we are dying, and with his help and his grace, we willingly endure on that same cross until the last moment of life" (Long Text 21).

Nonetheless, it is a stunning suggestion: that *whatever* suffering you and I might be undergoing, even the sort that flows out of our own mistakes, is in a real sense analogous to Christ's and is gradually uniting us with him. A magnificent picture emerges, one of creature and creator moving toward each other, kin in their suffering, immersed alike in the thirst for each other that Julian calls "love-longing."

Julian explains now that it is precisely this "one-ing" within us—Adam being the flesh and Christ the soul—that accounts for the unresolvable difficulties of earthly life. Bemusedly, she observes:

> During our lifetime here, we have in us a marvelous mixture of both well-being and woe. We have in us our risen Lord Jesus Christ, and we have in us the wretchedness and the harm of Adam's falling. Dying, we are constantly protected by Christ . . . so afflicted in our feelings by Adam's falling. . . . And now we are raised to the one, and now we are permitted to fall to the other.
>
> (Long Text 52)

The motif of mother and child is central to all the world's mystical traditions: even Buddhism, which Westerners tend to see as essentially cerebral in its emphasis on mental training, has as one of its central tenets the Buddha's own instruction, "Learn to love the whole world as a mother loves her only son." During the Middle Ages in Europe, the figure of the Madonna and child came to be very nearly as important as the crucifix itself. One of the most widespread devotions of the time was to imagine oneself as beholding, even nursing, the infant Jesus. A great many women mystics experienced this in dreams or visions. Julian of Norwich, however, went much further by attributing to *God*, specifically to Christ, the love of a mother for her child. A good many earlier mystics and theologians had touched upon the theme, including Augustine, Anselm of Canterbury, and Bernard of Clairvaux, but none had developed it as fully or appreciatively as she did.

Once you have read Julian's teachings on the motherhood of God (Long Text 57–64), it is relatively easy to look back across the work and see the elements that prefigured her triumphant declaration that "as truly as God is our Father, so truly is God our Mother" (Long Text 59). We have noted the imagery of clothing wrapped warmly about us, and the metaphor of the purse with its implied reverence for even the humblest bodily functions. Both of these occur in the first showing, and the Virgin

Mary appears there too—Mary as a young maiden, about the time she conceived. God would bring her before Julian twice more over the course of the showings. She is a wordless but commanding presence throughout.

Medieval writers regularly compared Christ's death throes to labor pangs. Even before Julian identifies Christ explicitly as a birthing mother, she establishes the connection through certain images, the most obvious of which derives from the biblical tradition that holds that after Christ's death a soldier pierced his side with a spear so that blood and water issued forth.[13] In the twenty-fourth chapter, Julian describes the Lord gazing into his side, through the wound, into "a fair and delectable place." Afterward, he brings to mind "the dear and precious blood and water which he suffered to be shed for love." To a woman, the suggestion is sufficiently explicit: in birth our waters break, our blood flows. The "fair and delectable place" within Christ seems recognizable enough, too, as the womb itself. All of these images coalesce at the point when Mary, as the mother of us all, becomes Christ: "So our Lady is our mother, in whom we are all enclosed and born of her in Christ, for she who is mother of our saviour is mother of all who are saved in our saviour; and our saviour is our true Mother, in whom we are endlessly born and out of whom we shall never come" (Long Text 57).

Julian has superimposed one figure upon the other; the "fair and delectable place" within Christ is heaven, but it is simultaneously the womb of the holy mother. From this point in the text onward, whenever she speaks of the Trinity, she is as likely to place "our Mother" in the second position as she is to designate Christ. Indeed, her devotion to the Trinity is intimately connected to her teaching on the motherhood of God.

It has been observed that devotion to the Trinity tends to intensify in the later stages of a Catholic mystic's development, and Julian's writings bear this out. She barely mentions the Trinity in the Short Text, but she brings it up repeatedly and emphatically in the Long Text. One could argue that she had been "educated" in the intervening years into understanding the doctrinal importance of the Trinity, but it seems to me more likely that the sheer capaciousness of the Trinity became increasingly attractive as her own experiential understanding of God expanded and accumulated. To say that God is three entities in one is to insist that *no* single conceptualization can encompass the divine. Dwelling upon the Trinity is thus an enormously liberating and "roomy" way of thinking about God, as Mechthild's boldly innovative evocations of the Trinity have already shown us. Indeed, it is in the context of a "celebration" of the Trinity that Julian's teaching on the motherhood of God first arises, in an absolutely natural, uncontrived way.

> For the almighty truth of the Trinity is our Father, for he made us and keeps us in him. And the deep wisdom of the Trinity is our Mother, in whom we are enclosed. And the high goodness of the Trinity is our Lord, and in him we are enclosed and he in us.
>
> (Long Text 54)

> So our Lady is our mother, in whom we are all enclosed and born of her in Christ, for she who is mother of our saviour is mother of all who are saved in our saviour; and our saviour is our true Mother, in whom we are endlessly born and out of whom we shall never come.
>
> (Long Text 57)

Julian's *experience* has taught her that maternality is as intrinsic to God's nature as majesty. In the course of her showings, she has found in God plenitude, fullness, and intense activity, and these are, for her, innately feminine qualities. God the Father may well be the foundation of all things, but God the Mother—Christ—busies herself about our needs: "The mother's service is nearest, readiest and surest" (Long Text 60). Christ "is working on us in various ways . . . for in our Mother Christ we profit and increase" (Long Text 58). God works "in mercy on all his beloved children who are docile and obedient to him" (Long Text 58), bringing us back at last "into our natural place, in which we were created by the motherhood of love, a mother's love which never leaves us" (Long Text 60). Lingeringly, tenderly, she touches upon all the aspects of motherhood, insisting that whatever an earthly mother does for her child, Christ does for all of us. "No one ever might or could perform this office fully, except only him" (Long Text 60).

When Julian identifies the feminine aspect of God as the more active, she is at variance with the Western norm, which tends to convey women as being passive by nature and receptive. In other traditions, however, in the very concept of God there is a union of the male and female principles and the designation of qualities as male or female can vary. In Hinduism, for example, the male principle is represented as the God Shiva and characterized as repose and stillness; the attributes of his consort Shakti, the feminine principle, are motion and energy. Every human being is understood to carry both these principles within herself, and the crowning moment in spiritual development is their convergence or wedding. Western mystics, too, often describe their experience in terms of a wedding—a union or re-union of the severed halves of one's own being. In drawing motherhood into the Trinity, Julian is accomplishing essentially the same thing, but with a difference that has made her more universally acceptable, for in her presentation the erotic overtones we find in some of Mechthild's and Teresa's writings are absent.

As theology, Julian's teaching on the motherhood of God is brilliant. On the personal level, it is enormously healing. For we cannot read her descriptions of maternal activity without reflecting upon our own experience within the maternal relationship, both as children and as mothers. For most of us, it would seem, that experience is exceedingly complex. We may feel our mothers were not all they might have been; just as frequently, particularly as we grow older, we begin to feel our own inadequacies as daughters. As mothers ourselves, we agonize endlessly over whether we are doing right by our children, and we grieve when we find ourselves estranged from them. We want them to be autonomous and we want them never to leave us, and even as we are sending out these wildly conflicting signals to our children, we are still getting them from our own mothers! All our life, it seems, whatever compromise we work out, some vestige of that conflictedness lingers.

Mystics, too, have had to struggle with the deeply loving connections they have felt with family and friends. Augustine wrote not only about his friends and his mistress, but also about his relationship with his mother Monica. Teresa of Avila was forever untangling the knots in her large family's lives. Julian, we must assume, had her own experience to reckon with—and whatever she learned in the process would have been augmented by what she had learned about human nature as a spiritual counselor. The healing balm she offers us in her teachings on the motherhood of God is the understanding that we need not grieve that our relationships here on earth are less than perfect. Life on earth is, after all, inherently flawed. Nonetheless, the rich promise that the maternal relationship holds out can finally be realized, because the mother we long for, and the mother we long to be, is within each of us. We can meet her there. Our own children, too, must eventually find the mother of their longings within themselves—and so must our own mothers, for "no one ever might or could perform this office fully, except only Him." Julian insists that "this fair lovely word 'mother' is so sweet and so kind in itself that it cannot truly be said of anyone or to anyone except of him and to him who is the true Mother of life" (Long Text 60).

She sets the final seal of reassurance, lifts away the last ounce of regret, when she writes, "In this I saw that every debt which we owe by God's command to fatherhood and motherhood is fulfilled in truly loving God." The two teachings that have so endeared Julian to modern readers, those on sin and forgiveness and those on the motherhood of God, are deeply intertwined. In the parable of the servant and the lord, Julian tells us that no matter how benighted our actions, every one of us longs to be good and to do the right thing. That in itself takes us a long way toward learning to forgive ourselves and others, but the teaching of the motherhood of God takes us even further, for it maintains that every human relationship finds its perfect fulfillment in the mystical experience. And what of the inadequacies we all feel toward those we love and who love us? the blame that keeps wanting to be put *some* place? Never mind. All will be well. We can forgive our mothers, our fathers, our sons and daughters, our partners and lovers, even ourselves, for all will be well!

WHEN Julian has completed her account of the first fifteen revelations, she pauses to recapitulate: "The first began early in the morning, about the hour of four, and it lasted, revealing them in a determined order, most lovely and calm, each following the other, until it was three o'clock in the afternoon or later."

She reminds us that all this while, the pain of her illness had been taken from her entirely. Now she says that when the revelations were completed, everything was hidden, and presently her sickness returned, "first in my head, with a sound and a din; and suddenly all my body was filled with sickness as it was before, and I was as barren and dry as if the consolation which I had received before were trifling."

An occurrence takes place now whose importance could easily elude us. Julian has experienced Christ's presence. She has seen him (her!) and spoken with him. From the very beginning of that experience, she guessed that its purpose was to prepare her to be tempted "by the fiend." And yet now, overcome by discomfort, she all but discounts the revelations. A priest comes to her and asks how she is. She says that during the day she was delirious, and he laughs heartily. She tells him she thought the cross she was looking at had been bleeding. Suddenly the cleric is serious, and at once Julian realizes her mistake. In effect, she is Peter, and she has denied Christ—though only once—and, in effect, the cock has just crowed. She berates herself, "See how wretched I was!" But she draws the conclusion she must: "Here you can see what I am in myself; but our courteous Lord would not leave me so." Like Peter, she will be all the more solidly "the rock" for having seen her own fallibility. "For my strength," in the apostle Paul's words, "is made perfect in weakness" (2 Corinthians 12:9, KJV). She rests until night, "trusting in his mercy," and then falls asleep. There ensues a long, cruel ordeal, but one from which we know she will emerge triumphant. The fiend's visitation is unforgettable.

> And as soon as I fell asleep, it seemed to me that the devil set himself at my throat, thrusting his face, like that of a young man, long and strangely lean, close to mine. I never saw anything like him; his colour was red, like a newly baked tile, with black spots like freckles, uglier than a tile. His hair was red as rust, not cut short in front, with side-locks hanging at his temples. He grinned at me with a vicious look, showing me white teeth so big that it all seemed the uglier to me. His body and his hands were misshapen, but he held me by the throat with his paws, and wanted to stop my breath and kill me, but he could not.
>
> (Long Text 67)

At one point Julian awakened, "more dead than alive." The people who were with her wet her temples, and "my heart began to gain strength." She smelled smoke and a stench, which no one else did, and now she realized that it had been the devil. Immediately, "I had recourse to what our Lord had revealed to me on that same day." She fled to it as to her source of strength, "and immediately everything vanished, and I was brought to great rest and peace."

Once again, "our good Lord opened my spiritual eye." God showed her her own soul, "as wide as if it were an endless citadel, and also as if it were a blessed kingdom, and . . . a fine city." In the midst sat Jesus, "a delectable sight," and when she had gazed long upon him, God said to her, "Know it well, it was no hallucination which you saw today, but accept and believe it and hold firmly to it . . . and you will not be overcome."

The devil returned "with his heat and his stench, and kept me very busy." She heard a confused mumbling that seemed to be mocking inattentive prayer. The distress continued all night and into the morning, ceasing just after sunrise.

Aʟʟ that Julian ever really sought, when she uttered the threefold prayer that prompted the showings, was union with God in love. She did not ask, initially, about the nature of good and evil, the significance of the Trinity, the fate of the damned, or any of the other mysteries that were ultimately opened to her. Not intellectual curiosity, but desire, was her starting point. Withdrawn from ordinary objects and focused intensely, her desire to grow closer to God had finally pierced the veil between this world and the other. This conjunction of love and the desire to know, as fundamental to medieval spirituality as it is foreign to contemporary thought, emerges beautifully in the last chapter of the Long Text:

> And from the time that it was revealed, I desired many times to know in what was our Lord's meaning. And fifteen years after and more . . . it was said: What, do you wish to know your Lord's meaning in this thing? Know it well, love was his meaning. Who reveals it to you? Love. What did he reveal to you? Love. Why does he reveal it to you? For love. Remain in this, and you will know more of the same. But you will never know different, without end.

Throughout the Long Text, Julian adjusted her account of the showings so that it would nourish ordinary Christians—the men and women who came to her, like Margery Kempe, because she "good counsel could give." Nowhere did she do this more "courteously" than in her final words.

> Do not accuse yourself that your tribulation and your woe is all your fault; for I do not want you to be immoderately depressed or sorrowful. For I tell you that whatever you do, you will have woe. And therefore I want you wisely to understand the penance which you are continually in, and to accept that meekly for your penance. And then you will truly see that all your life is profitable penance. This place is prison, this life is penance, and he wants us to rejoice in the remedy. The remedy is that our Lord is with us, protecting us and leading us into the fullness of joy.
>
> (Long Text 77)

Julian of Norwich speaks with rare directness to contemporary women. Her depiction of the mystical experience is so wonderfully "relational." Showings of Christ, yes—vivid, arresting, set forth in such concrete and realistic detail that they are absolutely credible. But more than that, Julian and God *talked*. And their conversation was not a mere exchange of courtly compliments, it was substantive. Julian was actively encouraged to raise her most provocative questions; she was taken seriously.

Julian's account of sin and forgiveness stands unexcelled for its compassion and its psychological acuity. Equally pleasing to modern readers are her teachings on the motherhood of God. But her greatest appeal for us could be the primacy she places on personal experience. She knows, and she knows she knows—not because of anything she has read in books, even holy writ, but because she has experienced it firsthand: her own "showings" are for her the ultimate touchstone of belief. Her confidence is extraordinary and contagious, all the more so for being tempered by episodes like that final encounter with "the fiend," through which Julian confides, in effect, "I know . . . and yet I know nothing more certainly than I do my own fallibility."

Saint Catherine of Siena

(1347–1380)

> A soul rises up, restless with tremendous desire
> for God's honor and the salvation of souls . . .
>
> — Saint Catherine of Siena,
> the *Dialogue* 25

> But as a flame burns higher the more fuel is fed it,
> the fire in this soul grew so great that her body could
> not have contained it. She could not, in fact, have
> survived had she not been encircled by the strength
> of him who is strength itself.
>
> — Saint Catherine of Siena,
> the *Dialogue* 48

CATHERINE of Siena is one of the most extraordinary women in European history, a spiritual teacher of tremendous magnetism who was also a powerful advocate for peace and reconciliation. Canonized soon after her death and made a "Doctor of the Church" in 1970, along with Teresa of Avila, she is among the mystics the church has honored most lavishly. Nonetheless, when we work our way beneath the legend—past the generic saintliness that surrounds the more "visible" mystics—we find ourselves in the presence of a blessedly eccentric individual who was as fully human and as vulnerable as we ourselves feel. So reluctant was she to display her supernatural powers, for instance, that as a distraught couple approached her cottage carrying their child, whom they believed to be "possessed," she climbed up on her roof and hid, muttering, "Alas, every day I am tormented by evil spirits: do you think I want anybody else's?" This, though on brighter days she would make light of the devil and her disciples' anxieties over his powers, saying, "Don't be afraid of the Old Pickpocket!"

Catherine was a contemporary of Julian of Norwich, and, like her, a visionary. But in other regards their lives could not have been more different. While Julian lived out her days in virtual anonymity, Catherine was one of those mystics who seem to have been singled out at birth, to their chagrin, to be God's own show-offs. Mandated to break through all ordinary constraints and shatter the laws of normalcy, these individuals are not merely saints, they are culture heroes and heroines as well, embodying the spirit of their people or region and reshaping its history. Catherine was Siena's beloved *beata popolana*, the people's own saint, who would bring a pope to heel. Saints are always identified by the town where they were born or lived, but the connection seems to have been particularly strong in Catherine's case. In her intensity she was said to be "like the wine of Siena—very red."

Catherine was declared "Doctor of the Church" for many reasons, prominent among which certainly was the *Dialogue*, which she wrote near the end of her life. The book is an exceedingly rich and complex work, and we could justifiably spend most of this chapter examining it, as we have done with the writings of both Mechthild and Julian.[1] In Catherine's case, though, we have a life to look at as well, amply documented and eventful, and it seems to me best to focus on that life, reasoning from my own experience that the more we know about Catherine herself, the better equipped we are to read the *Dialogue*.

CONSIDER, just for the moment, a young man, decent enough and resourceful, who is launched through no evident choice of his own upon a long and dangerous journey. Turning his back on family and friends, he sets out to retrieve something precious that has been lost and endures appalling hunger and thirst along the way. He passes through fire and water and incurs painful injuries. He learns to live without sleep, and his path takes him deep underground through the land of death. He is forced in any number of ways to overcome revulsion and horror. He receives the help of wise counselors and faces down demonic figures. Animals and birds come to his aid. His courage is rewarded. Magic rings come his way, enchanted staffs, and protective cloaks that keep him warm or invisible; a goddess becomes his personal guardian. (Athena, for example, kept a close lookout for Odysseus.)

Swordfights take place, and wrestling matches—a romantic dalliance or two—but ultimately the young man passes all the tests the story has imposed upon him. He reaches his destination, lays hold of whatever he has come for—a key, a seal, a crown—and returns triumphant to marry the princess and take charge of the kingdom. Somewhere along the way, lest he ever be tempted to think it was all only a dream, he will have picked up a scar or a slight disfigurement. . . .

Since time began we have been telling ourselves this story in every conceivable variation, as epic, myth, and fairy tale. We are comfortable with the narrative, amused to see it reiterated in contemporary films and novels, enthralled to find ourselves walking through it in our dreams.

Suppose, on the other hand, we are told of a *woman,* clever and at least passably pretty, who does not leave her home but submits herself to awesome fasts and vigils anyway. She is zealous with the leather thongs that monastic tradition calls "the discipline" and for a time girds her waist with a tight iron chain. She defies her family's plans for her marriage, allowing no personal relationship to obstruct her endeavors. She welcomes a disfiguring disease, cuts off her hair as well, and when her mother tries to distract her by taking her to a fashionable spa, she manages to slip away to the source waters for a bath so scalding hot she is badly blistered afterward. Her exasperated family assigns to her the bulk of the household work, and one day while she is turning the spit, she falls into ecstasy and rolls insensible into the embers but revives unharmed. She is attacked by demons but stands them off and is eventually able to evict them when they take over other individuals.

When this young woman prays, a white dove is seen to hover over her head. She, too, is given a guardian—not the goddess Athena but Mary Magdalene. Jesus comes to her in a vision and draws a beautiful scarlet garment out of the wound in his side. It is invisible to others, and it keeps her warm and comfortable whatever the temperature. She receives a betrothal ring from him too—again, invisible—and the gift of seeing into souls. Countless numbers of men and women seek her guidance, and before she dies she performs a great service for Christendom at large. . . .

Once again, the narrative is familiar in its basic outlines. This time, though, I believe most of us are *not* comfortable with it. The heroes of epic and fairy tale, we protest, do not deliberately inflict their trials on themselves; rather, they endure what they must, and the hero's fear and ingenuousness are half the charm of the story. The hardships Catherine of Siena survived—for she is the young woman in question—are not way stations in a fairy geography. They took place in the real world, and she imposed them on herself with a singlemindedness that is almost repellent to the modern reader. The supernatural elements of the story put us off, too, because they are also presented to us as a matter of fact.

Catherine's contemporaries, though, would not have found the story implausible or the heroine's behavior neurotic. They believed wholeheartedly in a noncorporeal world and in events that contravened normalcy. They would have accepted Catherine's insistence that in fact she was not the instigator of her ascetic practices but rather took her cues entirely from inner promptings that were just as real and audible to her as were all the mysterious counselors and oracles that steered the epic heroes along their path. The real issue for them would have been whether the promptings were from divine or demonic sources.

Out of sympathy to the modern reader's sensibilities, I have downplayed some of the more sensational aspects of Catherine of Siena's life. They are a hindrance to those of us who want to look at her inner life and at the kind of spiritual teacher she was. But if we can make peace with the miracles, the exorcisms, and the severe ascetic practices long enough to see them in the context of traditional quest literature, they make a remarkable kind of sense. Considered as a whole, as a *narrative,* they support the hypothesis a great many students of folklore and religion have proposed: that embedded in every human psyche there is a map to higher consciousness that in its essentials does not vary; that the individual who sets out upon that journey inward will describe it afterward in whatever idiom or symbolic language is available to her; and that her account will be only partially accessible to someone from another time or place. From this point of view, it seems reasonable to suppose that Catherine was compelled just as irresistibly as an Odysseus or Beowulf or Parsifal to survive certain ordeals and make certain discoveries, even if the whole adventure had to take place under her father's roof, *as it had to*, given that she was a relatively sheltered young woman living in a patriarchal society. Her story is highly indigenous—shaped profoundly by her Catholicism, but shaped too by the folkways of the Mediterranean culture in which she lived, many of which stretched far back into pre-Christian times.

With Catherine, we have an embarrassment of the kind of riches we longed for where Clare, Mechthild, and Julian were concerned. I have mentioned her *Dialogue*; we have letters as well, some three hundred and eighty-two of them written or dictated by Catherine, and a great many others written *about* her by contemporaries. Several accounts of her life were written by her chief confessors, advocates of her canonization. Additionally, because she took impassioned part in the public, political events of her time, we must be alert to the broader historical record itself. Right along with the richness, of course, comes a hoard of difficulties. All of those witnesses to her sanctity had preconceptions about how a saint could be expected to behave, and their testimonies tend to flatten out the quirky bits of the story that do not fit the prototype—exactly the parts of the story many of us would find most pertinent (we who live in an age of antiheroes and antiheroines). Then, too, it is not easy to understand the historical setting: the more we learn, the more complex it reveals itself to be.

CATHERINE Benincasa was born in 1347, just four years after Julian of Norwich, the twenty-fourth of twenty-five children. (This fact merits, if not comment, at least a respectful pause.) Her father was a wool dyer and prosperous enough to maintain a large home next door to the dyeworks. Indeed, the family name means "well-housed." One can see the house even today, carefully preserved by the Sienese. Built of solid brick with tile roofs, it rises three stories above the ground floor and has nine big windows across the front.

The little girl's vocation made itself known early. Returning home from a walk with her little brother when she was only six, Catherine had a vision of Christ wearing the papal tiara, a detail that prefigures the role she would later play in relocating the papacy from Avignon to Rome. She took a vow of perpetual virginity when she was only seven. She was

attracted from the outset to the Dominican order. The church and cloister of Saint Dominic were just up the hill from her family home, and she
spent a good deal of time there. Her brother-in-law's brother, who had
lived in the Benincasa home after being orphaned by the black death,
joined the Dominicans when Catherine was very young: this was
Tomaso della Fonte, who would be her first confessor. The tenor of life
in Siena was as turbulent as it was throughout fourteenth-century
Europe. War was the perennial backdrop—war between England and
France, between the emperor and challengers to his authority, war between the city-states, and war between neighborhoods and even families. From one generation to the next, feuds were passed on as tenderly
as heirlooms. Eventually, the church itself would split apart, making war
against itself and dragging its bewildered children into the fray. In a general atmosphere of divisiveness and hatred, the city of Siena was notorious for the virulence of its quarrels. As if in recurring, deadly chastisement,
the plague would sweep across the region at regular intervals, settling
old scores once and for all.

When we start to say of someone like Catherine, "but she was so *extreme*," we need to realize how extreme the times themselves were. The
spiritual precocity that had been a source of pride for Catherine's parents
became troublesome to them as she approached early adolescence. Her
mother, Lapa, began to instruct her daughter, "making her wash her face
and neck properly, keeping her hair combed and tidy" (*Life* 37). When
Catherine showed no interest in men, Monna Lapa turned her over to
her married sister, Bonaventura, to whom Catherine was deeply attached. Catherine went through the motions of coquetry and began to
slacken ever so slightly in her prayers. Suddenly, though, and shockingly,
her sister died in childbirth.

In the family's bereavement over the loss of Bonaventura—and of
the resulting loss to the clan of her husband and the alliance to his family that the marriage had ensured—they decided to procure a husband
for Catherine regardless of her wishes. Under the advice of a sympathetic
confessor, she chopped off her long golden brown hair. Enraged, her parents dismissed the maidservant and put Catherine to work in her place.
"Every day she was deluged with insults, taunts and jeers."[2]

Undaunted by her family's harshness, Catherine regarded them as
the Holy Family and rejoiced in waiting upon them, which must have

unnerved them at times as effectively as Mahatma Gandhi's open friend-
liness did his British jailers. She had had the luxury of a small room to
herself, but now, hoping to interfere with her prayers, the family revoked
the privilege. Their action had an effect counter to what they had hoped,
because now Catherine constructed for herself "a secret cell . . . an inner
cell which no one could take away from her" (*Life* 43). Now, even while
she moved around her family home, Catherine was given over more and
more to a deepening inner life.

In a larger sense, of course, by invoking the power of her own imagination Catherine was doing what human beings have regularly done
when confronted by forces they cannot control, forces that would crush
them or stunt them or strip them bare. Imagination seems to be a vital
component of genuine nonviolent resistance, for it allows us to hold on
to a positive view of ourselves no matter what the world tells us we are.

Certainly Catherine's image of an invisible cell of self-knowledge
is related to other kinds of invisible protective coverings that she mentions in her letters and the *Dialogue*. She speaks continually of being
"clothed in truth," for example, and of being "clothed in Christ's flesh,"
and I have mentioned the invisible protective garment Christ gives her.
But when she speaks of the cell of self-knowledge, we will see in a moment that she means much more than just the protection of one's spiritual identity against the harshness of life in the world.

The battle continued, as of course it must, because what mother
among us would not put up a fight if her daughter decided to sleep on
boards and stop eating? It was during this period that Monna Lapa took
Catherine to the baths at Vignone, only to have her seek out the very
source of the hot springs for her bath. It was about this time that
Catherine's father walked into the room where she was praying and saw
a white dove above her head, whereupon he decided the girl's vocation
was genuine and forbade anyone in the family to interfere with it. He told
her she could have her own room after all, that they would not force a
husband upon her—that yes, Jesus Christ would make a perfectly acceptable son-in-law—and that she could give alms as she chose from the
family's goods. She interpreted this last permission freely: her brothers
and sisters-in-law learned quickly enough to keep their rooms locked, for
nothing was safe when Catherine felt that the needs of the pauper at the
door exceeded theirs. Eventually, she would decide that the Benincasa

clan's prosperity was doing them no spiritual good and would appeal to God—successfully—to remove it.

Catherine had received indubitably clear signs that she was to join the Dominicans—not the cloistered nuns, but a tertiary order composed mostly of widows. Since the Sisters of Penance lived in their homes, open to public scrutiny, they were reluctant to admit a young, attractive woman. As luck would have it, though, she contracted a disease—chicken pox, perhaps—that left her badly enough scarred that the sisters decided she would not compromise their respectability.

The first stage of her struggle was now over. Catherine wore a habit with a white veil that marked her out as a *mantellata*, a daughter of Saint Dominic belonging to the third order. She had the full support of her family but also a door she could close upon them. She was free to give herself over completely to spiritual disciplines and she did so, rarely leaving her cell. Immediately, and magnificently, her contemplative life opened out, bringing her visions so powerful and voices so real that she feared they might not be coming from God at all. The Lord commended her prudence and instructed her: visions that come from God inspire fear at first, he told her, but then go on to fortify. Visions of demonic origin yield sweetness at the outset, but soon pain and nausea develop. The certain sign that a vision is from God is that it will always bear fruit in "a greater knowledge of truth in the soul" (*Life* 73). The mark of one who has had this kind of vision is humility:

> Do you know, daughter, who you are, and who I am? If you know
> these two things, you will be blessed. You are she who is not;
> whereas I am He who is. Have this knowledge in your soul and
> the Enemy will never deceive you.
>
> (*Life* 79)

The assertion "you are she who is not" sets off a whole battery of alarms for contemporary women. Very few of us regard a strong sense of self as anything but an asset; indeed, it is something many of us struggle hard to achieve. In this regard, it is helpful to observe that among the women mystics studied here not one gives evidence of having suffered as a child from what we would now call low self-esteem. On the contrary, these individuals appear to have been secure and unusually cherished by their families. Catherine was by all accounts her parents' favorite child, and so were Teresa and Thérèse. Mechthild specifies that her family loved her dearly, and it is plain that Clare's did too.

Despite the almost formulaic apologies for ineptitudes they describe as feminine, all of these women display quite a sturdy sense of self. I would suggest that the confusion lies in the notorious slipperiness of language where mystical expression is concerned and that Catherine's rather "bald" formulation is not essentially different from those we have already dealt with more easily. Mechthild spoke of the low places where grace could pour in, and Clare of the absolute poverty, within and without, that allows God to work through us. Julian argued that sin is necessary because it brings us to self-knowledge—knowledge of our own fallibility—which in turn moves us to seek God. Catherine, for her part, tells us simply that when we look inward long enough and hard enough to dispel any illusions we might cherish about ourselves, and when we manage to silence the voice that shouts "I am," then, in that silence, our deepest and truest self can speak. "Not I, not I," said the apostle Paul, "but Christ liveth in me."

Raymond of Capua, who later became Catherine's chief confessor, dearest friend, and foremost biographer, believed that the foundation of all she taught was laid in that first teaching, "Know that you are she who is not and I am He who is." Its corollary, he added, was the command that she should conform herself to Christ in his suffering and learn "to regard sweet things as bitter, bitter things as sweet."

Catherine was sixteen when she became a *mantellata,* and she lived in solitude for more than three years. She stayed in her cell for the most part, kept silent, and prayed, leaving home only to walk up to San Domenico for mass. Her reception at the church was not altogether enthusiastic, for often when she received Holy Communion she would burst into tears and loud sobs that would disturb the other worshipers. She stayed on for endless prayers, and often she would lose all consciousness of her body and stand leaning against one of the stone pillars, immobile, her face white, seeing and hearing nothing.

Sometime during her three years of solitude, there came a period when Catherine virtually haunted the church whenever it was open, for the cell that had been her heart's longing had become a terrifying place. Day after day now, whenever she entered her room, a terrible buzzing ensued, "like a maddening swarm of flies" (*Life* 93). Demonic voices wheedled and cajoled. Who did she think she was? Was she trying to commit suicide with all this fasting and mortification? It wasn't too late to turn back and take a husband, have children. . . .

Catherine knew better than to answer. She would tell her disciples much later that you must not discuss anything with the enemy; once he's got your attention, he's got you too. Nor was it a time for complicated devotions. Her one prayer throughout this time was, "I trust in the Lord Jesus Christ, not in myself." Like Clare, she consciously disavowed any illusion of personal strength.

The ante went higher, though. Now, on all sides of her room, she saw pairs of naked men and women coupling—howling and dancing, inviting her to join them. The experience was acutely painful to her, and it went on for days. Just when she needed him most, moreover, Jesus, the friend who had brought her so many consolations, seemed to have vanished. She struggled and through her prayers dispersed the horde over and over again, though only barely. At last, nearly exhausted, like the fairy tale heroine who suddenly recalls the magic formula, Catherine remembered that she was to accept "the bitter as sweet" and to embrace suffering as her Beloved had. Her bewilderment vanished and her strength returned. Now when one of the demons told her they would persecute her unto death if she did not give in, she laughed and said they could do as they liked; she might even find them entertaining!

Throw the bucket of water on the witch, and she dissolves. Name Rumpelstiltskin, and he falls through the floor cursing. Catherine had in a sense named her tormentors, too, by recognizing that they were permitted expressly to come and test her and that apart from that purpose they really had no existence. Like Julian of Norwich, she had learned to laugh at the devil, and of course as soon as she did, he and his companions vanished, defeated.

A bit reproachfully, though, she asked her Beloved, "And where were *you* when all that was happening?" He insisted that he had been in her heart the whole time. Catherine was not so sure. All she had seen in there were "ugly, filthy thoughts." But the Lord asked her whether those thoughts had given her pleasure. Absolutely not, she maintained, and he smiled, "But you see, if I hadn't been there, you would have found them most pleasurable" (*Life* 94). Later Catherine would implore her disciples to regard everything that happened to them as coming from God and as being ultimately for their own good. God is never closer, she promised them, than when we imagine him to be furthest away.

It is interesting that Catherine felt no need to destroy her tormentors. Rather, she struggled long and hard simply to distance herself from them. Much later she told her confessor, Raymond, that the really frightening thing about the demons had not been their mere presence, but their presence *inside her mind*. What she had to realize, then, was that *she* was not her mind. Once she did, and saw that they were just one more hardship she must endure along her way, she was able to objectify them and relax. Having mocked them, she tells us, she was never troubled again by impure thoughts of any kind.

Contemporary women have so many and such searching questions about the relationship between the spiritual and the sexual that we are particularly alert, when we read the lives and writings of women like Catherine—or Clare or Mechthild—to passages that would seem to reveal their attitudes and experiences. Unfortunately, these passages are exceedingly rare and probably too heavily "encoded" by time and place to tell us much.[3] This particular episode probably reveals something about how Catherine might have felt growing up in the atmosphere of a city that was apparently notorious for its licentiousness. But more interesting, it seems to me, is what we might call the "spiritual psychology" involved: the distinction Catherine has learned to make—which is not always spelled out as clearly in Christian mysticism as it is in Hinduism—between one's thoughts, which change with every moment, and one's deepest self.

Soon after this episode, Catherine tells us, the Lord told her why she would be subjected to suffering in every form: "I never give up trying to make you like me in so far as you are able to respond: I try to create within your soul too, in this life, what then took place in my body. . . ."

From this point on, the intimacy between Catherine and her bridegroom intensified to a degree Raymond of Capua warns us we might find "incredible and almost ridiculous." Sometimes Christ came to her alone, other times he brought his mother or Saint Dominic. Mary Magdalene accompanied him some days, and often the apostle Paul. Sometimes the two of them, Jesus and Catherine, would pace up and down in her cell reciting the psalms; evenings they would walk about in the rooftop garden. Her prayers began to converge around a single theme now: she asked for perfect love of her fellow human beings, such as Christ had felt, and perfect faith. On Shrove Tuesday 1367 (Mardi Gras, the last day before Lent), while the rest of Siena was in costume— dancing, drinking, and eating—her prayers were answered in the form of a betrothal. The ring she received was invisible to all but her. Her confessor describes a central diamond surrounded by pearls, but Catherine herself tells us the ring was made of the circumcised flesh of the infant Jesus, and this seems more fitting in a sense, for she was quite literally "putting on Christ's flesh."

On another occasion, after Catherine had been praying "for a clean heart," the Lord appeared and removed her heart. In a few days he brought it back—except that it was his heart, not hers, and it beat a good deal more loudly than hers had! After this she felt herself to be loving others with Christ's own heart. The process that she would describe at the beginning of her *Dialogue* was well under way now. "The soul is united with God, following in the footsteps of Christ crucified, and through desire and affection and the union of love *he makes of her another himself*" (italics mine).

Nothing in us would be shocked if at this point Catherine had left her family home for a hermitage, losing herself in the sweetness of her contemplative life. Instead, sometime before her twentieth birthday, and to her grief, she learned that her time of solitude was over. Instead of coming into her cell as he usually did, she tells us, Jesus positioned himself one day outside its door and told her to come out, too. From now on, she could love him only by loving others. "The service you cannot do me you must render your neighbors." She must learn to see her Beloved in everyone. "Your neighbors are the channel through which all your virtues come to birth."

This is surely the pivotal moment in Catherine's life. She probably did not hesitate at the threshold of her cell, for hesitation was not in her nature, but what we know of her life after that moment could well have given her pause. Before her lay thirteen years of all-consuming labor in the service of humankind. She would die in Rome at barely thirty-three years old.

Catherine's intimate friends were probably hard-pressed to perceive a pattern in those years; she was so determinedly available to life that she was jostled from one crisis to the next, resolving a neighbor's domestic quarrel in one letter or interview, addressing the most far-reaching ecclesiastical and political dilemma in the next. From our own vantage point, though, her life appears to have progressed in a clear pattern of widening concentric circles as her field of attention expanded steadily outward.

"Go, it is dinner time," said Christ. "Go and join them" (*Life* 107), and Catherine walked out into the first circle, the affectionate uproar of her large extended family. Some faces were not even familiar, for new sisters-in-law and children had arrived during her three years of solitude. The wife of one of her eldest brothers, Lisa Colombini, became her first disciple.

Catherine took upon herself the full range of the family's needs. She was no longer the strong girl who, as her mother had boasted, could carry a donkey's load of grain to the attic storage room. Extensive fasting had halved her weight and her strength. But she carried out a full share of the household work, and at night while everyone slept she collected their linens and washed them. Her silence broken, she spoke amiably but more often listened, and everyone remarked on the intensity of her attention. Her father died around this time, and Catherine, seated with him, displayed that disconcerting joyousness that mystics so often do on these occasions; she said she had clearly seen him pass over into paradise. Later, burying six nieces and nephews who died of the plague, she was heard to murmur, "Here are six anyway that I don't have to worry about."

Soon her sphere of influence widened. As a *mantellata,* she was expected to nurse the ill and infirm, and she did so now, zealously, at two charitable hospitals in Siena. Free to move about unremarked in her black-and-white habit, she went out each day and took the worst cases—the most irascible patients with the most repellent conditions—treating them as though they were of the Benincasa clan itself. Lest anything inhibit her compassion, she took drastic steps to combat her own revulsion. She admitted later to having been helped throughout this work by a special gift from God: the gift of being able to see the beauty of each soul, whatever the exterior.

Now a second older matron attached herself—another *mantellata.* Alessia Saracini was an aristocrat, and she undoubtedly helped Catherine become knowledgeable in the political realities of Siena. She and

Catherine's sister-in-law Lisa accompanied the much-younger woman everywhere, protecting her from the growing attentions of the towns-people.

Again, in the normal course of things, Catherine's field of attention widened and she was drawn out into a still greater circle as the community at large became aware of her gifts of counseling and mediating. Mothers of violent sons, wives of philandering husbands, or often the womenfolk of two feuding families or two sides of one feuding family would come to Catherine and beg her to intercede. The stories are so many and so convergent—of hardened sinners or world-weary skeptics who had only to come into her presence to fall down sobbing and go off to confession immediately, their lives profoundly and permanently reversed. Her power to do this seems to have had everything to do with the way she looked at you, the enormous interest and understanding that glowed out of her huge, dark eyes. There would come a day when she was criticized severely for permitting people to fall onto their knees in her presence. She looked blank and then laughed, "I am so busy reading their souls that I have no idea what is happening to their bodies!"

Catherine's light was not permitted to remain even briefly under a bushel basket. Supernatural events of all kinds began to take place. She would not live forever, and her teachings needed to get out fast. The people of her region were passionate, earthy, and highly impressionable, and the miracles were wonderfully effective in bringing them into her presence. Once they were there before her, she could carry out what was for her the real miracle, which was to open their hearts and minds to God.

And there was the matter of her death—her putative death, at any rate (*Life* 192ff.). Sometime before 1374, she gave every appearance of having died. For four hours, according to many witnesses, she stopped breathing. For a long time before this she had been in an ecstatic state, and at last she began to pray continuously to be taken "from this body of death" and fully united with God. "I did not obtain this," she told Raymond later, "but I did finally manage to get Him to communicate the pains that He had felt to me, in so far as I was able to bear them." This only heightened her own love and desire, and at last—her words are extraordinary—"My heart could bear it no longer, and the love became as strong as death: then the heart broke in two."

She was not speaking figuratively. She felt her heart had actually broken and that her soul was set free. Raymond asked what she saw, and she answered, "Everything in the other world that is to us invisible." But to her anguish, the Lord sent her back into the body. "For the good of souls" she had to return to the world. "I shall be with you always," her Beloved promised, but she must carry out his work. Later, she could never speak of the experience without bursting into tears. "I saw the hidden things of God," she would recall, "and now I am thrust back again into the prison of the body."

When Catherine said that her love became "as strong as death," she drew the phrase from the favorite Scripture of medieval mystics, the Song of Songs. "Set me as a seal upon thy arm . . . for love is as strong as death." The context in which she uses them, though, gives the words a very specific meaning. Her desire to be united with Christ had become so strong that it literally pulled into itself what we think of as "the life force." So complete was her absorption in God that all the vital processes were suspended. Her heart stopped beating, respiration ceased, her body grew cold and motionless. Physically she had died, but it was no true death, for there was no break in consciousness—not death, this, but love at its most intense pitch, and just as strong.

RAPIDLY, Catherine became a court of last resort for the quarrelsome Sienese as well as the surrounding countrypeople. There was nothing ethereal about Catherine's spirituality. She shrank from nothing; she could bring to the most virulent blood feuds the same clear-eyed compassion with which she dressed the most appalling wounds and cancers.

She needed badly to speak of God; when she could, she was observed to be radiant and alive, but when she could not, she became feeble and listless. She was as eager to have her companions around her as they were to be there. They were her *bella brigata,* and Catherine was their *dolcissima mamma.* This was fine with her, for she had received her charge from God. "Daughter, conceive and give birth! Give birth to a race of men that shall hate sin and love Me with a great and burning love." When she wrote to one of the young men in her circle, a particularly moody one, she urged him to come soon, for his mamma had plenty of milk for him![4] (Raymond was more decorous. He wrote that she was truly their "mamma," that she carried them all within her womb, but also that she fed them with the bread of sound and true doctrine.)

Catherine's fasting intensified throughout this period. When she was twenty-five, through no apparent desire or effort of her own, she stopped eating altogether and continued in this way until her death nine years later. Catherine's *inedia* (failure to eat, for whatever reason) is well attested, and certainly there were plenty of skeptics around who would have disproved it if they had been able. The condition was not something she willed. Distressed at the attention her fasting brought her, she begged God to allow her to eat normally, and she tried every day to choke something down—a few leaves of raw lettuce even—but her body would reject the food immediately. This was not to be construed as evidence of profound sanctity, she insisted, or ascetic heroism on her part. It was simply God's will. In her confessor's firm and carefully chosen words, "It would be wrong to think that it was by any kind of effort or experience or habit of a natural kind that she reached this state, or that anyone else could do such things. . . . Fullness of spirit overflows into the body, because *while the spirit is feeding, the body finds it easier to endure the pangs of hunger*" (*Life* 53, italics mine).[5]

Catherine is of course not alone, historically, in having fasted for long periods. Even in modern times, some individuals have survived on the Host alone for much longer than medical science would deem possible. One way to account for her *inedia* might be to suggest that she did not eat beyond a certain point in her life because she *could* not, because by this time her whole being worked in only one direction: she could only give. The same pattern governed her sleeping and waking. She slept, usually, about half an hour out of the twenty-four. She had begun staying up most of the night years earlier on behalf of her Dominican brothers—watching over them, in effect, and protecting them as they slept. But now her charges were far more in number. As the circle of her love expanded beyond her household, beyond Siena itself, everyone within that circle became her child, quite literally. To her way of thinking, all her children were desperately ill, and she could not leave their bedsides.

Catherine is the prime exemplar of the deeply spiritual women of her time who had discovered a mysterious reciprocity between their own fasting and their capacity to feed others. *Fasting* is here taken in the largest sense to mean restraint upon all one's desires for personal comfort. *To feed* is also meant in the largest sense: Catherine could multiply loaves with the best of them, but spiritual nourishment was her real concern. Her own appetite was for souls, and she was quite graphic in this regard, urging Raymond and others in her letters to them, "This is how we learn to enjoy eating souls. Souls are a food so sweet and mild that they make us fat, till we can enjoy no other food. I tell you, here your weak teeth will be so strengthened that you will be able to eat big mouthfuls as well as small!" (Letter 9).

As her concerns widened, personal interviews were not enough. Requests for her advice were coming in from far away. She was delighted when the young poet Neri di Landoccio asked to be taken into her spiritual family, and soon after that a polished young aristocrat named Stefano Maconi. "You can write my letters!" She was a tireless correspondent; the two young men worked hard for their spiritual bread and butter.

In 1374, when she was twenty-seven, Catherine was called to Florence by the Master-General of the Dominican order. Whatever the ostensible reason it was clear they wanted to examine the young tertiary who had won such a following. Far from censuring her, they were so impressed by her sanctity that they assigned to her spiritual family a Dominican superior. This is the point at which Raymond delle Vigne, later known as Blessed Raymond Capua, entered her life. He would be her personal confessor and spiritual director, her dearest friend.

One of the most beautiful phenomena in the history of Christian mysticism is the intense and mutually supportive friendship that can spring up between its men and women contemplatives. The relationship between Raymond and Catherine ranks among the sweetest of these friendships. Raymond came from one of the most distinguished families in Florence, a learned and aristocratic man who enjoyed considerable prestige within his order. No stranger to feminine spirituality, he had directed a convent of Dominican nuns at Montepulciano for two years and had just completed a biography of that convent's own Blessed Agnes. Though careful and slow to form his full assessment of Catherine, he was instantly alert to the possibilities, and once he was certain about her stature, he was her devoted follower for life.

Raymond's story of Catherine is documented assiduously, telling us in each chapter exactly whom he had consulted when he was writing about events that took place before he joined her. It is as appealing for what it tells us about him, though, as for what it tells us about her. He has left us an unwitting self-portrait of that very special "type" of the period, the learned priest who understood that genuine spirituality had nothing to do with erudition and who could see in the deeply devotional women mystics of the period the embodiment of Christ's teachings. With charming gusto, he relates story after story about how effortlessly Catherine punctured the arrogance of various men—rich, learned, powerful—and brought them into the circle of "Caterinati."

From Florence, Raymond accompanied Catherine back to a Siena struck by disaster. The plague had returned. Civic life was at a standstill, and one-third of the population would die by autumn. Delle Vigne threw himself unhesitatingly into the care of the sick and dying, working alongside Catherine for weeks, until one day he himself awoke with a fever and the telltale swelling in the groin. Growing weaker by the moment, he staggered into the Benincasa's and asked that Catherine be sent for. Hours passed, and at last she came, acting, he complained later, as if she were in no hurry at all. She merely touched his forehead, then knelt and prayed for a full hour and a half. Without speaking, she prepared some food and fed him. He slept, and when he awoke he was fit again. Catherine would perform a great many healings, but this episode is unusually endearing, for it carries with it echoes of a tradition as old as time: when you save someone's life, that life is in a sense yours.

To comprehend even vaguely the direction Catherine's life now took, one must to have some grasp of the political realities of her time and place. First, Pope Clement V had left Rome upon his election in 1309—some twenty-eight years before Catherine was even born—and taken up residence in the town of Avignon, in Provence. The political turbulence of Rome and the Romans' resentment of papal authority had made the Holy City increasingly inhospitable to the papacy. The south of France was as pleasant then as it is now—the food and wines as inviting, the climate as comfortable—and Clement was himself a Frenchman from Bordeaux. If some were disturbed that the church had severed itself from its historic roots, others were just as grateful for a quiet atmosphere in which to carry out the daily routine of judicial business, and in the assessment of historian Robert Southern, "The papal court was now mainly a place where business was done."[6] Clement V was not the first pope to live away from Rome, but it was under his papacy that the exiled church at Avignon began to be called Babylon, since the excesses of every conceivable kind were practiced there, financed by enormous amounts of money from the sale of indulgences. From the top down, the clergy was in a sorry state, all the more so since a great many unqualified individuals had been brought into holy orders just to fill the gaps left by the plague.

Italy itself, a loose grouping of independent city-states, was being administered by papal legates from France, officials with little understanding of the people. Tensions had been growing for some time, but finally in 1375 Florence actually declared war against the papacy, joined quickly by most of the other republics. The indefensibly corrupt state of the clergy was a powerful rallying point for the "Tuscan League," but the Florentines themselves were no angels. Cynicism pervaded the entire conflict.

Catherine's grief at the state of things crystallized into four basic objectives. First, she appealed to the pope—Gregory XI by now—to return to Rome. Second, she urged him to initiate sweeping clerical reform, beginning at the top. Third, he should make peace with Florence, behaving magnanimously and setting an example of forgiveness. Finally—and we flinch at this—he should launch a crusade. Even the first of Catherine's aims seems questionable to most of us today. Does it matter that much where the church makes its headquarters? Many of Catherine's contemporaries felt that it did, but for few of them did the issue have the life-and-death urgency it did for Catherine. To understand why she felt as she did, we must remember that for her, the essential Christian act is to receive suffering joyfully on behalf of others and thereby make of oneself "another Christ." That the papacy left Rome for the gracious ease of Avignon meant it had abandoned the voluntary suffering—literally, the blood and the bones—of its first martyrs, and repudiated the very heart of Christianity. A crusade that might win back the Holy Land would have had the same kind of significance for her as returning the pope to Rome—a retrieval of the church's own historic identity and, more than that, a restoration of continuity with the act of supreme self sacrifice, the crucifixion. She reasoned, too (erroneously, it would seem to most of us), that a crusade would convert a great many Muslims to Christianity.

Catherine's other motive was understandable enough, if shortsighted: she wanted to get the fighting out of Italy. For generations now, mercenary armies had been helping the Italians themselves to lay waste to the countryside. Where her imagination fell short, of course, was in failing to consider fully the impact of another crusade on the Muslims. Hers was a lamentable failure, but it is not unique in the lives of mystics, reminding us that these individuals are finally only human and subject as we all are to the perceptual limitations of their own cultures. Perhaps we will be in a better position to criticize Catherine's mania for a crusade when we ourselves have begun to deal constructively with the youthful energies, combative for want of direction and opportunity, that fuel gang warfare in so many of our own inner cities.

From 1375 until her death in 1380, Catherine was in Siena for only brief spells. A wealthy convert gave her a castle outside of town to use as a convent, but she resided there, from what we can gather, less than a month. Over and over she was called away—to Pisa, where she would preach a crusade and struggle in vain to keep the city from going over to the Florentine side. To Florence twice, with the understanding she was negotiating a peace with the papacy—again, in vain, for the Florentines were merely using her to buy time. To a castle at Rocca d'Orcia in the mountainous regions outside Siena for six months, where she and her "family" made peace—successfully in this case—between warring branches of one of the city's first families. To Rome, finally, in 1378, where she would remain throughout the last two years of her life.

Wherever she went, throngs of men and women crowded around her. The pope issued a special bull in 1376 requiring that three priests accompany her at all times to take the confessions of the multitude that would suddenly ask for the sacraments when they laid eyes upon her. During her stay at the castle in Rocca d'Orcia, four more priests would have to join them to deal with the "rivers of men and women" Raymond says poured down out of the hills just to see her. Vividly, he describes his own as well as his two co-workers' exhaustion as they heard confessions well into the night with no break for dinner.[7]

Despite her desperate efforts, which included a steady stream of letters to everyone involved, the war between Florence and the papacy continued until 1378. The crusade Catherine sought never happened. Clerical reform would eventually take place, and her own followers would play important roles, but not until long after her death.

Pope Gregory XI did indeed return the papacy to Rome, and it is clear that Catherine's insistent appeals had much to do with getting him there. "I am begging you," she wrote imperiously, "I am *telling* you" (Letter 63). But her joy at his arrival in Rome turned bitter almost immediately. He died in March of 1378, and his successor, Urban VI, managed things so badly, despite all of Catherine's passionate warnings, that in September the cardinals elected another man pope—another Clement—and the Great Schism was under way, with incalculably far-reaching destructive effect. Catherine remained loyal to Urban, and it was at his request that she came to Rome. She had predicted the schism. Raymond had come to her one day weeping over the defection of Italian cities to the Tuscan League, and Catherine had told him, dry-eyed, "This is milk and honey compared with what will follow, for the clergy themselves will rebel and divide the Church."[8]

During her stay at Rocca d'Orcia, Catherine had begun composing the *Dialogue*, so called because it consists of four petitions to God, each followed by God's reply and then Catherine's prayer of thanksgiving. She completed it in October of the following year, just before she was called to Rome. She is said to have dictated most of it while in an ecstatic state: three people worked in tandem, writing as fast as they could, to get it all down. It is written in Italian, and it is deeply vernacular, earthy and concrete, replete with metaphors drawn from ordinary life ("We are kneaded into Christ!"). Its central metaphor is of Christ as the bridge: humanity at one end, divinity at the other, uniting at the center in the figure of Christ. The image reminds us of "flow" in Mechthild, wherein ontologically distinct entities merge imperceptibly into one another. Indeed, the coming together of humanity and Christ is her abiding concern. "If you will love me and keep my word," the Lord promises at the very beginning of the book, "I will show myself to you, and you will be one thing with me and I with you."

The *Dialogue* is Catherine's spiritual compendium; everything she had learned about the life of the spirit is here. It is not an easily approachable work. Its tone is unremittingly intense, and the structure is complex. The first petition is on behalf of Catherine herself, and the second asks for the reform of the church; the third is concerned with the welfare of the whole world, especially regarding peace, and the last is for divine providence in all things. Within this framework, Catherine moves across a broad range of topics, to dazzling though sometimes bewildering effect. Even if one grasps the overall format of the treatise, there is a relentlessness about it that forces one to read it slowly or in small bits. We sympathize readily with Raymond, who admitted to having nodded off sometimes in the midst of Catherine's inspired talks. "My dear man," she would say loudly as she shook him awake, "do you really want to miss things useful to your soul, just for the sake of sleep? Am I supposed to be talking to you or the wall?" (*Life* 55).

Toward the end of the *Dialogue*, writing from Siena by now, Catherine records God's words: "Sometimes I let the whole world be against the just, and in the end they die a death that leaves worldly people stunned in wonder" (*Dialogue* 283). Indeed, the final days of the great spiritual teachers are nothing like those of the hero in the traditional quest narrative. You can look for a long time before you find a saint's life rounded off with a happy ending, and Catherine's is true to form. No matter who is telling the story—and at least a hundred biographers have—Catherine's last months take place under a dark sky, heavy with storm clouds. They are pervaded with her grief: grief at the terrible destructiveness of war and schism, grief at the futility of her own efforts to stave it all off, grief at the failure of people close to her to live up to her hopes. When she came to Rome, several key members of the *bella brigata* balked at accompanying her. They would come later, they promised, but months passed, and they still lingered in Siena. Most troubling was the paralysis of her personal secretary, Stefano Maconi. Her most valued supporter, Raymond, had preceded the party to Rome, but Catherine had no sooner joined him there than he was snatched away; the pope had charged him to preach a crusade against Clement. They had barely said their tearful good-byes when she found herself writing him indignant letters, for out of justifiable fear of ambush he failed to cross the border into France. Catherine could not abide cowardice.

Urban's behavior, meanwhile, did little to persuade anyone he was the true heir of Saint Peter. Cruel and arbitrary in his judgments, he would turn out to be one of the most hated men to wear the papal tiara. Word reached Catherine that men and women of real sanctity had transferred their loyalties to Clement VII in Avignon. All around Rome itself, meanwhile, ferocious fighting was taking place. Urban himself went from bad to worse, appointing a new set of cardinals whose lives were far from exemplary and systematically destroying every opening for peace with his explosive temper. "For the love of Christ crucified," Catherine wrote, "restrain a little those hasty movements of your nature."[9]

By the first days of 1380, Rome was filled with rumors of plots to assassinate Pope Urban. Catherine was living with her spiritual family in a house provided by the pope about a mile from Saint Peter's. They spent most of their day in prayer, taking on kitchen duties by turn and begging alms as needed. They were joined each day by new friends; Rome had its own *caterinati*.

Late in January, just after writing a letter to the pope, Catherine fell down in a dead stupor, as though she had suffered a stroke. To Father Raymond, she wrote afterward that once again her soul had left her body—not, this time, to taste joy, but to enter direct combat with the powers of darkness. She implored God on behalf of the church and its children to reverse the direction things were taking, and when after two days and two nights she returned to consciousness, she believed God would. For her part, she would walk every day to Saint Peter's to hear mass.

"You know that this is impossible for me," she wrote Raymond, for her physical condition had deteriorated appallingly, "but in obedience to Him everything has been possible." At dawn every morning she could be seen, "a dead woman," in her own words, walking to Saint Peter's "to labour in the little bark of Holy Church." She remained there all day, "without food, even without a drop of water. . . . My life is hanging by a thread." And that thread stretched out so long. We can scarcely believe how many months she survived, this woman who had not eaten or slept for years, who suffered in every part of her body. On the third Sunday in Lent she was kneeling in prayer at Saint Peter's. Before her was a depiction in mosaic of a famous scene from the Gospel according to Matthew. A tiny ship carrying the apostles is being buffeted by a terrible storm when Christ appears, walking toward them across the water. Peter flings himself out of the boat to go to Christ, then panics and starts to drown. Christ reaches out to steady him, rebuking him for his little faith. By the time they reach the boat, the storm is over. As Catherine looked at the picture, she suddenly felt that the boat itself, Holy Church, had been lifted out of the picture and placed, the full weight of it, upon her shoulders. She sank to the ground, losing the use of her legs, and was carried back home. For weeks she would linger on, in virtual paralysis and terrible pain. Hearing how far she had sunk, poor Stefano Maconi was suddenly galvanized. On horseback he flew to Rome, in time to receive her blessing and hear her whisper "Join the Carthusians."[10] On April 29, surrounded by those who held her most dear, Catherine Benincasa, *beata popolana*, was released "from this body of death."

For as long as I have been studying the lives of mystics, I have struggled with the mystery of the terrible suffering that engulfs the men and women of God in the last days of their lives. It is mysterious, but perhaps it is plain as day, too. From the moment when Christ told Catherine she would be "another him," a process was initiated that could have only one outcome—the passion itself. When we love someone deeply, we do experience their suffering as our own. If Catherine's love really did expand to include more and more human beings—all of Christendom, finally—then she was opening herself to more and more pain as well. Her life was a miracle of inclusion. Raymond said of her, "Catherine carried the whole church in her heart." Reading her letters, one sees that she really did think of herself as a mother—birthing and lactating—throughout her apostolate. She truly was like someone pregnant, her love and her consciousness expanding outward until finally she could not contain any more love or any more pain, and the physical part of her simply had to fall away, just as the husk of a seed falls away when the seed has swollen to the point of giving new life. "I am bursting," Catherine wrote on one occasion, "and cannot burst!" (Letter 70). In the words of the Gospel according to John, "Except a corn of wheat fall into the ground and die, it abideth alone: but if it die, it bringeth forth much fruit" (John 12:24, KJV).

It is with Catherine of Siena that I think we see most clearly just how far-reaching can be the force of a mystic's personality, or "charisma," to fall back upon a woefully misused term that simply means "holy spirit." She was so passionate in her convictions and in her affections, so fully engaged in life as to belie conventional assumptions about sainthood and what it means to renounce the world. Her remarkable warmth—that intensity, red like the wine of Siena—seems to me to give credence to the notion that in the fully realized human being, sexual energy is transmuted into a force—a field of forces, even, that nourishes, heals, and galvanizes all who enter it.

There is a charming postscript to Catherine's death. Among her many friends in Rome was a woman named Semia, a widow with five grown sons (*Life* 341ff.). Semia had been too busy at home to visit Catherine and did not know how far her health had deteriorated. Nonetheless, Semia unaccountably had a beautiful dream in which she spoke with Catherine and witnessed her ascension into Heaven. On waking, Semia realized she had overslept. The last mass was over and she had yet to get her sons' lunch on the table. She began preparing the meal, hurried and distraught, when she heard bells from a nearby convent and realized she could still attend mass after all. Exhilarated by her dream-vision, though still unaware of its meaning, she flung off her apron and chanced it, murmuring to herself that if she got there in time, it would be proof of Catherine's grace. Of course she did, and on her way back she met her sons hurrying home and asking if their lunch was ready. "Only a minute," she said, stalling for time as she ran into the kitchen. There it all was, the bread and meat sliced, the soup simmering away, the cabbage chopped and ready to be added. Catherine had paused on her way out of this life, Semia concluded, to make a quick pass through a friend's kitchen.

Saint Catherine of Genoa

(1447–1510)

And the state of this soul is then a feeling of such utter
peace and tranquillity that it seems to her that her heart,
and her bodily being, and all both within and without
is immersed in an ocean of utmost peace; from which
she shall never come forth for anything that can befall
her in this life. And she stays immovable, imperturbable,
impassible. . . . And she is so full of peace that though
she press her flesh, her nerves, her bones, no other thing
comes forth from them than peace.

— Saint Catherine of Genoa,
Life, Chap. 18[1]

❦

GENOA *la Superba*. The proud city, Genoa. It is a tough city, too, a
seaport town peopled now as then by wealthy businessmen and
sharp characters. Like any busy international port, its streets are
always full of sailors on shore leave and resident operators, ready to take
their pay: the barmen and prostitutes, the pickpockets, shopkeepers, and
drug dealers. As you walk or drive from the harbor into the city itself, you
pass through slums that have been there for hundreds of years. Beyond
these are the elegant marble palaces of Genoa's aristocracy, many of them

museums today. Genoa shared with Venice the commercial rule of the Mediterranean. It was an exceedingly wealthy city. You can still see the magnificent cathedrals where Catherine and her family worshiped. The hospital she administered was still standing and still in use until American incendiary bombs destroyed it in 1944.

The story of Catherine of Genoa is brought forward regularly as proof that one need not be a cloistered nun to be a saint. Caterina Adorna was not only a lay person, she was married, and she worked for most of her adult life at a huge city hospital, holding positions at every level from the most menial to the directorship. At the same time, she is not one of those saints whom we suspect of having been whisked through the process of canonization for reasons that have little to do with the inner life.[2] She was a mystic of the highest stature, revered during her lifetime and ever since. Her teachings are among the most sublime in the European Catholic tradition. Passages like the following have the purity and otherworldliness of the *Upanishads:*

> I see without eyes, and I hear without ears. I feel without feeling and taste without tasting. I know neither form nor measure; for without seeing I yet behold an operation so divine that the words I first used, perfection, purity, and the like, seem to me now mere lies in the presence of truth . . . Nor can I any longer say, "My God, my all." Everything is mine, for all that is God's seem to be wholly mine. I am mute and lost in God.
>
> (*Life* 50)

Catherine was indeed a full-time working woman, and that was unheard of among women of the aristocratic class into which she was born. Her tender and tireless service to the city's poorest inhabitants is still honored by the grateful Genoese. Nothing in the hospital escaped her notice: her books were kept accurately to the florin. She was nonetheless "wholly absorbed in secret delights" so often that a small room had to be set aside in the hospital where she could hide herself. She would be found there prostrate, "like one dead," her face covered with her hands, and she could not be roused, even by a loud cry. Yet, her biographer tells us, if at such times someone called her in genuine need, she would come forth immediately, "with a glowing countenance, like a cherub"(*Life* 40).

Between her calling as a contemplative on the one hand and a caretaker on the other, we are to understand, no real conflict ever occurred, because the voice of someone "in genuine need" would have been the voice of Christ, issuing from her fellow creature as audibly as from the depths of her own consciousness. Her work and her contemplative life were one and the same.

Catherine of Genoa holds out a rare and precious gift, it seems to me, for contemporary women. But that gift has little to do with her having been married or director of a hospital. It has to do, rather, with the unfolding of her. For in order to become the tremendous figure she was, she had first to free herself from severe chronic depression and quite literally turn her life around. In a setting that was not the least bit supportive of her need to do so, she had, in effect, to reinvent herself, and I believe that her achievement can inspire anyone who has endured even some degree of what she did.

More than any of the four life stories we have looked at so far, Catherine's has a strong element of the classic conversion narrative. This is worth noting because, as we have observed, the typical pattern for women saints is not so much conversion as "steady state." Their male counterparts sowed wild oats aplenty (Augustine and Francis, for example), but women saints are generally portrayed as starting out pious and only getting more so over time. Catherine's departure from that norm reflects in part the far-reaching changes that all of Europe was undergoing: the Middle Ages, with its monolithically normative view of existence, was over. With the rise of humanism, an increasingly diversified picture of human existence had begun to emerge. As we will see, the hagiographers' views of Catherine were still heavily shaped by traditional assumptions: the old idealizing grid is still in place in their accounts. Nonetheless, a great many untidy, intractable, and delicious bits of personal data have slipped through, and they raise all kinds of intriguing questions.

My favorite Catherine story plants her squarely in our mind's eye, flushed, defiant, and fairly crackling with the life force. We are not told when the episode took place, but it was obviously at a point when Catherine's reputation for sanctity had been well established. It seems that an unidentified friar preacher took it upon himself one afternoon to say that he was freer and better prepared to love God than was Catherine. After all, he reminded her, when he had taken his vows (which Catherine, of course, had not), he had renounced everything. He was wedded, therefore, to religion, and she to the world.

Catherine was not the sort who paraded her sanctity, so it is hard to imagine what might have prompted such a rude challenge. She did not take it sitting down, but up on her feet, fire in her eye—in fact, fire all over the place. The narrator tells of "an ardent flame of pure love" that seized her and "inflamed" her heart. "Fervently" she exclaimed, "as though beside herself":

> If I believed that your habit would add one spark [!] to my love, I would not hesitate to tear it from your shoulders piece by piece, if I couldn't get hold of it any other way. Whatever you merit more than I, through the renunciation you have made for God's sake, and through your religious life, which lets you go on winning merit from one day to the next, I don't seek to obtain; these are yours; but that I cannot love God as much as yourself, you can never make me believe.
>
> (*Life* 94)

She spoke with such passion that her hair burst from the band that confined it (picture those broad cloth bands in Renaissance portraits that come right down to the forehead) "and fell disheveled over her shoulders."

To onlookers, Catherine seemed "like a mad woman." The narrator describes them as *"stopefatto, e sodisfatto,"* literally, stupefied, and satisfied ("satisfied," I believe, in the quasilegal meaning of being instructed or answered). The depth of her feeling has thrilled them, but so, too, has her sheer magnificence: she *is* the truth she has uttered. "Love cannot be checked," the narrator adds, "and if checked, it is not pure and simple love."

Writers of the period were nothing if not allegorists: Catherine's unruly hair, a lovely bit of "stage business," becomes a telling detail. To have burst as it did, it must have been of the thick, springy, gleaming kind that Titian painted, and later, Rossetti—the kind of hair that goes where it will. Catherine's very hair becomes, then, metaphorically, love that is too strong to be checked.

This must have taken place in public somewhere, because Catherine is said to have spoken again upon reaching her house. Under her breath, she murmured, "Even if I were in a camp of soldiers, I could not be prevented from loving you. If the world, or if the husband could impede love, what would such love be but a thing of weak and contemptible power?" (*Life* 95)

Strong language this, for she is not saying "a whole army couldn't keep me from loving you" or anything so delicate. In the fifteenth century, a woman would have turned up in a military camp for only one reason. To paraphrase, then: "You think my being married keeps me from loving God as much as I could? Why, if I had as many 'husbands' as a camp follower, it wouldn't abate my love for God."

But we are not to think for a moment that the depth of her devotion reflects any particular merit on her part, for she adds, "I know by what I have experienced that divine love can be conquered or impeded by nothing. It conquers all things." *All* things.

REGRETTABLY, as far as we know, Catherine herself did not write. A considerable body of teachings has been attributed to her, but all of them were written down by close followers twelve years after her death (though they were working from extensive notes and dictation they had taken during her lifetime). This situation is frustrating, but there is such a marvelous consistency in the voice that emerges from this material, and such authority and magnificence in the teachings themselves, that scholars have chosen to accept them as essentially accurate.

Three works are generally attributed to Catherine "and her friends." One is a biography. Much of this is in direct quotes; it appears to have been compiled by her closest disciples from the notes they had all taken of conversations with her over the years. The second appears on first perusal to be a theological discourse on purgatory. Long treated as such, it has been called *Purgation and Purgatory*. In fact, though, it is Catherine's description of her own inner states, using purgatory as a kind of extended metaphor. The third is a three-part work entitled *The Spiritual Dialogue*. The first section of this work is a crisp allegorical dramatization of Catherine's inner struggles: of the soul coming to grips first with the claims of the body and then with those of a subtler figure called self-love. In the second section, the allegory fades out and we get, instead, a more factual account of Catherine's spiritual transformation. The third section is something of a hodge-podge, but is mostly a description of Catherine's last days.

From these three works is drawn all that we know of Catherine's life and teachings. Scholars acknowledge that at any point we could conceivably be reading the interpolation of a follower, but the consensus is that the men who compiled the teachings were self-effacing enough on the one hand, and unimaginative enough on the other, not to have tampered wildly with what they had actually heard and seen. Besides, many of Catherine's other followers were still alive when these works were published, and none apparently took issue with their contents.

Are there textual criteria by which one might distinguish Catherine's own utterances from editorial interpolations or paraphrases? One of Catherine's most devoted scholar-admirers, writing at the beginning of this century, suggested that as we read the prose, we should note the rhythm. Long years studying the writings of mystics had convinced him that the perceptions of an illumined person tend to be expressed "in rhythmical periods."[3] This might sound fanciful, but I am inclined to agree. The marvelously melodic prose of Julian of Norwich or Richard Rolle, for example, lends weight to the theory. I wonder, too, whether vividness of language might not be another strong criterion. It seems almost inconceivable that the careful, reverential devotees who compiled Catherine's teachings could ever have invented the earthy Genoese tone of lines like, "I see myself more covered with secret sins than a cat is with hairs" (*Life* 81).

Catherine was born in 1447 into one of Genoa's wealthiest and most distinguished families, the Fieschi. Most of northern Italy's aristocracy fell into two great and battling tribes, the Guelphs and the Ghibbelines. These were the same warring clans that had torn Dante's Florence asunder and forced the poet into lifelong exile from his beloved city and the same that had thrown Francis's and Clare's Umbria into bloody turmoil. Two hundred years after Clare's death, the feud still simmered. The Fieschis were Guelphs, and the young man Catherine would be compelled to marry was a Ghibbeline, but inherited family quarrels would be the least of that couple's problems.

Of Catherine's childhood, little is known except that she kept to herself and was extremely devout. She began to do penance when she was eight years old; she slept on straw with a block of hard wood in place of a pillow. Her biographers tell us that, like Mechthild, she had a powerful spiritual experience when she was just twelve. "God in his grace bestowed on her the gift of prayer, and a wonderful communion with our Lord, which enkindled within her a new flame of deep love, together with a lively sense of the sufferings he endured in his holy passion" (*Life* 20).

"The gift of prayer" suggests the capacity for what Teresa of Avila would call "recollection" and possibly even "the prayer of quiet": the ability, in any event, to become deeply absorbed in prayer. The second part of the experience, a powerful sense of identification with Christ crucified that included firsthand knowledge of both his suffering and his love, had been sought by mystics throughout the Middle Ages, including Julian of Norwich and Francis of Assisi. What actually happened to twelve-year-old Catherine is obviously not meant to be seen as comparable to the stigmata that Francis received or to Julian's sixteen "showings." We receive, the mystics tell us, according to our capacity, and Catherine was far from being the enormously capacious soul she would one day be. Nonetheless, we must recognize that for this young girl, life on the ordinary level could never have looked the same again.

Catherine asked just a year afterward to be received into a local Augustinian convent, and her confessor supported the petition. The mother superior demurred, though; thirteen was just too young, and anyone who has lived with a thirteen-year-old, or even *been* one, can surely understand her reluctance. Besides, the convent had already received her older sister, and as we will see in the case of Thérèse of Lisieux, that can be worrisome to cloistered communities.

One of the rubrics of the spiritual life is that when our heart's desire is thwarted, it is because God has something even better in mind for us. This would prove true for Catherine, but only after a good long while. For the time being, life continued to slide downhill. Just a year after she was denied admission to the convent of Our Lady of Grace, her father died. She was now in the custody of her eldest brother Giacomo, and he contracted her in marriage to Giuliano Adorno, member of another highly placed Genoese family with whom the Fieschis were bitterly estranged. When her uncle the archbishop married the two—motivated, no doubt, by a genuine desire to heal the feud—Catherine was just fifteen and a half.

Giacomo's decision is understandable in several senses. Catherine's beauty was widely acclaimed, and a beautiful girl of good family would have had excellent market value in a society that was virtually all market.

There may have been strong financial reasons for seeking reconciliation with the Adornos. Fifteen was not an indecently early age for marriage at that time, and after all, what could he have known of the real nature of his strange little sister, so given to prayer—she of whom we learn almost nothing but that "she led a very simple life, seldom speaking with anyone"? He might even have thought marriage would draw her out: particularly marriage to a live wire like Giuliano.

But there, we really cannot let him off the hook. For surely Giuliano's character would have been apparent enough in the relatively small world of Genoese high society. Profligate and irascible at once, he is said to have had a singularly weak character. Catherine's mother does not appear to have objected to the marriage, a fact that biographers have noted with some bitterness.

It is reasonable to wonder why Catherine went through with the marriage. Others in her position found ways to escape, and the hagiographers cannot extol them highly enough—those like Catherine of Siena who cut off their hair or others who went out and contracted smallpox on purpose. There was Christina of Markyate, for that matter, who hid herself for several years in a hermit's cell, in a closet the size of a linen chest.[4] There *are* ways, and surely the spirited woman we met a few moments ago was resourceful enough to have found herself one. Young Catherine was not able to extricate herself, though, because she had not yet become that spirited woman. I think it is fair to guess that she felt suspended, quite literally, between two worlds. She had glimpsed just enough, that day when she was twelve, to blight any pleasure she might have taken in an ordinary life. The door to that other world, though, the one she was born to inhabit, had swung open for only an instant before slamming shut again. She had been denied entrance into her sister's convent, and her betrothal, coming right after the loss of her father, must have felt cruelly consistent: her destiny was to be determined by others.

To put it differently, and positively, as hindsight encourages us to do, a process had been initiated: Catherine's transformation was well under way, but it was working itself out well below the surface level of consciousness. Her conscious life was not yet touched. On the face of things, she was just a young and very sheltered girl who had always been obedient, and she acted now, as far as anyone could have seen, out of that obedience.

Nothing is recorded of Catherine's first five years of married life except that she spent them in a state of extreme depression and withdrawal. Her husband proved to be "entirely the opposite of herself in his mode of life" (*Life* 22). He gambled, he partied, he spent money too freely. He had a mistress, in fact, and an illegitimate child of whose presence Catherine would learn only when the money ran out. One chronicler says Giuliano had five natural offspring, but vilifying the poor fellow became almost an obsession with Catherine's more creative chroniclers. Adorno's own mother mentions little "Thobia" in her will, as does Catherine, but neither mentions the hypothetical other four children. In any event, more damning evidence than a natural child or two is needed before we can make Giuliano out to be the Caligula of his age.

In the light of Giuliano's eventual conversion and its apparent sincerity, I think we can put a gentler reading on these years than Catherine's biographers have done. The couple was, after all, so badly matched. It would have taken an extraordinarily sensitive, patient, and kindly man to win over this young woman into any conventional version of marriage. One imagines a disastrous wedding night and many disastrous nights to follow—a settling in, eventually, to patterns of mutual avoidance: all this, and surely, on one or both sides, acute loneliness. "She was a most pitiable object," says her biographer. "She lived in a solitary house, alone, to satisfy him, and never went out except to attend mass, and then return as quickly as possible, for she would endure anything rather than give pain to others" (*Life* 151).

After five years, by age twenty, Catherine seems to have shaken herself—friends and relatives helped with the shaking—into an effort to make the best of her situation. For the second five years of her marriage, then, she tried to lose herself in "external affairs and feminine amusements": the equivalent, one guesses, of fashion shows and bridge parties. This worked about as well as one might expect for someone of Catherine's depth; at the end of the experiment, she was unhappier than ever. Catherine was twenty-five now and so troubled by "the opposition of her husband's disposition to her own" that one day she went to church and called on her patron saint to help her: "Pray to God for me, oh, St. Benedict, that for three months He may keep me sick in bed" (*Life* 22).

It is a peculiar prayer. Catherine has not asked to experience a sickness unto death, as Julian had, who has just asked to be left to herself for a while: "Not tonight, dear, I have a headache," but for three months running. A more guileful woman would have invented an illness; Catherine had to beg God to give her one, and, indeed, some unnamed debility confined her to her room for the specified period, beginning around Christmas 1472.

The pivotal day in Catherine's life was March 22, 1473, and it was her sister Limbania who provided the means of transformation. Limbania was a nun at the convent Catherine had tried to enter. Grieved at Catherine's condition, she brought her to the convent to meet her own confessor, a man of such sanctity that Limbania hoped Catherine would respond. Catherine let herself be taken there, insisting, though, that she was too distraught to make a confession. Fine, her sister said, then just ask for his blessing.

Perhaps timing is everything. Perhaps Catherine would have had the same experience if she had stayed home pacing in her garden, in the manner of Augustine. But there is another way of looking at these narratives that brings out the value of the small, precious services human beings can render one another, the ways we can be channels of grace for one another, even unwittingly. By that kind of reading, Catherine's sister and her confessor can take some credit. For Catherine had just knelt before the man when the floodgates of her heart opened out. She received a "wound to the heart" from God's "immense love" and, at the same time, full and overwhelming awareness of her own misery and the "defects" in herself that had brought it on; full awareness, too, of the inconceivable *goodness* of God.

Not as ideas, we must realize, but as facts did this new awareness force itself in on her. Knowledge of God's love always comes, Catherine said later, "in a rush" and not through any action of our own will or intellect; it is all the recipient can do to bear the impact. No sooner had Catherine knelt before her sister's confessor than he was called away. Alone, she murmured over and over to herself, "No more world. No more sins." "No more Catherine," she might have added, for the woman she had been was no more.

But what are the sins and defects she is repudiating? Had her first twenty-six years really been so riddled with iniquity? Had she not been more truly victim than wrongdoer? Arguably so, but in Catherine's time, melancholy and *accidie,* or despair, were not considered afflictions merely. They entailed choice. However slender Catherine's literary back ground might have been, she probably was familiar with Dante's description of the souls in hell who had succumbed to the sin of *accidie*. Invisible, they can be detected only by bubbles on the surface of mud: "Wedged in the slime, they say: 'We had been sullen in the sweet air that's gladdened by the sun; we bore the mist of sluggishness in us: Now we are bitter in the blackened mud.'"[5]

There is a terrible anonymity in the image, a literal return to primal ooze. Hope and good cheer are virtues of the spiritual high road, while despair and melancholy express the individual's refusal to take another step.

If we are still not convinced, if "sin" for us seems to connote more active forms of wrongdoing than Catherine exhibited, we would perhaps do well to ponder the suggestions of certain theologians writing today who are women.[6] If women had been writing theology all along, they wonder, would there not be considerably less emphasis on sinful tendencies like abuse of power, arrogance, pride, and the other more conventionally male problems? Would correspondingly more attention be paid to the sinful dispositions that plague women specifically? Negation of one's self, for instance—the refusal to *become*—the "sin" of spending your entire life reacting to circumstances from one moment to the next without ever forming a resolve or moving toward a goal.

With regard to Francis and Clare in particular, I have spoken of what it means to "make oneself zero" by gradually withdrawing all desires from short-term personal satisfactions and unifying them—focusing them all into a single driving need, the need, quite simply, to see God. There is all the difference in the world between this effort, called "self-naughting" in the Christian tradition, and its deadly counterfeits—belittling oneself, for example, or submerging oneself in demeaning or merely trivial relationships so as to beg the deepest questions of existence. Have the priests and confessors who have counseled women through the ages been sufficiently sensitive to that difference? Could it be that the wise abbess or anchoress might have been more astute in this regard?

Call it what you will, then—sinfulness, neurosis, or plain stupor— Catherine cast it off entirely in that first incandescent moment. She was one passionate resolve now and barely aware of her surroundings. Unaware that anything had happened, the confessor returned. Catherine managed to postpone her confession for a day and went home. With-drawing to a private room, she exclaimed, "Oh, Love, can it be that you have called me with such love and made me to know in one instant that which tongue cannot utter?" For days she labored to take in the enormity of what she had seen, and in a few days it came upon her again—that same double awareness, of bliss and suffering, but fused now, and em-bodied, in a vision of Christ crucified. She would carry that vision be-fore her mind's eye always, and it would hurl her into a life of heroic service—to Christ living in the tormented shapes of thousands upon thousands of suffering men, women, and children.

I have treated that visit to her sister's confessor as the turning point for Catherine, and on the face of things it would seem that divine grace, biding its time up until now, intervened at precisely that moment. But it sheds some light on the mysterious interplay between grace and the in-dividual's own striving to recognize that in a funny, backhanded way, Catherine had actually taken initiative to turn her life around well before that crucial day in spring. When her biographer describes her plea for three months' complete bed rest, he relates it to the profound exaspera-tion to which her marriage had reduced her. There is another way to look at the episode, however. Her request for a temporary reprieve from everyday life had been honored, and you could reasonably say "by God"; but you could say with equal accuracy "by her very own self" and for her very own reasons. At junctures like this, there may be no real distinc-tion. For in a sense all that Catherine was asking of Benedict was *con-finement*—I use the word in its fullest sense—because deep inside the awareness was stirring that something was about to happen. Childless after ten years of marriage, she was about to give birth at last to herself.

Sunk deep in misery as she had been, then, and perilously self-absorbed, Catherine had nonetheless acted that winter with an instinc-tive wisdom. She had moved into silence, allowed a receiving silence to grow within her. She had listened with every cell of her being. The pat-tern is archetypal and heroic. The seeker of light moves down and down and down, leaving every familiar support behind, until she can go no fur-ther. She waits in silence, all comforts refused, until, at long last, there dawns the Light. The Word. Birth. "I live no longer," Catherine would exult soon afterward, "but Christ lives in me" (*Life* 28). At the critical moment, we note, Catherine was actually kneeling before her confessor, like Mary at the Annunciation. (The Feast of the Annunciation was, in fact, only a few days away.)

Catherine's life confronts us over and over again with formidable paradoxes. One of these is that while she knew herself to be completely united with God from that first moment, she would nonetheless spend the rest of her long life undergoing an arduous process of purification, a process that began that very first day. Much of it would take place within, as an "interior fire," but much of it went on during her daily life, too, in the work to which she felt herself called. She used an arresting and markedly feminine metaphor to describe that work: "The Spirit wanted [her] to work with human misery as if [she] were kneading bread, and even, if need be, to taste it a bit" (*Spiritual Dialogue* 130). The "bread" of human misery is by inference the torn flesh of Christ crucified: "Take, eat, this is my Body."

To explain that paradox—the co-existence in her experience of the most intense joy conceivable with the worst pain imaginable—Catherine compares her state to that of souls in purgatory, whose condition was an article of faith to Catholics of her time. They may appear to be suffering terribly as they undergo what Dante called "the fire that refines," and in a real sense, Catherine acknowledges, they *are* suffering, but only because of the flaws in themselves that delay their full union with God. Their suffering is limited, contained, and offset by the absolute certainty that in the course of time they *will* know that union. Central to all of Catherine's teachings is what she calls Pure and Simple Love, which makes itself felt as fire. The imagery is magnificent:

> When God sees the Soul pure as it was in its origins,
> He tugs at it with a glance,
> draws it and binds it to Himself with a fiery love
> that by itself could annihilate the immortal soul.
> In so acting, God so transforms the soul in Him
> that it knows nothing other than God;
> and He continues to draw it up into His fiery love
> until He restores it
> to that pure state from which it first issued.

These rays purify and then annihilate.
The soul becomes like gold
that becomes purer as it is fired,
all dross being cast out.

Having come to the point of twenty-four carats,
gold cannot be purified any further;
and this is what happens to the soul
in the fire of God's love.

(*Purgation and Purgatory* 79–80)

To imagine God's love as fire does not come naturally to those of us reared on conventional renderings of hell's fiery furnace. But for the poet Dante, for example, hell was not characterized by flames or smoldering embers, but by icy cold, immobility, a frozen cavern at its deepest levels, housing monstrous incarnations of self-will. Fire, on the other hand, had more to do with warmth and light and love.

Catherine acknowledged fully that it hurt to be refined by fire. She described herself as looking, in those first weeks, "more like a frightened animal than a human being" and added that "the pain of enduring that vision of sin was as keen-edged and hard as a diamond" (*Spiritual Dialogue* 118). And yet, she insisted there was no real suffering in this pain because once you have submitted yourself entirely to God's will, and all you really want is to be drawn up into God's love, you accept everything that happens along the way. If there is no resistance to the divine will, there is no sorrow either.

Stunned at seeing the distance between herself and the purity she had experienced, Catherine wanted nothing now but to remove every impediment. Following what her biographers call her "conversion," or her "second conversion," there ensued a four-year period of adjustment. She imposed on herself the whole traditional range of austerities. She prayed for six hours a day; she abstained from meat and fruit and sprinkled bitter herbs on other foods; she wore a hair shirt, walked about with her eyes cast down, withdrew from conversation with friends (she was by nature, we are told, very sociable). She tried to stay awake at night but found that God would not let her! Her fasts were notable.

Her course of action—this purgation or "washing away"—is mirrored in a great many mystics' lives. By imposing all manner of strictures on the external life, over which one *can* exert some control, they appear to be seeking to counterbalance the tremendous storm that is taking place within, which is not at all under the individual's control. The intense sobriety of asceticism is imposed to offset the almost unbearable joy arising within. Purgation is an attempt to harmonize, or align, the whole person at the physical, emotional, and intellectual levels, adjusting for the far-reaching changes that have taken place deep within. The particulars of this process, admittedly, do not bear close examination; they are sometimes raw and extreme and foolishly life threatening. There is a point along the way of purgation at which guidance from someone who has already been through it can be critical, and too rarely in the lives of Western mystics has such a mentor appeared, someone who could temper their excesses as Francis did Clare's and protect both their physical and mental health. And yet we must tread lightly here and not rush to judge, for the very times these people lived in seemed to require excess in ways I think we do not. Catherine did survive this period, and, weakened as she was by fasting, Clare did meet the goals she had set for herself.

At the end of four years, all of Catherine's mortifications ended abruptly. "Her mind became clear and free, and so filled with God that nothing else ever entered into it" (*Life* 39). Curiously, however, for the next twenty-three years, through no volition of her own, she found herself fasting throughout Lent and Advent. These were complete fasts, when she took only a beverage of water, vinegar, and salt. She made light of them and in fact tried to eat, but could not. Far from suggesting that anyone else undertake such fasts, she shrugged them off and said there was no particular spiritual merit in them. During these periods she was, if anything, more active, and she slept better than at any other time.

One gropes to understand: Were these bouts of *inedia* a kind of regular and almost "automatic" reenactment of that balancing and compensating impulse described above? We get the impression that even after the four-year period of intense asceticism, something like that "battening down" process continued throughout her life in direct proportion to the intensity of her ecstatic experiences.

In all of Catherine's references to this period, one can be put off by her passionate repudiations of self. "Lord, why do you illumine a soul so rank—an enemy who continually flees from you, an obstinate, sensual soul?" But it has always to be borne in mind, and not only with Catherine but also with Augustine, Teresa, and others, that when they talk this way, the real focal point is not "wretched me," but rather, "incredible God." It is in the light of revealed truth, love, and beauty that our human and quite ordinary flaws appear so very dark, and the mystic has come to have full confidence that in time those flaws really will be mended. Their tears, their wordless sighs have nothing to do with self-pity or self-deprecation at all, but *relief*. To paraphrase: "I've been abysmally wrong, and I grieve for that. I *need* to grieve for that. . . . But my world is bright, for I am surrounded and embraced now by limitless love. The past is over. I will go now where love leads me."

And love did lead Catherine, right out of her privileged place in wealthy Genoese society and into the streets of the city's most desperately poor quarters, where she cared for syphilitics, lepers, plague victims, and many more. To guide her in her work and her spiritual life, God gave her two pieces of instruction. First were the three "nevers": "My daughter . . . Never say I will or I will not. Never say mine, but always ours. Never excuse yourself, but always accuse yourself."

Standard issue, these three practices, for the spiritual aspirant of any time or place—simple, yet powerful strategies aimed to reduce, little by little, the tyranny of "I" and "mine."

The second piece of instruction was also threefold. It is as if Catherine had asked God to distill the whole of Christ's teachings into three words or phrases so concise they would come to mind in any circumstances (in the most appalling tenement room, at the bedside of the most wretched death imaginable). First, God told her to extract from the "Our Father" the phrase *fiat voluntas tua*, "Thy will be done." Second, she was told, "From the 'Hail Mary,' take the word *Jesus*, and may it be implanted in your heart, and it will be a sweet guide and shield to you in all the necessities of life." Third, out of all the Scriptures, she should seize upon one word. The word, of course, was *love*. Love was to be her one support, and with it she would go on her way "direct, pure, light, watchful, quick, enlightened, without erring, yet without a guide or help from any creature" (*Life* 40–41).

The first instruction is a kind of gloss on the advice never to say "I will" or "I will not": we can let go, we are to understand, because a wisdom much deeper than ours, and a love much wider, is at work. The second piece of instruction is most interesting, because it advocates the use of a holy name—a *mantram,* in effect. "Hesychasm," or the repetition of the short prayer "Lord, have mercy upon me," is widely practiced in the Russian and Greek Orthodox traditions, but there is no universally recommended counterpart in Catholicism.[7] And yet we suspect the practice has been undertaken by many mystics in the West. Saint Bernard of Clairvaux spoke of the "energizing word," and in the hymn "Sweet Is the Remembrance of Jesus" he declared Jesus to be "a sweet song in the ears, in the mouth wonderful honey, the spiced wine of heaven in the heart."[8] The anonymous English treatise called *The Cloud of Unknowing* seems very close in spirit to Catherine:

> And if thou desirest to have this intent lapped and folden in one word, so that thou mayest have better hold thereupon, take thee but a little word of one syllable. . . . Such a word is this word God or this word Love. Choose whichever thou wilt, or another; . . . and fasten this word to thy heart that so it may never go thence for anything that befalleth. . . . With this word thou shalt smite down all manner of thought under the "cloud of forgetting."[9]

Late in her life, Catherine bent over the bed of a devout woman who lay dying, a member of the Third Order of Saint Francis. She was in great pain and with considerable difficulty was trying to speak. "Call Jesus," Catherine urged her, and when she saw her trying—saw, in the words of the biographer, "that her mouth was as it were full of Jesus"—she could not refrain from kissing her, thus, it was believed, contracting the fever herself. Christ and the name of Christ had become one for her.

The third piece of instruction needs no comment: I would observe only that the description of how Catherine would proceed if she went on her way with love as her only support, "direct, pure, light," is a lovely summary of everything her supporters ever said about her—and that it is most fortunate we have their testimony, to offset her own bleak assessments of herself!

In association with a charitable organization, the Ladies of Mercy, Catherine began to work in Genoa's slums. She quite literally had seen God. She knew herself to be joined to God more surely than most of us know our names. But before she could love and serve God unrestrainedly, embodied as a syphilitic or a leper with foul-smelling sores, she would have to overcome her very human repugnance. Like Catherine of Siena, she took heroic measures, shocking measures: "She cleansed their houses from the most disgusting filth, and she would even put it in her mouth, in order to conquer the disgust it produced. She took home the garments of the poor, covered with dirt and vermin, and having cleansed them thoroughly, returned them to their owners" (*Life* 45).

Swiftly now, the circumstances of her external life bent and gave way. A few months after her conversion, her husband went bankrupt. Some accounts claim he had reduced them to utter poverty, but the records of a town run by bookkeepers make it plain theirs was only a relative poverty, a reduction in wealth that was undoubtedly a great relief to her, insofar as it removed them from the social strata they had lived in and from all the obligations that that life had entailed. Would she have been as free to give herself over to her charitable works if they had not lost their fortune? Not, one guesses, without a struggle. And Catherine does not seem to have felt obliged to honor her husband's feelings. A Giuliano chastened by bad luck was, at last, just the Giuliano she needed!

Remarkably enough, Giuliano underwent a conversion. Some sources give credit for this to Catherine and the unflagging sweetness with which she supported him during his financial crisis. He joined Francis's Third Order, which was a step that had concrete financial consequences: it meant you would never participate in a lawsuit, for example, and that you would stay out of disputes over inheritance. Soon, Giuliano joined Catherine in her work among the poor.

Upon his conversion, Giuliano received his own piece of divine instruction. Catherine's biographer writes, "The Lord gave her this grace, that he placed in the heart of her husband the idea that they would live together as brother and sister." It is nowhere recorded that Catherine raised any objection. The fact of Giuliano's mistress and child are believed to have surfaced about now. "Heroically," says the chronicler, Catherine bestowed affection and money on the young girl. Some sources say she actually adopted her and helped the girl's mother gain admission to a cloistered community.

The exact timing of all these events is not known. Some accounts make it sound as if they all took place in one afternoon, like the last act of an opera by Verdi or Puccini. Probably, though, they unfolded over a year or two. And while one appreciates the biographer's lavish praise of Catherine's largesse and heroism, it is important to remember that at this period in her life, she was really living on another plane altogether, so absorbed in her expanding inner life that husbands, mistresses, financial disasters, and the like were relatively peripheral. One reasons that since she was at last free of the constraints her family and station in life had placed upon her, her heart quite naturally opened to the plight of a woman and child living under far more severe constraints than she ever had, for as mistress to a man suddenly dispossessed, little Thobia's mother would surely have had to degrade herself even further.

From the formal grandeur of the Adorno palace, Giuliano and Catherine moved to a smaller house near the Pammetone Hospital in a neighborhood inhabited mostly by *tintori,* the dyers of cloth. The house had a garden and a large dining room. Thanks again to those wonderfully thorough record keepers—a notary public in this case—we even have a description of the home as it appeared when Catherine died. The editor of the critical edition of Catherine's teachings, who discovered this description, writes in a kind of rapture that is one part devotion and one part archaeological enthusiasm:

> Here is the hearth, the wide dining and reception room, furnished with two broad chairs covered with leather, shoulder high as was fashionable at the time. Here a wide table with three feet and a stately chest of drawers that contained the crockery and the table linens, fragrant with lavender; and against the wall a precious Manger on a table, with the coat of arms of the Fieschi.
> Here is the bedroom where Catherine and Giuliano lived together for long years in a noble exercise of voluntary chastity. . . . [Our editor may be missing a beat.]
> Here is the wide bed furnished with two mattresses, covered with scarlet featherbeds. Here is the divan on which Catherine, overcome by love, often rested.[10]

Catherine and Giuliano would live and work together side by side for another twenty years. In 1479 they were invited to work at the huge Pammetone, and they remained in service there, without pay, for the rest of their lives. Catherine held positions at every level, from the most menial to director (1490–1496) of the entire hospital. It was during these years that she demonstrated the seamless unity of her two lives—the active and the contemplative—for which the church has particularly honored her.

WHEN Catherine's *Life* tells us that she nursed more out of zeal than compassion, contemporary readers are bound to recoil. Have we come this far only to find that our worst fears were well founded? that these individuals are essentially *unnatural?* "Thou hast commanded me to love my neighbor," says Catherine at one point, "and I am unable to love anyone but thee, or to admit any partner with thee: how then shall I obey thee?" (*Life* 104), and God replies: "For the welfare of the neighbor thou shouldst do all that is necessary for his soul and body. Such a love as this is sure to be without passion: because it is not in himself but in God that the neighbor should be loved."

In other words, it is not love itself that is to be eschewed, but particular love and exclusive love. If Catherine sets herself to doing for her fellow creatures only what body and soul require, she will be in no danger of entering the kind of entanglement that might impede her union with God. Indeed, she will be doing what is best for others, too, because rather than trying, even unconsciously, to attract them or "bind them" to herself, she will be pointing them toward their own real identity.

Charitable work is sweetened for most people by "warm feelings," but it was not for Catherine. To ensure complete annihilation of self-will with regard to friends, relatives, and patients, the Lord issued a blanket command: "You will love everyone without love" (*Spiritual Dialogue* 129). She begged God on another occasion to deepen her emotional resources, saying, "To do this work well, love is needed," and God conceded to her "a certain corresponding love, but only when it was strictly necessary for the work" (*Spiritual Dialogue* 132).

It *is* austere, this life and teaching, about as gentle and comforting as a breeze off Mount Everest. Catherine was absolutely uncompromising with herself and those who would emulate her. She had had a good look at what she wanted and knew it was worth worlds more than any temporary satisfaction. She fairly begs us to grasp the difference between pleasures and joy, between the finite and the infinite. There is nothing wrong with "creatures" as far as they go: they simply do not go far enough. They cannot assuage our deepest hungers, and this, she taught, is as it should be, for "were man to find peace on earth, few souls would be saved—the soul would transform itself into earth, and there it would rest" (*Spiritual Dialogue* 103).

Considered more or less in the abstract, the concept of detachment has pure and cleansing associations, and we can acknowledge its appeal. But when detachment is placed before us, embodied, *as a woman caring for others,* I think we are less comfortable. Of our care givers, and ourselves in care-giving roles, I think we expect, ideally at least, something resembling unconditional and unstinting love: the compassion and tenderness, in short, of a mother, a perfect mother. Consciously, we might know this is unrealistic, a child's fantasy of how life ought to be, but the expectation persists and shapes our behavior throughout life. We are hurt when we do not meet it in others; we feel inadequate when we cannot muster it ourselves.

The mystic's response—and I think this is Catherine's real point in speaking about love that is "without love"—is that our dream is not impossible at all. There is nothing infantile or unrealistic about it, for such unconditional love does exist. Our only error is in thinking we can extract it from someone else or dish it out *from* ourselves in our present limited state. The source of such love, the *minne-flut* Mechthild experienced, is deep within; it is God's love, and once we have tapped into it, it can pass *through* us to others. To the extent that Catherine has gotten her own feelings and designs entirely out of the way, she is a perfect instrument of a love far more abundant and all-seeing than any she could have mustered on her own.

It should be clear by now that through no fault of her own Catherine of Genoa is in fact *not* the role model most married women of today are looking for. Hers was a loveless marriage—loveless in the stormy early years but loveless, too, as far as we can gather, in the later and more tranquil times. She endured it. Some will find solace in that and even inspiration. Many more of us, though, when we seek out married saints or mystics, are looking for hard evidence that a woman can have a partner and/or a family and still realize her full spiritual identity. Our questions are not abstract; they arise out of our own struggles. Some of them have to do with time—when do we meditate, for example? But more of them have to do with love itself and the depths to which our emotional resources are tapped in even the most successful relationships. The bare facts of Catherine's life provide little help in either regard. But it may be that her teachings on love "pure and simple"—detached love, that is, which looks always to the spiritual well-being of the other—are the essence of what we are looking for.

One would so like to think that once Catherine and Giuliano undertook their life of service together their marriage took a turn for the better—that they enjoyed a quiet companionability as they worked and that a certain sweetness slipped gradually into their relationship. The warm wording of Giuliano's will suggests that from his point of view there was such a sweetness. He left Catherine his remaining fortune "to provide the means for her continuing to lead her quiet, peaceful, and spiritual mode of life." Of her feelings about him, though, we know virtually nothing, and the one glimpse we are given is not altogether reassuring.

Giuliano became gravely ill during the early months of 1493. As he neared death that fall, a terrible "impatience" seized him, and Catherine feared for his soul. She went into an adjoining room and "with tears and sobs" prayed, "I beg of thee this soul. I pray thee give it to me, for thou canst do it." She prayed for half an hour until an inner voice assured her she was heard. On returning to her husband's room, she found him calm, patient, ready to submit to God. After his death, she confided to one of her followers: "My son, Giuliano is gone: you know his eccentricity, which caused me so much suffering during his life, but before he passed away, my sweet Love assured me of his salvation" (Life 150).

Immediately after speaking, she visibly regretted it. After Giuliano was buried, friends tried to say what was obvious to them: that his death had surely relieved her of great trials and oppressions. This was surely indelicate, and she gave them the nonanswer they deserved. Stiffly, one imagines, she replied she was not conscious of it. All things were the same to her, and she only cared to do the will of God.

I have heard it said that the illumined man or woman typically looks back in full gratitude upon the individuals who had made their lives most difficult, viewing them in retrospect as instruments of their salvation. All our wishful thinking aside, it seems quite likely that Catherine felt this degree of tenderness toward Giuliano, but very little more. Her biographer may well have been presenting Catherine's own view of things when he wrote: "God, who in his goodness would not leave his chosen one to place her affections on the world and the flesh, permitted a husband to be given her entirely the opposite of herself in his mode of life" (*Life* 22).

The last ten years of Catherine's life, though, from 1500 to 1510, have an unprecedented glow about them. One of her most devoted scholars speaks of this period as her "Indian summer." Human companionship and even guidance were finally permitted her. Up until then, Catherine had carried out her entire spiritual struggle without human aid or comfort. Now she was given a spiritual director of rare sweetness and sensitivity, Don Cattaneo Marabotto, her successor as director of the Pammetone Hospital. She never questioned that Father Marabotto was God's gift to her, and for his part, he knew himself to be nothing but a channel of grace, for he never knew what he was going to say to her until the moment arose. Marabotto, who contributed much of the material in her *Life*, thought of himself more as her disciple than her guide. And yet, there were times when he was able to guess what was on her mind and relieve her of its burden without her saying a word. At one point, she claimed that a heavenly perfume came from his hand—he could not smell it—that nourished and strengthened her. "At a glance," she marveled, he seemed to understand her inner state. In all of the Catherine literature, there are no more winningly human words than those in which she begged Marabotto to spend more time with her (as director of the Pammetone, he undoubtedly had his hands full):

It seems to me that God has given you the care of me alone, and that you ought not to attend to any one else, for I have persevered during twenty-five years in the spiritual life without the help of any creature, but now that I cannot endure such interior and exterior conflicts, God has sent you to me. If you knew how terribly I suffer when you are absent, you would rather remain with me in my trials than go in search of any recreation.

(*Life* 146)

The appeal is so unguarded a child could be speaking. Most touching of all, though, are her closing words: "But I would not ask you not to go."

More disciples materialized during the years, among them a young businessman named Ettore Vernazza, who devoted his short life to charitable works in and about the Pammetone. For the first time, Catherine began haltingly to express something of what she had experienced, protesting all the while that everything she said felt like a lie. Seeing that she would never write down anything, Marabotto and Vernazza tried to record all that she told them. One of them confessed at the end of the *Spiritual Dialogue* that the task was the hardest he had ever carried out. Easy enough to make a literal transcription, but nearly impossible to answer the central question her life posed: "In one instant she was made perfect. . . . For this reason she never knew how to give any account of the way to obtain perfection."

The truth is, we can perhaps be grateful that someone other than Catherine herself was responsible for setting down what we know of her. She was so severe with regard to herself, and her teachings were so austere, that the glimpses we get of her in the *Life* form an all-important corrective. The Catherine that her devotees knew was clearly a woman of unstinting sweetness and warmth, radiance and peacefulness, humor and affection.

She received a young widow about this time, too, as a spiritual daughter—one of those devoted caretakers that seems often to enter the life of a mystic during the very last days. And Catherine's last days were drawing near. Sometime in 1509 she received "interiorly" the awareness that her death would be long, drawn-out, and exceedingly painful. She shrank in terror at first but composed herself and then endured nine months of what must have been perfect hell. The malady was mysterious; doctors could not treat it. She suffered by her own account interior fires that alternated with terrible cold. At one point she asked her attendants to throw open the windows, for surely the whole world must be on fire.

The progress of Catherine's demise is recorded in the *Dialogue* in excruciating detail. Religious writers of the period loved a good death, and hers was extraordinary. Once again, we find ourselves pulling back in horror. It is never acceptable, the suffering of every kind that is so often heaped upon the purest and best as they leave the earth. We struggle to make some sense of it, and we wonder what it has to do with us.

Perhaps it is this. I have heard it said of the great sequoia trees, the giants that go on forever, that their cones burst and scatter their seed only under the intense heat of a forest fire. The analogy suggests itself, because typically during the last days of a great mystic's life, a great many very ordinary people converge—in silence, in awe, drawn there without being able to say why, but altered forever by the experience—so that when they go back to their everyday lives, they go, to use a biblical phrase, "bearing witness."

Catherine had said all her life that love conquers all things. To see her now, undergoing ferocious torments and yet remaining all the while unbroken, often exultant, seemed to prove it. "They beheld heaven in her soul, and purgatory in her agonized body" (*Life* 162).

Catherine regained consciousness now and then during her final trials. She was heard laughing and saying that she had been playing with the angels. Another time, she spoke "like a person in health, and told others they must not be troubled on her account for she was happy, but they must strive to do right, for the ways of God were very strait." And of course, she had chosen the straitest of ways, for she knew it would lead her to freedom. It was not a question of "faith" in our usual sense. "So clearly do I perceive thy goodness," she maintained, "that I do not seem to walk by faith, but by a true and heartfelt experience."

For our final glimpse of this magnificent woman, the deathbed is altogether wrong. The image of the glass casket where her flesh and bones are preserved in the hospital chapel in Genoa is even worse. Here, then, instead:

It is late summer, 1493, and Catherine is forty-six. Giuliano Adorno is dying. The plague has struck Genoa, the most virulent attack ever. The wealthy have fled to villas and estates in the country, where they will wait it out. Before the summer is over, four-fifths of the people who have stayed in town, mostly the very poor, will die. Catherine, of course, has stayed on. She is in her third year as director of the Pammetone Hospital. Victims of the plague have poured into the hospital, filling to overflowing its beds and even the field behind the hospital. Catherine has requisitioned sails from the shipyards and has had a vast series of tents constructed there behind the great Pammetone. She has organized teams of doctors, nurses, and Franciscan tertiaries, and all summer long, the historians of Genoa tell us, she has overseen them as they ministered to the sick and dying. It is for this summer in particular that the city holds her in abiding love and reverence.

Catherine had a sense of humor, a startling, dark, wild kind of humor that emerges here and there in the *Dialogue,* and I wonder whether some mornings as she looked out across that field full of dying men and women and children and heard their pitiable voices—saw the canvas sails flapping overhead—I wonder whether, standing there exhausted before the day was even begun, she ever let some incongruous comparisons slip into her mind. Was this a fleet of ships bound for another world, and she its weary admiral? Or was it a macabre garden party, and she the hostess? Never mind, she would have said, catching herself up. Out amongst them. Not her guests, not her passengers or even her patients. Her children, rather. A drink of water here, a consoling handclasp there, and always, "Call Jesus. . . . Call Jesus."

Saint Teresa of Avila

(1515–1582)

The important thing is not to think much but to love
much; and so do that which best stirs you to love.

> — Saint Teresa of Avila,
> *Interior Castle* 4.1.7

Let nothing upset you,
Let nothing frighten you.
Everything is changing;
God alone is changeless.
Patience attains the goal.
Who has God lacks nothing;
God alone fills all her needs.

> — The "Bookmark Prayer" of Teresa of Avila

TRADITION has it that on the morning Teresa of Avila was leaving her home to join a convent, a gentleman saw her climbing into the carriage and could not resist making an appreciative assessment of her ankles. "Take a good look," she is said to have called out merrily (and cryptically, for she had not told anyone but her brother she was going), "that's the last one you'll get!"

Apocryphal perhaps, but not out of character. No mystic, and no saint, is more thoroughly accessible than Teresa of Avila. There was not a conventionally pious bone in her body, but as to goodness itself, the deep-down goodness of someone you could live with all your days and never grow weary, she was that kind of good. Much of what characterized the lives we have been looking at is absent from Teresa's. She did not go in for physical mortifications, believing that genuine mortification consists in the elimination of self-will—a task she thought best accomplished in living with others. She was a notable cook and a superb conversationalist. She performed very few miracles and no real exorcisms, unless you count the time she persuaded an errant country priest to give up his mistress. And really, when you consider the circumstances—all those long soulful talks at her sister's farm: she a beautiful young novice and he a man of the cloth whose chastity had already proven fragile—she was certainly playing with fire. She did that rather a lot.

On other counts, though, Teresa matches up well with the rough composite picture that has begun to take shape. Like Clare, she saw absolute poverty as a cornerstone for the contemplative life. She tried to make it mandatory for the Reformed Carmelite convents she founded but could not because several of her foundations were in regions so remote and poor they had to have endowments from wealthy patrons and patronesses—instruments of God who would give Teresa easily as many headaches as *reales.*

Like Clare, too, Teresa wrote her own rule, the *Constitutions,* and it conveys the same consistent respect for her sisters and their vocations that Clare's had. She gave them guidelines for discreet change of confessors when necessary and insisted that each nun have her own cell, regardless of her dowry, which no one could enter without the prioress's permission. The document also reflects her unflinching knowledge of human nature, of the kind of temptations it is unfair to place before a young woman, no matter how strong her vocation appears to be, and of the temptations that a prioress, too, must face down: like the application of an unqualified entrant with a munificent dowry; or the oldest lure in the world, that of power itself.

Like all the women we have looked at, Teresa was a visionary. Unlike any of them, though, except perhaps Mechthild, Teresa's visions placed her life in terrible jeopardy. The Spanish Inquisition was fully operative at just the moment when word of her raptures began to circulate. If she had failed to persuade her directors that her visions were from God and not the devil, she could have been burned at the stake, and for many reasons the scales were tipped against her.

And yet such was her courage that even as she was writing her *Autobiography* to explain her experience to hostile critics, she maintained, "without doubt I fear those who have such great fear of the devil more than I do the devil himself." (*Life* 25.22).

For sainthood as it is usually imagined, Teresa of Avila was utterly, almost comically, unsuited. And yet, for the specific work she was to carry out, she was supremely well equipped. Her adeptness at getting people to like and admire her (particularly men), and the delight she took in doing so, would seem to have fitted her badly for a cloistered life. And her passion for words was surely excessive—words written, spoken, sung, bantered, and riddled with, spun out into marvelous metaphors that let her say even the hardest things with dazzling ease. Both these liabilities, though, proved priceless assets: Teresa's reform succeeded, and sainthood came along almost as an afterthought, the last best joke from a woman who loved to amuse.

Teresa's spiritual journey was exceedingly difficult, for institutional as well as personal reasons. Life at the Convent of the Incarnation, where she first professed as a Carmelite nun, very nearly defeated her vocation. It was her own painful experience there—gratuitous pain she thought no young spiritual aspirant should suffer—that moved her to reform the Carmelite Order. She was a passionate advocate for young women and fought tirelessly to create environments within which they could be free to turn inward. I say *women,* but her reform extended to the Carmelite monks as well, spearheaded by her close friend and ally, John of the Cross.

Teresa's calling had to do, above all else, with mental prayer. Contemplative prayer had worked a miracle in her life, and she was determined to make that miracle available to others. One of those individuals who is unaccountably gifted as a contemplative, she knew nonetheless that her discovery of that hidden track inward, and her having been able to follow it into full, ecstatic awareness of God, was sheer grace. Her very unsuitedness for this gift seemed to her proof of God's infinite mercy. (Surely, therefore, Teresa reasoned, the world should know how wayward she had been in the early days: surely they should not, insisted her scandalized spiritual directors, who steadily edited out every written attempt she made to tell us. When absurdly salacious rumors about her began to circulate when she was sixty, she laughed and said no matter; God and everyone else had concealed the genuine misdeeds of her youth, so there was a certain justice in her being falsely accused now, as an old woman.)

To love without loving, as Catherine of Genoa had been commanded, is difficult enough; to teach without teaching is at least as confounding an assignment, and this was what was required of Teresa. Forbidden because she was a woman to preach or even to comment on Scripture, she nevertheless did function as a spiritual teacher for the last twenty years of her life, writing four books and hundreds of letters, poems, and "diversions"[1] in a voice that resonates with the authority of profound personal experience, but which is continually interrupted by the graceful disclaimers she knew she dared not omit.

Early biographers of Teresa loved to compare her with her seven *conquistador* brothers: while they conquered huge territories in the New World and came back laden with its treasures, she conquered the vast realms of the spirit—the world within—and brought forth a different kind of treasure. Today, one shudders even to recall what took place when the young men of Spain reached the Americas. We may still slip and refer to the ancient civilizations they destroyed there as "the New World" (I have in my teaching and have caught some heat for it, too), but we are trying to unlearn the arrogance implicit in the phrase. The whole brutal fact of colonialism is so grievous that very few of us can respond warmly to metaphors for the spiritual journey that have to do with subjugation or looting. In fact, the growing sensitivity of today's historians to issues of racial and cultural oppression has reshaped considerably the way scholars look at Teresa and her milieu. The complexity of her own and her city's religious and ethnic background is recognized now, and her story is all the more fascinating because of it. We should begin her story, then, with something of that background—brushed in with large strokes.

Spain had been effectively cut off from most of the great flowering of Catholic mysticism that had taken place in the rest of Europe during the thirteenth and fourteenth centuries, because for nearly eight hundred years the country had been in a state of internal war. In 1492, the last Moorish stronghold fell at Granada, and Spain became officially—obsessively, one might add, and aggressively—Christian. Moors continued to live in Spain but under increasingly restrictive conditions—pressured to convert to Christianity and forbidden to use Arab names or make marriage contracts in accordance with their ancient laws. They were finally expelled altogether in 1610. Jews, however, were forcibly expelled immediately after Granada fell; none could stay in Spain who did not convert to Christianity. *Judaeo-conversos* who were suspected of practicing their ancestral religion were subject to arrest by the Inquisitors. Some of those found guilty were burned at the stake; others might have wished they had been, too. In Toledo, for example, in 1485, after one Juan Sanchez confessed publicly to the "crime" of reversion, he and his children were marched through the streets of the city in penitential procession, dressed in yellow garments marked with black crosses, visiting all the cathedrals in turn while the citizens of the town threw stones, spat, and cursed them—not just once, and not twice, but every Friday for seven weeks.

In the same year that the Moors were defeated and the Jews expelled, as if to confirm the sense of "manifest destiny" that the fall of Granada had inspired in Ferdinand and Isabella, Christopher Columbus "found" the Americas and, in them, a seemingly boundless source of new wealth. Part of this wealth would finance the building of a great university at Alcala, a brilliant showcase of Renaissance humanist scholarship. The founder was Ximenes Cisneros, the queen's confessor, a Franciscan monk who drew much of his own inspiration from the mystical and devotional writings coming out of northern Europe. Cisneros saw to it that these were translated into the vernacular, printed, and made available throughout Spain. He welcomed the Christian humanism of Erasmus in particular, with its emphasis on interior prayer, direct personal experience of God, and affective piety.

A form of spirituality spread rapidly across Spain now that felt quite new and appealed to lay people as well as monastics. The Franciscans were particularly responsive. One of them, Francisco de Osuna, wrote for those who would practice mental prayer a manual called *The Third Spiritual Alphabet*. This was the book that launched Teresa, at twenty-three years old, on the wide, deep waters of her own contemplative life.

Spain stood open to the outside world for only fifty years. By the middle of the sixteenth century, the Protestant Reformation was well under way in northern Europe, and in 1559, when Teresa was forty-four, enclaves of so-called Lutherans were discovered in Seville and Valladolid. Shocked, and determined that Spain should remain the bastion of Catholic orthodoxy for Europe, King Philip II moved swiftly to cut off all outside influences. He closed down presses and issued lists of proscribed books that included nearly everything written in the vernacular, particularly books about mental prayer. The Inquisition bore down on heresy in every imaginable expression, particularly Protestantism and the religious hysteria associated with "illuminism." The *alumbrados,* or "illuminists," advocated direct, ecstatic contact with God for lay people as well as professional religious. As a movement, illuminism embraced the whole gamut of seekers, from the genuinely holy to those who by dint of their visionary experiences felt themselves to be above all laws.

True to its anti-Semitic roots, the Inquisition operated under the certainty that *conversos* were particularly vulnerable to heresy and demonic possession. *Conversos . . .* and women. There could not have been a worse moment for rumors to begin leaking out of the Convent of the Incarnation, rumors of a nun practicing mental prayer who was experiencing raptures—a woman who loved books, and who was known by some to be of *converso* origin.

Alonso Sanchez was a young boy in 1485 when he walked through the streets of Toledo with his father, bewildered, surely, at the wrath of the righteous citizens who stoned them and cursed them and spat upon them for practicing their ancestral faith, the same faith, after all, that Jesus himself had practiced. Soon afterward, to place Toledo and its memory firmly behind them, Juan Sanchez moved his family to Ciudad Real, changed their name to "Cepeda," and came eventually to Avila, a city known for its proudly held tradition of religious tolerance. Whether the family continued to practice as Jews is unknown. To all appearances, they were Catholics.

By the year 1515, Alonso was about forty. A tax-gatherer, he was "Don Alonso de Cepeda" and married for the second time. He had two children by his deceased wife, and now his second wife, a beautiful young girl named Beatriz de Ahumada, had given birth to two sons. On March 28 of that year, her first daughter was born—Teresa de Ahumada y Cepeda.

Realizing that Teresa was as Jewish by ancestry as she was Christian alters our perspective in several regards. Toward the father who resisted so stubbornly Teresa's desire to join a convent, we feel a rich sympathy, and we recognize the irony in her brothers' emigration to the Indies (one of the few options that would have been open to *conversos*) to bring the inhabitants into the True Faith.[2] We understand, too, why Teresa herself never fell into the error of thinking you can convert anyone by force.

Like many of its citizens, Avila itself was a kind of *palimpsest,* a city of overlays. "Abula," it was called originally, when it was a Roman and then a Visigothic settlement high on the central Castilian plateau. Captured from the Moors in the eleventh century, it was populated and built up by settlers from northern Spain and France and surrounded by massive walls that were built in part by Moorish prisoners of war. Obsessed with lineage and honor, the citizens of Avila attached enormous importance to whether one's family was among those first settlers. Later, that obsession would expand and concern itself with "purity of blood" as well. As the religious tolerance of Avila's past weakened in the atmosphere of mistrust promoted by the Inquisition's fresh new wave of activity, any strain of Jewish or Moorish blood in one's lineage came to be ground for suspicion and avoidance.

Even by the standards of a society that kept its women very much at home, Dona Beatriz, Teresa's mother, was an outright recluse. She was beautiful, Teresa tells us, quiet, intelligent, and "a great invalid." Weakened by relentlessly frequent pregnancies (the first when she was barely thirteen), she spent her time reading chivalric novels and sharing them with her children. The books were passed back and forth in secret; Don Alonso did not approve. Teresa and her older brother Rodrigo co-authored one of these when they were teenagers. The manuscript has never surfaced, but one loves to think of her at work on it—an aspiring writer long before she wrote the books she pretended to write with such reluctance, and only under obedience! Beatriz died at thirty-three years old, giving birth to her ninth child. Teresa was fourteen. Don Alonso was left in sole charge of what could only have been an exceedingly unruly brood, and trouble was literally right around the corner.

Teresa was described throughout her life (even at fifty!) as being unusually attractive—vivacious, nicely shaped, with dark, curly hair, expressive hands, large, dark eyes, and full, curving lips. As a young girl, she spent her time in exactly the ways Catherine of Siena had refused to: "I began to dress in finery and to desire to please and look pretty, taking great care of my hands and hair and about perfumes." (She would always be a fanatic where cleanliness was concerned; not for her the asceticism of the unwashed body and habit.) She loved, always, to make people like her. Only a teenager, barely recovered from the loss of her mother, she must have been exceedingly vulnerable.

The Cepeda y Ahumada home shared a courtyard with another family, a relative's, with its own loosely governed ensemble of children and teenagers. It was inevitable that the two tribes would merge and play and be very silly together, and that at some point a romance of sorts would flare up. The boy is never named, and of course nobody knows how far things actually went. But Teresa refuses to make light of the episode, saying that her behavior was such as to have placed her father and brothers in danger, meaning that she came close enough to losing her honor that they might have had to defend it. She believes her father never really knew anything for certain, but as soon as it could be managed with discretion, he placed her in a strictly governed convent school, Our Lady of Grace. Messages from her cousins kept coming in through the wall for a time, but soon they tapered off, and to her astonishment, Teresa realized she was happy. She had loved the attentions of her cousins, loved the intrigue and the flattery. But it seemed that another Teresa was trying to make herself known, one to whom the extreme calm of the place and the order and the focus, the tremendous *seriousness* of it all, was deeply if inexplicably welcome.

Teresa began now to consider whether she might actually join a convent, and she asked the nuns to pray that her way might be made clear. But clarity refused to come. After a year and a half in the convent school, though, she felt herself to be much improved, "Still I had no desire to be a nun, and I asked God not to give me this vocation; although I also feared marriage." One assumes this fear must have had something to do with watching her mother weaken and finally die bearing all those children, but Teresa's reluctance to marry probably had other sources. In the *Way of Perfection,* she addresses her daughters vigorously: "They say that for a woman to be a good wife toward her husband she must be sad when he is sad, and joyful when he is joyful, even though she may not be so. (See what subjection you have been freed from, Sisters!)" (*Way of Perfection* 26. 4). Even as a young girl, Teresa probably realized that submission to authority would never be her strong suit. (She was a great one for changing confessors when they did not see things her way.) But then, would not the same lack of docility presumably rule out a religious vocation as well? Deeply conflicted, Teresa began to have fainting spells and high fevers. Her father brought her home again.

Several years passed while Teresa lived at home and helped her father raise her younger siblings. (She would go on looking after their well-being, and their children's, to the end of her days.) Gradually her vocation strengthened. She would not enter Our Lady of Grace, though, with its strict enclosure, but the Incarnation, whose atmosphere she knew to be considerably more relaxed. Her father refused, but when Teresa was twenty she presented herself at the convent anyway, dowered rather shakily with a will signed by her brother Rodrigo, who was off to join his brothers in the Indies and kindly bequeathed all the gold he would presumably win there to his beloved sister. Alonso relented, forgave his daughter—she was always his favorite—and provided an ample dowry.

Accommodations at the convent varied according to one's means. The poorest nuns slept in a dormitory; Teresa was among those who had a suite of two rooms and a kitchen. (Much later, when she felt herself called to leave the Incarnation and found a new convent in complete poverty, she wins our hearts by admitting to having dragged her feet just a little because "the cell in which I lived was just what I wanted" [*Autobiography* 32.10]). Looking back upon this period, Teresa tells us that she entered the convent out of fear and not love. Fear, she says, of hell; fear of the weakness of her own character and where it might lead her if she remained in the world. Unfortunately, her choice of the Incarnation, made out of a humble assessment of her own limitations, placed her in serious jeopardy. Vehemently, she would write later how grievous it was "that many who desire to withdraw from the world . . . and flee worldly dangers, find themselves in ten worlds joined together without knowing how to protect themselves or remedy the situation" (*Autobiography* 7.4).

The so-called Primitive Rule of the Carmelite order was ancient and strict, but it had been mitigated by Pope Eugenius in 1432. The modified rule did not require, for example, that nuns renounce their worldly possessions before entering the convent.

Although many of the individual nuns at the Incarnation were well-to-do, the convent itself was poor and overcrowded. So many young men had gone the way of Teresa's brothers, leaving so many marriageable young women behind. Counting servants and nuns' live-in relatives, some two hundred women were packed inside the convent walls. Scant wonder the prioress permitted her daughters to visit their families whenever they chose and thus eat at someone else's expense.

Visitors to the convent were welcome for the same reason. They often brought sweets or a bag of fruit. Sometimes these guests were widows wishing to be edified or prayerful young girls pondering a vocation, but more often they were men-about-town looking for an afternoon's pleasant conversation, perhaps even a harmless flirtation. Overall, the atmosphere seems to have been that of a sorority "at-home" or even a *salon*. Few of the nuns were as effective in the role of hostess as the vivacious Teresa. To her dismay, she found herself surrounded by exactly the sort of temptation she was least able to withstand.

In short, men.

Let us be clear from the outset, though: Teresa never blamed men, categorically, for her problems. She maintained, in fact, that the chief concern of her daughters should not be to avoid men, but to avoid giving God displeasure. All her life she would enjoy warm friendships with a great many men, among the dearest, her brother Lorenzo. Besides, what she was dealing with now may not have been a direct threat to her chastity (though we cannot rule that out—scandals did occur, assignations took place, young novices went home pregnant), but rather the hypnotic spell of pure triviality, the intoxicating fun of holding forth wittily. Such a small thing, but in the words of her friend John of the Cross, "It makes little difference whether a bird be held by a slender thread or by a rope; the bird is bound, and cannot fly until the cord that holds it is broken."[3]

Her confessors were of no help, for they failed to see the dangers in the situation. One suspects they did not take the vocations of the nuns that seriously to begin with.

Helpless, discouraged, Teresas took the only available course of action: she got sick. Again, she came home, so ill this time that her family arranged to have her treated by a famous healer who lived in the countryside near her married sister Maria's farm. On the way to Maria's, she stopped for a day or two at her uncle Pedro's farm. He was a deeply religious man, and, sensing the depth of her troubles, he gave her copies of certain books. Among these was the *Spiritual Alphabet,* and Teresa could not stop reading it. She began to pray in accordance with its guidelines and experienced immediate results. At last she had found a blade sufficiently keen-edged to sever those "slender threads." Mental prayer would be the sharp, shining difference between a Teresa powerless to move forward and a Teresa who would make history.

The treatments she would be undergoing were extremely aggressive. She would need, first, to regain a certain amount of strength. For months she rested at her sister's farm, watching the seasons change, reading her books, praying, and counseling the local priest, whose open liaison with a village widow had made a mockery of himself and his office. Teresa persuaded him finally to give her the copper amulet that his mistress had given him. Once she had thrown it into the river, he regained his freedom. Writing later, she clearly felt ambivalent; she realized that in order to draw him back to God, she "showed him more love," which in turn "prompted him to love me greatly." He died just one year after they met, and while she insisted that his affection for her was not wrong, she said, too, "There were also occasions on which, if we had not remained very much in God's presence, there would have been more serious offenses."

Her vitality at low ebb, Teresa nonetheless made rapid progress in prayer. She experienced what she would later call the prayer of quiet, wherein "the soul begins to be recollected and comes upon something supernatural because in no way can it acquire this prayer through any efforts it may make. . . . In this prayer the faculties are gathered within so as to enjoy that satisfaction with greater delight. But they are not lost, nor do they sleep . . . " (*Autobiography* 14.2). On occasion, she may have known the prayer of union, during which, she explains, all the faculties are united in themselves and with God. Glimpses only, these experiences were probably the reason she survived the months to come . . . for the treatments did not help her. She fell finally into a profound coma and lay for four days without moving. Almost everyone believed she had died, but her father would not let them touch her body. "The child isn't dead," he kept repeating. At last, after four days, she opened her eyes—with difficulty, because someone had placed wax on the lids. So weak now and in such pain that she had to be carried about in a sheet, Teresa asked that she be taken back to her convent to recover or to die. It was eight months before she could move, another two years before she was able to crawl on her hands and knees. A few months after that, she could walk. Her recovery was full, though her digestion was damaged for life, probably by the harsh measures taken by her would-be healer.

Her recovery was deemed miraculous, but the greater miracle, by her own tally, was the change in her father. Sometime during her illness in 1537–1538, she had given him books on mental prayer and urged him to take it up. Within five years or so, "he was so advanced that I praised the Lord very much." He underwent severe trials, she tells us, "with the deepest conformity to God's will." He came often to see her, "for it consoled him to speak of the things of God" (*Autobiography* 1.7.11).

One might assume that Teresa's near-death experience would be the turning point in her life, that she would never again be as vulnerable to the petty claims of ordinary existence. But this was not the case. Her story has its own twist, for which generations of seekers have been grateful.

Once again, Teresa found herself back at the parlor of the Incarnation, holding court. She was better company now than she had ever been. Her charm and humor had new depth, for her miraculous recovery, the long months of solitude and prayer, had left their mark. She was eager to talk about mental prayer and to lend out her books. Given her setting, Teresa looked very good indeed. "They had great confidence in me," she later recalled sadly. As long as she was ill and throughout her recovery, Teresa had made steady progress along the path she had laid out for herself. But the easy, tolerant atmosphere of the Incarnation closed in around her again like a dense fog: long, dilatory conversations in the convent parlor passed over imperceptibly into the barely sublimated eroticism of what Dorothy Sayers called "talking piffle." And indeed, among the parlor "regulars," there appears to have been one in particular—he remains nameless—whose attentions began to undermine her spiritual practice. "The whole trouble lay in not getting at the root of the occasions and with my confessors who were of little help. For had they told me of the danger I was in and that I had the obligation to avoid those friendships, without a doubt I believe I would have remedied the matter" (*Autobiography* 6.4).

The word *occasions* means "occasions of sin." A nun or monk is expected not only to avoid wrongdoing, but also the situations that conduce to it. The sin in question here is subtler than concupiscence itself;

it has to do with one's mental state. Teresa had experienced enough of the deeper stages of mental prayer by now to have known that no one can enter those deeper stages whose attention and desires are not completely unified. Now when she tried to "shut herself within herself," as her method of prayer required, she merely shut within herself "a thousand vanities." Finally, it became unbearable, and she stopped trying. She would recall later,

> It is one of the most painful lives, I think, that one can imagine; for neither did I enjoy God nor did I find happiness in the world. When I was experiencing the enjoyments of the world, I felt sorrow when I recalled what I owed to God. When I was with God, my attachments to the world disturbed me. This is a war so troublesome that I don't know how I was able to suffer it even a month, much less for so many years.
>
> (*Autobiography* 8.2)

Ironically, her father's spiritual life was gathering force as rapidly as hers was drying up. She pretended to him that her health problems made it impossible for her to pray as she once had. One of the most painful passages in her writings occurs when she describes how the good old man started cutting short his visits once he saw how much they had diverged. He fell ill during this period and, in 1543, he died, "in the middle of the creed, reciting it himself." He displayed, Teresa tells us, joy in dying, but for "the great sorrow he felt in not having served God, and that he would have liked to be a friar; I mean, he would have chosen one of the strictest orders."

Knowing what we do of Alonso (Sanchez) Cepeda's childhood, we must struggle to make sense of his last years. Teresa is not describing a grudging, last-minute capitulation, but a wholehearted embrace of the faith whose adherents had subjected him to the worst imaginable humiliation.

I would offer the following explanation.

We must remember, first, that practitioners of mental prayer represented a marginal population within the church. They were regarded by many as subversive, or at least potentially so. Christians of the time were expected to see in the performance of the Mass, particularly the moment when the Host was elevated by the officiating priest, as the sublime center of their spiritual lives. Contemplatives, who claimed to have direct, unmediated experience of God, and not necessarily during the Mass, constituted a distinct challenge to the church insofar as it was centered upon ritual and run by priests. As a *converso,* Alonso was already marginal, and probably somewhat anticlerical, so he would have been relatively comfortable in this "church within a church."

Second, we must recognize that loving identification with Christ crucified was set forth as an ideal for all Christians. Who might be expected to identify more readily than one who had himself walked through city streets bearing the cross on his own back—emblematically, at least—and been stoned and spat upon for practicing his ancestral faith (or at least, being a member of a family practicing that faith)? With that dreadful piece of street theater, chilling in its anticipation of Nazi Germany, might not the Inquisitors have sabotaged their own intent? For who but Christ himself had admonished, "Inasmuch as you do it unto the least of these, you do it unto me"? Surely, then, from one point of view the Inquisitors themselves had become the tormentors, the crucifiers, and the Sanchez family the crucified.

What I am suggesting is the possibility that, like many Christians today, Teresa's father felt he had found his own track into his own Christianity. Through mental prayer, he may well have experienced a peace, an acceptance, deep within himself that allowed him to put terrible memories behind him and to align himself with Christ's own perspective: "Forgive them, Father, for they know not what they do." The "they" could have included all of the "establishment" Christians who had hurt him and his family in a thousand ways we will never know. It has been observed that the emphasis on Christ's humanity—his having rendered himself up without resistance to authorities and the fact that his body was broken and bleeding—allowed women in particular to identify with him at a very deep level. I would submit that much the same process might have taken place for Alonso Sanchez Cepeda.

I first came to this interpretation prompted by the words—I have heard them often now—of a friend, a priest whose entire ministry is to people with AIDS. Asked sometimes about his response to certain official church policies toward which he is opposed, he smiles with all the patience and all the sadness in the world commingled and says, "Yes, but that isn't *my* church." Only after I had thought through the relevance of this position to what might have been Teresa's father's did I remember an episode she relates that took place just before his death.

> His main sickness was a very severe pain in his shoulders which never left him. Sometimes it hurt him so much that it was an agony for him. I told him that *since he was so devoted to the memory of when the Lord carried the burden of the cross* that His Majesty thought He would like to make him experience something of what He suffered with that pain. This comforted my father so much that it seems to me I never heard him complain again.
> (*Autobiography* 1.7.16, italics mine)

Teresa was twenty-three when illness forced her to leave the Convent of the Incarnation. She was nearly forty now, and would undergo what her biographers call her second conversion, an event that many of them have described as semi-miraculous—abrupt and arbitrary: one minute Teresa was walking past an image of the crucified Christ recently placed in a corridor of the Incarnation, and the next, they tell us, she was on her knees, sobbing, repenting of nearly twenty years' indifference, and begging God to strengthen her once and for all. In truth, this sudden conversion had been a long time in the making.

Within a year after her father's death, late in 1544, his confessor had persuaded Teresa to resume interior prayer and to take communion every fifteen days, which meant, of course, that she must also confess at those same intervals. Not that she had begun to pray again right away, and not that when she did, the benefits were immediate. "Very often for some years I was more anxious that the hour I had determined to spend in prayer be over than I was to remain there" (*Autobiography* 8.7). She felt "unbearable sadness" at entering the oratory. Only the courage God gave her "more than women usually have" sustained her. Oddly, though, she began to notice that she found herself, at the end of the periods of prayer she had begun most reluctantly, "left with greater quiet and delight than sometimes when I had the desire to pray."

Steadily, then, over the years, she had begun to rally her inner forces. For the floodgates to have burst so dramatically that day before the image of Christ, the waters had to have been rising for some time.

From that moment onward, the things that had been hardest for Teresa became almost effortless. The parlor exerted no pull on her now, and she went eagerly to her hours of prayer. A new warmth, that of genuine charity, sprang into her relationships with the other sisters. And with wonderful timing, someone gave her a copy of the *Confessions* of Saint Augustine. She wept for days upon reading it. Here, at last, was a narrative that made sense of her own history. Here was someone else who had received abundant grace from God but held it all at arm's length. "Give me chastity, Lord," Augustine had prayed, "Give me continence . . . But not yet!" (*Confessions* 8.7).

There is a lovely sweetness and flurry and breathlessness about this period in Teresa's life. For no sooner did she start to avoid the "occasions" she speaks of so delicately than she began to receive "delights and favors" from God. Quite without her seeking them, she experienced raptures, moments when she was lifted up out of herself and into God's presence. She was a bride, swept off her feet now by the attentions of the lover she had half-consciously longed for ever since she and her mother read chivalric romances together. She felt his presence now, accompanying her everywhere. Asked by her directors how she knew he was there, she explained "In the dark, when someone is close by, you just know he's there. . . ."

It seemed to Teresa now that "mental prayer . . . is nothing else than an intimate sharing between friends; it means taking time frequently to be alone with Him who we know loves us" (*Autobiography* 8.5). The turning point for her was the moment "when I saw Him as one with whom I could converse so continually" (*Autobiography* 37.5). The elusive promise of intimate communication, heart open to heart, that had kept pulling her back into the parlor was fully realized now. During her first rapture, she heard the words "No longer do I want you to converse with men, but with angels" (*Autobiography* 24.5).

From her new vantage point, she could look back upon her former turmoil with serenity and powerful insight.

In every favor the Lord granted me, whether vision or revelation, my soul gained something. . . . The vision of Christ left upon me an impression of His most extraordinary beauty, and the impression remains today; one time is sufficient to make this imprint.

I had a serious fault that did me much harm; it was that when I began to know that certain persons liked me, and I found them attractive, I became so attached that my memory was bound strongly by the thought of them. . . . This was something so harmful it was leading my soul seriously astray. After I beheld the extraordinary beauty of the Lord, I didn't see anyone who in comparison with Him seemed to attract me or occupy my thoughts. By turning my gaze just a little inward to behold the image I have in my soul, I obtained such freedom in this respect that . . . it would be impossible for me . . . to be so occupied with the thought of anyone that I couldn't free myself from it by only a slight effort to remember this Lord.

(*Autobiography* 37.4)

One cannot break attachments by force, Teresa discovered; they are the expression of an inner hunger. When that hunger is assuaged, attachments will fall away with almost no effort on our part.

Feminist theorists today are intrigued by the connections in women's lives between language and power, between the effort to "find one's voice" and the attainment of a stronger sense of identity. From this perspective, it is fascinating to find that Teresa distinguished between her two worlds—the old one of the parlor and the new interior one—in terms of language. Of the nuns in Saint Joseph, her first reformed convent, she wrote, "Their language allows them to speak only of God, and so they only understand one who speaks the same language; nor would they in turn be understood by anyone who doesn't" (*Autobiography* 36.26). She speaks even more emphatically in *The Way of Perfection*:

God is your business and language. Whoever wants to speak to you must learn this language; and if he doesn't, be on your guard that you don't learn his; it will be a hell. . . And you cannot know as I do, for I have experience of it, the great evil this new language is for the soul; in order to know the one, the other is forgotten. The language involves a constant disturbance from which you ought to flee at all costs.

(*Way of Perfection* 20.4)

What kind of language is it that involves "constant disturbance"? Simple enough: "Don't let your conversation be of the sort in which you ask, 'Do you like me?' or 'Don't you like me?'" So much for the courtly love tradition, and so much for the parlor of the convent of the Incarnation.

The raptures of this period ceased after a time, and friends noticed this. When they asked her about it, Teresa smiled and answered, "I've found a better way to pray." She would move beyond the need for raptures, but she remained grateful always for having had them because they had given her the detachment that her work would require—detachment from all things, including the admiration and affection of others she had always needed so desperately. She would never again look outside herself for joy or security because she had found the source of all joy and security within.

Teresa had kept her mother's name when she made her profession as a nun, but now Teresa de Ahumada became Teresa of Jesus.

THE reform of the Carmelite Order began the summer of 1562 with the founding of the Convent of Saint Joseph, carried out in dire secrecy and announced only after the fact. Stung by the implied criticism of their own spiritual practice, the nuns of the Incarnation—and their families—could be counted upon to protest mightily. Grilles and veils would be firmly in place; there could be no compromise with the lax ways of places like the Incarnation. Teresa knew well how delicate is the seedling of spiritual awareness and that it needs to be fenced around carefully. At her insistence, the convent would have no endowment, news that infuriated the citizens of Avila.

The convents of Avila had been organized up until then to serve the dynastic families of the town in a variety of ways, providing a home for superfluous daughters, but also functioning as a kind of long-term insurance program for the aristocracy's honor and afterlife. Endowments, that is, came with stipulations. Memorial chapels built at a convent in someone's memory would be decorated conspicuously with the family's coat of arms. One man's will left an elaborate altar to the Incarnation, provided one of the sisters be on her knees before said altar praying aloud for him twenty-four hours a day: twenty-four nuns, in daily rotation, praying aloud, because how else could the family be sure their investment was being honored? Abolishing arrangements of this sort effectively removed the city's daughters from the service of the dead and placed an altogether new value on their life of prayer and, in effect, on the young women themselves.

So began the tremendous work of the reform, initiated by God and directed at every juncture, Teresa maintained, by God's voice.

Up to this point in her life, we have been able to accompany her step by step. From here onward, though, it is impossible. It is a bit like coming up over a rise and seeing a whole city spread out before you. The tempo of her life accelerates, and crowds of people swarm into it. There are minor characters of every kind: princesses and hermits, wandering ascetics and querulous town officials, problematic nieces, stingy brothers-in-law, strong-willed prioresses, and microminded inquisitors—but major protagonists, too, like John of the Cross, whom she called "the Father of my soul."

Juan de la Cruz was twenty-five when they met, and she was fifty. He was a Carmelite, but he had practiced the Primitive Rule of his order all along and was about to become a hermit until she dissuaded him, which she did with ease, because it seems that he recognized her stature as quickly as she did his. Barely five feet tall in *physical* stature, emaciated, described as very dark, with a broad forehead and burning eyes, he too came of *converso* stock. He would be the cornerstone of her monastic foundations and her strong right arm in managing the convents as well. They loved one another dearly, and yet in certain ways they probably never understood one another. "My little Seneca," she called him, referring to his logical and stoical outlook. He was never comfortable with her alacrity in heeding God's voice. Marcelle Auclair, one of Teresa's most insightful biographers, put it this way: "For her, to love was to act. For him, to love was to immerse oneself completely in contemplation."[4]

Tracing out the terrible poignancy of their relationship, Auclair observes, "The strength of refusal of John of the Cross, his despairing sweetness, made Teresa, in her relations with him, more virile than her character was in reality and perhaps even a little brusque. . . . Without thoroughly understanding it, John admired Teresa's astonishing adaptability to all circumstances, her talent for worldly business, the way she was at home in joy as in trials, her natural energy in action; Teresa of

Jesus esteemed at its super-terrestrial value 'this soul to whom God communicates his spirit.'"5

We would know more of their relationship; it is so clearly paradigmatic of the mixed delight and exasperation with which the best of men and the best of women confront one another even now. Sadly, though, we cannot know much more than we do, for John realized one day that there was still one thing to which he was attached. He took out his bag of letters from Teresa, which he had carefully preserved, and burned them, every last one.

Hundreds of Teresa's letters *have* been preserved, though, and they allow us to see the fine shadings of many of her relationships and the close contact she strove to maintain with all her foundations. Before her death at sixty-seven, she would found seventeen Discalced Carmelite convents and four monasteries. (*Discalced* means, literally, unshod. The nuns wore rope sandals, in keeping with their return to the original rule of their order.)

Teresa's seventeen foundations were scattered across the length of Spain, separated by rugged mountain ranges with only the vaguest semblance of roads. Year after year, in deteriorating health, she set out to make one after another of these foundations, traveling in covered donkey carts with wooden wheels, laying over at filthy inns, and forced to rely on ignorant or treacherous guides. One of our favorite glimpses of her comes out of these travels. Crossing a river swollen with spring floods, her party tried to float their wagons across on rafts. The cables broke, and all their supplies swirled off downstream. Pushed very close to the limits of her patience, Teresa turned her attention inward and heard her Beloved assure her, "This is how I treat my real friends. . . ." "Then it's no wonder," she murmured in reply, "that your Lordship has so few!"

Harsh as her travels were, things often got even worse when she reached her destination. Few towns were eager to receive a new community of nuns, no matter what God was supposed to have told Teresa, particularly when the nuns came in without endowment. It took the full force of Teresa's personality to set those convents in place and keep them there. Problems arose within the convents, too. The time frame God gave Teresa did not always allow for adequate formation of the nuns who would live there or even of their prioresses. She was continually having to resolve disputes and quiet scandals, in person or by mail.

Nor did the Mitigated Carmelites take the reform of their order lying down. In the monasteries, bouts of armed violence took place. John of the Cross was kidnapped at one point and imprisoned for nine months at the Toledo monastery of Mitigated Carmelites. All of this time, moreover, Teresa was under the intense scrutiny of the Inquisition.

Her health declined by the year. A physician examining her when she was sixty-two declared he could find no focal point for her ailments, for her body was an arsenal of diseases: rheumatoid arthritis, a weak heart, terrible digestion, "quartan fever" (which was a form of malaria), a broken shoulder that was so badly set it had to be broken and reset and never really stopped hurting, and, at the end, throat cancer. All of this and recurring, acutely uncomfortable sensations in the head, as of waterfalls passing through.

Her letters are punctuated with reassurances to those who loved her that she was "getting better" and "not in so much pain now." Writing to a friend after her brother Lorenzo's death, she reflects that she is four years older than he had been, "and yet I never quite manage to die."

Fully absorbed in the work entrusted to her, she dragged her body about with her, only half-aware of its condition—a beat-up old garment that admittedly needed replacing.

I have downplayed Teresa as a miracle worker, but in view of the difficulties she faced, her literary output was surely little short of miraculous. Its volume alone would be impressive, but its originality and sheer brilliance vindicate completely her having been declared Doctor of the Church. She is simply the best. No one writing in the Catholic tradition has made the practice of interior prayer more comprehensible.

Teresa wrote the *Autobiography* under orders to set forth exactly what her spiritual practice and experience were. Even as she wrote, she was effectively on trial, because her visions and raptures were widely known. Seldom has a fledgling writer been given such a perilous first assignment or for such a hostile audience. The Dominicans, who ran the Inquisition, were for the most part *letrados,* "learned ones," who believed that theological studies provided the only knowledge one could have of God in this life. (The Dominican who had been Teresa's father's confessor was obviously an exception.) Deeply suspicious of mental prayer, they saw it as "a screen for Protestant pietism and other forms of heterodox belief, and as a means of avoiding the control of the Church hierarchy."[6] The *Confessions* of Augustine gave Teresa a framework upon which to model her own account, but they did not give her a literary *voice*. That she had to invent. She would of course write in the vernacular, because she knew no Latin anyway, but in fact she adopted an extremely down-to-earth, idiomatic *extra*vernacular vernacular. She wrote, her contemporaries remarked, exactly as she spoke, interrupting herself, sounding almost harebrained at times, flinging ellipses about on every page and wishing aloud that she had six hands to write down everything that came into her mind when she was particularly inspired.

A story is told about the women of Avila that should help us appreciate Teresa's mode of discourse. The episode took place one day during the time of the Reconquest.[7] The men of Avila were away at war one day when Moorish troops surrounded the city. Led by the royal governor's wife, the women put on their husbands' second-best armor and took to the battlements, where they made a thunderous racket. The enemy vanished, terrified, unaware that the great clatter and bang was not of swords and shields, but of pots and pans. When the men came home and heard the story, they were so impressed they offered the women full citizenship and the right to vote in the city council, which the women gratefully declined. It has been suggested that this last detail is a later embellishment, added as a male rationalization for the complete exclusion of women from political power. I would disagree and suggest instead that women astute enough to have done what they did also knew better than to think that in the absolutely masculine atmosphere of a wartime city council, women's modes of discourse would have been any more effective than their kettles and frying pans would have been as weapons against the Moors.

Teresa knew better, too, and I think that is why she took pains not to adopt a literary style that in any way resembled that of the *letrados*. She would not meet her critics on their ground and set herself up to be judged by their criteria. Instead, she fashioned a language for herself that fell so completely outside their professional paradigm that it effectively disarmed them.

There is a wonderful directness and simplicity about her style, despite its syntactical convolutions. Her imagery is so vivid: of the Franciscan hermit-saint Peter Alcantara, she observed, "He was very old when I came to know him, and so extremely weak that it seemed he was made of nothing but tree roots" (*Autobiography* 27.17). To describe a particular "neither-here-nor-there" state of being, a "foolishness of soul," she says, "It doesn't seem that the soul feels anything. I think it goes about like a little donkey that's grazing" (*Autobiography* 30.18). And to the delight of anyone who has tried to practice mental prayer, "This intellect is so wild that it doesn't seem to be anything else than a frantic madman no one can tie down" (*Autobiography* 30.17).

With concrete and understandable language, Teresa describes the subtlest of inner experiences, and nowhere more skillfully than in her famous treatise on the stages of mental prayer regarded as "four waters" (chapters eleven through twenty-one of the *Autobiography*). Implicitly, she is addressing herself to a controversy that arises regularly in spiritual circles, Christian or otherwise. In her time and place, the two positions were represented by the *recogidos* and the *dejados*. Both believed, in contrast with the *letrados*, that one can have direct, unmediated knowledge of God through contemplative prayer. The *dejados* based their religious practice on self-abandonment: all exterior devotion was scorned in favor of interior passivity and inspiration. The *recogidos* developed systematic methods of interior prayer that would permit the soul to withdraw ultimately from everything created so as to be penetrated by God. They remained much closer to orthodoxy.

From the perspective of the powerful *letrados*, the distinction between a *recogido* and a *dejado* was academic; to Teresa, it was of paramount importance. Fully aware of the dangers of undisciplined interior prayer, she knew, too, the miraculously transformative power of mental prayer rightly practiced. She knew it was fundamental to Christianity itself.

What is remarkable about her presentation is that while she places herself unequivocally on the side of the *recogido*, she manages at the same time to acknowledge the correctness of the mystic's impulse to abandon human efforts and place herself entirely in God's hands, so long as this "letting go" takes place at the appropriate stage in spiritual development. She constructs a comfortably inclusive solution, in other words, to what most of her contemporaries were perceiving as a dilemma.

It is telling, I think, that when Teresa broaches her metaphorical plan, she fairly turns herself inside out apologizing for her presumption, going far beyond the disclaimers women mystics so often make:

I shall have to make use of some comparison, although I should like to excuse myself from this since I am a woman. . . . Seeing so much stupidity will provide some recreation for your Reverence. It seems now to me that I read or heard of this comparison—for since I have a bad memory, I don't know where or for what reason it was used.

(*Autobiography* 11.6)

Who but the cruelest opponent could find fault with anyone who finds so much fault with herself? Teresa knows very well that the explanation she is about to give is inspired; the "aw, shucks" posturing is pure rhetoric.

The garden of the human soul, she explains, is on barren soil and full of weeds, but "His Majesty" pulls up the weeds and plants good seed. God plants the seeds, she emphasizes; it falls to us to water the plants. Teresa identifies four ways to do the job, each of them symbolizing a level in prayer.

Beginners in prayer draw water from a well, and it is hard work, for to recollect their senses they must overcome the habit of distractedness. They must strive to consider the life of Christ, and the intellect grows weary. "It will frequently happen to him that he will even be unable to lift his arms for this work and unable to get a good thought." The watchword here—as for all of Teresa's life—is *determination*.

The second way to water one's garden is by turning the crank of a waterwheel and using a system of aqueducts. The waterwheel requires less effort and corresponds to the prayer of quiet, when the soul has begun to be recollected. One's arms still get tired, but the water is higher in that "grace is more clearly manifest to the soul." Water, we realize, *is* grace. One is "nearer the light" at this stage, so the intellect has greater clarity. Teresa herself has found, for example, that although she does not know Latin, she is able now to penetrate the meaning of Latin prayers.

The third water comes into our garden from a river or spring. Our part is simply to direct the flow. The Lord himself becomes the gardener. The prayer here is "a sleep of the faculties," wherein "the water of grace rises up to the throat of this soul." The joy of this stage Teresa characterizes as "a delightful disquiet." The soul is given over entirely to God now, and it bears fruit that the soul can eat and grow strong upon and then, with God's permission, distribute to others; the soul is Mary still, but now it is Martha as well, engaged in both the contemplative and active life.

The fourth and final stage in prayer is that of union. Teresa offers no symbolic equivalent at first and says she had been at her wit's end to know how to describe it until she went to Communion and God gave her the image: the fourth water is rainfall, "heavenly water that in its abundance soaks and saturates this entire garden"(*Autobiography* 18.9). Exuberantly now, she swings into her disquisition: "Well, now . . . The soul becomes so courageous that if at that moment it were cut in pieces for God, it would be greatly consoled. Such prayer is the source of heroic promises . . . the beginning of contempt for the world" (*Autobiography* 19.2).

In fact, she extends the metaphor: "If the soil is well cultivated by trials, persecutions, criticisms, illnesses, and if it is softened by living in great detachment from self-interest, the water soaks it to the extent that it is almost never dry. But if it is still hardened in the earth and has a lot of briers . . . and is still not removed from occasions, the ground will dry up again" (*Autobiography* 19.3).

She can no longer contain herself, cannot keep pretending to speak about souls in general. The memory of her own experience explodes into the scheme she has constructed so objectively. Through her carelessness, she explains, the garden of her *own* soul had dried up completely—was "as lost." And yet, God had rescued her. No one, therefore, should consider herself lost, "For tears gain all things: one water draws down the other."

By degrees, then, as our prayer deepens, we move from the stage where we must strive with all our powers to the moment years later when we can and must yield ourselves up entirely into God's hands. True abandonment is right and proper, but it can take place only when we are in full possession of ourselves: you can't give what you don't have. Immediately after this treatise, Teresa issues a strong warning against a practice she knows was commonly advised in certain books on prayer. To reach the highest stages, some believe, one should "rid oneself of all corporeal images," because they are an "obstacle or impediment to the most perfect contemplation." Teresa objects strongly, and she bases her objection on her own experience. "To withdraw completely from Christ or that this divine Body be counted in a balance with our own miseries or with all creation, I cannot endure." If God wants to suspend our faculties and lift us beyond everything created, fine, God has reasons. But otherwise—and this is a centrally Teresian position—"It is an important thing that while we are living and are human we have human support." It is in precisely this area that she and John of the Cross would have their difficulties.

Plainly, Teresa loved to write, loved it so much that she knew she was spiritually "at risk" every time she took up her pen; its pleasures were more of those "slender threads" John of the Cross had warned against. I would guess that it was as a protective discipline, therefore, comparable to the ashes Francis sprinkled over his supper, that Teresa abstained from editing what she wrote: no second thoughts, no final polish. She would write, rapidly and, whenever possible, not really even be the one writing.

> The little time at my disposal is little help to me and so His Majesty
> must come to my aid. I have to follow the community life and
> have many other duties since I am in a house which is just begin-
> ning. . . . As a result, I write without the time and calm for it, and
> bit by bit. I should like to have time, because when the Lord gives
> the spirit, things are put down with ease and in a much better way.
> Putting them down is then like copying a model you have before
> your eyes. But if the spirit is lacking, it is more difficult to speak
> about these things than to speak Arabic, as the saying goes, even
> though many years may have been spent in prayer. As a result, it
> seems to me most advantageous to have this experience while I am
> writing, because I see clearly that it is not I who say what I write;
> for neither do I plan it with the intellect nor do I know afterward
> how I managed to say it. This often happens to me.
>
> (*Autobiography* 14.8)

Teresa's second book, the *Way of Perfection*, was written soon afterward. Thanks to fussy church authorities, her daughters could not lay hands on her *Autobiography*, and they needed advice on mental prayer. She agreed readily, and she wrote in a voice that is singularly warm and intimate; exhorting her readers one minute and teasing them without mercy the next.

She teases her sisters, but she teases those learned men, the *letrados,* even more (and we must remember that she counted many friends among them). There is no question here of finding her voice: she speaks with utter confidence. The formulaic apologies for opening her mouth are clearly tongue-in-cheek, almost a parody of themselves. For example: "There are so many good books written by able persons for those who have methodical minds . . . that it would be a mistake if you paid attention to what I say about prayer" (*Way of Perfection* 19).

She persists: "As I say, there are books in which the mysteries of the Lord's life and Passion are divided according to the days of the week, and there are meditations about judgment, hell, our nothingness, and the many things we owe God together with excellent doctrine and method concerning the beginning and end of prayer" (*Way of Perfection* 19.1).

Her playfulness is indisputable. Feigning innocence, she explains that she herself is only writing for those who have "souls and minds so scattered they are like wild horses," knowing full well that no one with a shred of self-knowledge or humility would pretend *not* to have such a soul or mind.

This preamble to Teresa's teachings on prayer does not in fact occur, though, until halfway through the *Way of Perfection.* Knowing that her readers are anticipating instruction in mental prayer that is esoteric and abstruse, she holds them at bay—again, playfully—while she tells them all manner of things that would not seem to be pertinent at all. She reminds them that "prayer without ceasing" is mandated in their primitive rule, and she insists that everything else about their way of life must work to promote such constant prayer: "If prayer is to be genuine it must be helped by these other things; prayer and comfortable living are incompatible."

Nothing about technique, then, and nothing about ascetic disciplines as they are normally understood. Instead, she identifies three things that will bring the peace that is indispensable for real prayer: "The first of these is love for one another; the second is detachment from all created things; the third is true humility, which, even though I speak of it last, is the main practice and embraces all the others" (*Way of Perfection* 4.4).

There has got to be love for one another, she explains. Mental prayer cannot be focused entirely on God if one's mind is disturbed by

small irritations, and "there is nothing annoying that is not suffered easily by those who love one another" (*Way of Perfection* 4, 5). And yet, that
love has to be regulated. Excessive love, or "particular friendships," bring
their own train of distractions: "Feeling sorry about any affront to the
friend; desiring possessions so as to give her gifts; looking for time to
speak with her. . . . The silly things that come from such attachment are
too numerous to be counted" (*Way of Perfection* 4.6). Her instructions to
the nuns on how to extricate themselves from such friendships, though,
are exceedingly kind. One must proceed "delicately and lovingly."
Indeed, in tacit acknowledgment of the deep need most of us, even the
most ardent aspirants among us, have for human friendship, she goes
on to paint a glorious picture of what friendship can be—spiritual
friendship, that is, in which the friends are concerned only for one another's spiritual well-being.

> It will seem to you that such persons do not love or know anyone
> but God. I say yes, they do love, with a much greater and more
> genuine love. . . . In short, it is love.
>
> (*Way of Perfection* 6.7)

Such a friend cannot be happy, she explains, if the other is not making progress toward God. Even if the other is seen to suffer, this can be
borne cheerfully if it is hastening his or her growth in God. She wishes
that she herself had such a friend.

Her second concern is closely related to this ideal kind of friendship.
It is detachment, without which a sister "will not possess freedom of spirit;
she will not possess complete peace." Again, it is a question of what busies
the mind throughout one's waking hours, spilling over inevitably into
one's prayer. Undue attachment to relatives, for example, is a source of
endless agitation, but so, she insists, is attachment to oneself—to one's
aches and pains, for example. "Hardly does our head begin to ache than
we stop going to choir, which won't kill us either. We stay away one day
because our head ached, another because it was just now aching, and three
more so that it won't ache again" (*Way of Perfection* 10.6).

Not that she leaves herself out of the blame: "In my case He granted
me a great mercy in my being sick; for since I would have looked after my
comfort anyway, He desired that there be a reason for my doing so."

The endpoint of detachment is the threshold to that "freedom of spirit" mentioned above, "interior mortification," but the term is transformed in Teresa's handling so that it has little or nothing to do with bodily penances. It is acquired, she says, "by proceeding gradually, not giving in to our will and appetites, even in little things, until the body is completely surrendered to the spirit," and she adds firmly: "You will say that these are natural little things to which we need pay no attention. Don't fool yourselves, they increase like foam" (*Way of Perfection* 12.8).

With regard to humility, she speaks in particular of the temptation to make excuses for oneself, and admits to serious culpability on this score herself. (While he was acting as her confessor, John of the Cross remarked one day, "You have a fine way of excusing yourself!") Urging her daughters to learn how to be silent when they find they've been condemned without fault, she concludes with endearing regret: "In these great things I have not been able to test this myself, for I have never heard anything evil said of me that I didn't see that it fell short. . . . I am always happier that they speak about what is not true of me than the truth" (*Way of Perfection* 15.3).

Once she has dealt with these vital preliminary matters, she gets down to work with gusto. "Don't think that what I have said so far is all I have to say, for I am just setting up the game, as they say." After all, she goes on to explain, if you can't set up a chessboard, you can't be expected to know how to play. "Well, you will reprimand me because I am speaking about a game we do not have in this house, nor should we have it. Here you see the kind of Mother God has given you, that she even knows about this vanity" (*Way of Perfection* 16.1).

She has such fun in this particular book. She apparently feels no need for solemnity and no need to handle her audience with kid gloves. Adamantly, she prepares her daughters to deflect interference from ignorant spiritual directors: "If they tell you that the prayer should be vocal, ask, for the sake of more precision, if in vocal prayer the mind and heart must be attentive to what you say. If they answer 'yes'—for they cannot, otherwise—you will see how they admit that you are forced to practice mental prayer and even experience contemplation if God should give it to you by this means" (*Way of Perfection* 21.10).

Sweetly reasonable but utterly firm, and that tone characterizes her entire disquisition. By it she says there *is* nothing esoteric about contemplative prayer. She sets up a kind of staircase that demonstrates how smoothly and inevitably one stage of prayer gives way to the next. After all, when we practice vocal prayer with the appropriate intensity of concentration, she asks, don't we find ourselves growing silent as we give more and more attention to the words? And that's all that mental prayer is in the early stages. Similarly, she maintains, through the intervention of divine grace the prayer of quiet arises just as naturally out of mental prayer. Just so, again through infused grace, when one has learned to enter the prayer of quiet and remain there for long periods, keeping all one's love and will focused upon the Beloved, the prayer of union will take its place. And let there be no doubt: contemplative prayer is the birthright of women as well as men. She knew the real strengths of women and believed God did too.[8]

Indeed, one of Teresa's great gifts to the literature of mysticism was her formulation of a language for describing mental prayer that departs in many ways from traditional imagery. To convey what she means by recollection, for example, she does not speak of fighting off distractions (as in the old "warriors of God" model), but rather of dispelling them by moving more and more deeply into the presence of Christ, "in intimate conversation." As we exert this effort, the senses will quite naturally close down. She strikes a marvelously homely metaphor to convey the process:

> We will understand, when beginning to pray, that the bees are approaching and entering the beehive to make honey . . . When the soul does no more than give a sign that it wishes to be recollected, the senses obey it and become recollected. Even though they go out again afterward, their having already surrendered is a great thing.
>
> (*Way of Perfection* 28.7)

The image of a beehive—a vessel, as it were, closed off to the world, silently filling up with honey—evokes images of women's bodies, particularly pregnant women's bodies. Immediately after invoking it, Teresa conjures up others of a similar nature: "Let us imagine that within us is an extremely rich palace, built entirely of gold and precious stones. . . ." Then, speaking of women in particular,

All of this imagining is necessary that we may truly understand that within us lies something incomparably more precious than what we see outside ourselves. Let's not imagine that we are hollow inside. And please God it may be only women that go about forgetful of this inner richness and beauty.

(*Way of Perfection* 28.10)

Finally, she marvels that "He who would fill a thousand worlds and many more with His grandeur" would enclose himself in something as small as the human soul, "and so He wanted to enclose Himself in the womb of His most Blessed Mother."

What she has done in this brief cascade of metaphors—the beehive, the palace of gold, the womb of Mary—is to place a newly positive, even radiant, valuation on images of enclosure. The Carmelite, silent in her convent, with its strict new vows of enclosure, is making honey, is delighting in God's company, is carrying the infant Jesus within her just as Mary had. Within a few pages, prompted surely by these lovely metaphors, she writes,

The soul is like an infant that still nurses when at its mother's breast, and the mother without her babe's effort to suckle puts the milk in its mouth in order to give it delight. So it is here; for without effort of the intellect the will is loving, and the Lord desires that the will, without thinking . . . understands that it is with Him.

(*Way of Perfection* 31.9)

As images of silence and containment and inner richness accumulate, we come to understand implicitly why Teresa spent so much time talking about humility, detachment, and love for one another. The inwardness she is dwelling upon with such enthusiasm is hard to come by in an atmosphere of wrangling and contention: to a great extent, the individual's mental state will be no better than her community's.

Teresa proceeds to explain mental prayer through a line-by-line commentary on the Lord's Prayer, loading each word with marvelous depth of meaning and asking her daughters to recite the prayer to themselves at least once each hour.

The special charm of the *Way of Perfection* is, I think, its intimacy. She had written her autobiography for an audience composed in part of her most stern critics, and she would write the *Interior Castle* for virtually anyone who wished to practice mental prayer (only as a matter of form, I believe, and knowing it would still be prudent for her to at least pretend not to be a teacher of meditation, did she address that book to the members of her convents). But the *Way of Perfection* has all the immediacy of informal discourses transcribed on the spot right there at Saint Joseph's. Her insistence on spending so much of the book on themes whose relevance to interior prayer might not be immediately obvious denotes the confidence of a seasoned spiritual teacher.

The *Interior Castle* was written in 1577, about fifteen years later than the first two books, when Teresa was sixty-two. It is certainly her master work. In contrast to the *Way of Perfection,* with its informality and intimacy, this is a more formal book, whose audience is only nominally limited to her spiritual daughters. "It's nonsense," she insists as usual, "to think that what I say could matter to other persons," but by this time she is "La Santa" to all of Spain and "La Madre Fundadora," revered by King Philip II himself—and she knows it.

She begins: "Consider our soul to be like a castle made entirely out of a diamond or of very clear crystal, in which there are many rooms" (*Interior Castle* 1.1.1). The simile becomes a sustained and subtle allegory for the deepening of contemplative prayer. The castle has seven "dwelling places" representing seven stages in prayer.

Lovers of Christ are told of this lovely castle within but don't seem to believe it: "All our attention is taken up with the plainness of the diamond's setting or the outer wall of the castle; that is, with these bodies of ours." Given the excessive emphasis Western culture has placed upon the physical appearance of women, Teresa's remark has special force for women readers now, but probably did then, too.

> It seems I'm saying something foolish. For if this castle is the soul, clearly one doesn't have to enter it since it is within oneself. How foolish it would seem were we to tell someone to enter a room he is already in. But you must understand that there is a great difference in the ways one may be inside the castle. . . .
>
> (*Interior Castle* 1.1.5)

There are *levels* of consciousness, it would seem, a neat twist on "My father's house has many mansions."

Teresa is in full possession of her skills as a writer now. Little trills of satisfaction punctuate her prose: "I don't think I've ever explained it as clearly as I have now!" (*Interior Castle* 4.3.2) and "That was right on the mark, for I don't know how to say it better" (*Interior Castle* 5.1.6). The first three dwelling places are initiatory. They have to do with "settling down" into mental prayer. The fourth includes the prayer of quiet and represents a transitional phase between the natural and supernatural. The fifth is characterized by the prayer of union and the soul's "death" and subsequent new life in Christ. She compares this death to that of a silkworm and maintains that when the soul dies in the cocoon (which is God), it is reborn, transformed, as a white butterfly. The sixth dwelling place takes longer to describe than any of the others. Great favors come here, but it is essentially a time of spiritual torment, of purification and preparation for the seventh and final stage. Recognizing the strictures on women as teachers, we can appreciate the caution Teresa employs when it is time to describe the seventh "dwelling place," but her preamble is nonetheless remarkably convoluted:

> It seems that a creature as miserable as I should tremble to deal
> with a thing so foreign to what I deserve to understand. . . . For it
> seems to me that others will think I know about it through experi-
> ence. This makes me extremely ashamed, for knowing what I am,
> such a thought is a terrible thing.
>
> (*Interior Castle* 7.1.2)

She cannot say she has not experienced the seventh dwelling place, because of course her commentary makes it clear she has been living there for some time, but to say so will bring the Inquisitors on the run. So she manages not to.

With each of these books on prayer, Teresa is also writing about her own life—"composing a life," in a real sense. We saw in the *Way of Perfection* how she placed a wonderfully positive valuation on images of enclosure and how deeply feminine those images were. With *Interior Castle* enclosure becomes synonymous with freedom, just as it had proven to be, paradoxically, for her and the women who followed her into reformed Carmels. In the innermost chamber of that castle, she tells us, at the center of the labyrinth, one discovers complete freedom. The irony, of course, is that Teresa herself enjoyed relatively little of the freedom that comes of being completely enclosed because she spent most of her last twenty years out on the road, trying to ensure that it would be there for others!

Entry into that last dwelling place is marked by an extraordinary vision of the Trinity that takes place "in the extreme interior" of oneself. One experiences that vision constantly, Teresa explains, and yet, her normal diverse duties go on uninterrupted.

> And it seemed to her, despite the trials she underwent and the business affairs she had to attend to, that the essential part of her soul never moved from that room. As a result, it seemed to her that there was, in a certain way, a division in her soul. And while suffering some great trials a little after God granted her this favor, she complained of that part of the soul, as Martha complained of Mary.
>
> (*Interior Castle* 7.1.10)

"Heaven in her soul," they had said of Catherine of Genoa, "and purgatory in her agonized body." Of one living in this last dwelling place, Teresa says, simply, "Its life is now Christ." Love without limit, we understand her to mean, and pain without surcease.

The journey inward has been a romance as well: at the fifth dwelling place, Teresa introduces the metaphor of courtship, followed by betrothal at the sixth, and marriage at the seventh. The conflation of metaphors is wonderful, reminding us that all along, for Teresa, mental prayer has been "intimate conversation with one who loves you."

Teresa lived and worked in an atmosphere that was arguably as complex and crazymaking as our own, shaped by the presence of a rabid "religious right" whose obsession with ideological purity, and means of ensuring it, remind us at times of the McCarthy era in the United States. She was forced to conceal so much: her Jewish antecedents, her early peccadilloes (whatever they might have been and how little concerned *she* was to conceal them), the raptures that marked the turning point in her spiritual life, and—most irksome, perhaps—the force of her quite re-markable intellect.

On paper her task sounds simple enough: to reform a contempla-tive order. Over and over, though, what should have been simple turned into a nightmare of rancorous contention. I have drawn comparisons be-tween Catherine of Siena and Gandhi, but perhaps he and Teresa are even closer in spirit. Dazzled by Gandhi's mastery of nonviolence as a tool for political reform—the acts of civil disobedience and the extended fasts—most commentators overlook his knack for compromise. Without caving in on essentials, he knew how to draw opponents over by giving way in small things. He knew how to find the few areas where conflict-ing interests happened to overlap and then to enlarge them little by painstaking little. He was never abstract, always personal. Teresa oper-ated in much the same way, drawing to her cause and into her affections individuals who did not always seem worthy of that honor. She did so for the same reason Gandhi would: the work at hand was far too urgent to be postponed until perfect men and women came along to undertake it.

Teresa did not move unscathed through that last twenty years. She made mistakes and did not always admit them in time. Her loyalty to old friends sometimes blinded her to their faults. (Writing in defense of one of those old associates, she broke off finally and admitted, "I could be bought for a herring!") Like Francis of Assisi, she had to witness fierce di-visiveness within her own order. Worst of all, perhaps, she was not al-ways sure herself what she was meant to do next.

She thought she knew, in the spring of 1582, that she was to found a convent in Burgos. God's Voice seemed to be telling her so.

"Granada," John of the Cross insisted. Her locutions had always made him uneasy, as had her raptures. To him, they belonged to a level of mystical development Teresa should have left behind.

"Burgos," she maintained, and they argued into the night. He left early the next morning, and they never saw each other again. She went on to Burgos, to found a convent in unbelievable turmoil, and was nearly killed in a flash flood of unprecedented destructiveness.

Weary, bruised, and heartsore, Teresa was finally released from life that fall, far away from her beloved Saint Joseph's, out on the road again, in obedience not to a call from her Beloved but from a duchess who wanted Teresa present when her grandchild was born. It was a nightmarish journey, during which she was subjected to unspeakable accommodations, little or no food, and intense hostility expressed by one of her own prioresses along the way—a genuine Golgotha. Near its end, word came that the baby had entered the world under his own steam. "God be praised!" Teresa said, "they won't need the saint!" She died a few days later, on October 4, 1582.

It grieves us to think John and Teresa parted at odds. It is to his credit that after she died he shouldered the full responsibility of continuing the reform of the order; he set aside the strictly contemplative life he would have preferred to carry out the work into which she had drawn him. When he had tried to persuade her to do just the opposite—come in off the road and give herself over to prayer—I suspect he was moved out of friendship as well as religious conviction. It must have hurt him to see how exhausted and ill she was and how much wrangling surrounded her; he wanted peace for her, and transcendence. But Teresa's path was her own, and absolutely of a piece with her nature. To ask a woman to abandon converse with God, a woman for whom the very meaning of interior prayer was "sweet talk" at its most beguiling? Inconceivable.

"Who are you?" her Beloved had asked her one afternoon.

"I am Teresa of Jesus," she had murmured, "and who are you?"

"I am Jesus—of Teresa."

Saint Thérèse of Lisieux

(1873–1897)

Instead of becoming discouraged, I said to myself:
God cannot inspire unrealizable desires. I can, then, in
spite of my littleness, aspire to holiness. It is impossible
for me to grow up, and so I must bear with myself
such as I am with all my imperfections. But I want to
seek out a means of going to heaven by a little way, a
way that is very straight, very short, and totally new.

> — Saint Thérèse of Lisieux,
> *The Story of a Soul* 207

Love is nourished only by sacrifices, and the more a
soul refuses natural satisfactions, the stronger and more
disinterested becomes her tenderness.

> — Saint Thérèse of Lisieux,
> *The Story of a Soul* 237

T HE diversity of the women we have looked at is impressive. "Be
ye perfect" does not seem to have meant "Be ye indistinguishable one from another" at all. And yet, in an important sense these
women *were* also visibly, almost eerily, one and the same. Most of what
sets one apart from another has to do with temperament, personal circumstances, and the special gifts the church calls charisms. Put all of this
aside, and you are left with a Julian, for instance, who could slip almost
unrecognized into the life of a Clare or a Teresa, for the core of her

being—an all-consuming desire to become one with God—is indistinguishable from the core of theirs.

Suppose, then, that one were to take this "prototypical" woman mystic and place her for the sake of experiment in still another setting—in the region of Normandy, for example, late in the last century, in an intensely pious family of the rising bourgeoisie. How would she fare? What would her unfolding look like, and to what particular task would she devote herself?

The answer to these questions is the brief but extremely well documented life of Saint Thérèse of Lisieux, who died at twenty-four in the Carmelite convent she had entered at fifteen. Object of some of the most excessively sentimental devotions in Catholicism, she is also the author of some of the most embarrassingly precious prose in that tradition. And yet she was also the woman of whom Dorothy Day, founder of the *Catholic Worker,* wrote admiringly, "Always she was praying that she would see things as they were, that she would live in reality, not in dreams."[1] For Day, the sheer concreteness of Thérèse's teachings swept away the abstractions of Marxist theory and allowed her to place her own work for social justice and reform in the context of a richly devotional spiritual practice.

Of all our subjects, Thérèse may be the easiest to overlook or misconstrue. She writes like the precocious but very narrowly educated schoolgirl she was. And yet, if you can complete her book and go about your business, certain passages will begin to come back to you— things no ordinary schoolgirl would ever say. Near the time of her death, Thérèse reassured her sister Marie that "Papa le bon Dieu" knew how to deal with his "little baby." Marie asked, "Are you then a baby?" Thérèse paused, grew serious, then said, "Yes, but a baby who has thought a great deal, a baby who is very old." Over and over, we see in Thérèse this fascinating incongruity—this plainly imperfect fit between the bright, well-brought-up child of the middle class on the one hand, and the "old soul," on the other, so intent on shedding every obstacle to spiritual awareness that she is just barely in the body.

Sometimes when we are getting to know a particular mystic or saint and we observe the precise dovetailing between the individual's gifts and the work she carries out, it is tempting to imagine a kind of divine placement office functioning behind the scenes to be sure that if a pope needs to be brought into line or an order reformed, the right person is sent out to do it. But sometimes, too, when we ask "Why her? . . . Why there? . . . Why then?" another sort of answer suggests itself. If we begin to regard the entire roll call of saints and mystics as a kind of introductory course in sanctity itself, as it is tempting to do, then each individual man or woman of God appears to have come along expressly to tell us at least one thing about that state of being—one thing that no other can tell us so well. I would like to take this approach to Thérèse of Lisieux and try to determine, once the reader is reasonably familiar with her life and writings, just what Thérèse adds to the testimonies we have already heard.

In Thérèse we are privileged to see for the first time an extremely close view of the earliest years of a mystic-in-the-making. The brevity of her life, balanced by a profusion of letters, diaries, and testimonies, allows and even compels her biographers to examine exhaustively episodes that would have been passed over in a phrase if one were dealing with a longer life. This is fortunate, because as it turned out, every smallest thing that happened to Thérèse seems to have counted, in one way or another, in the process of her transformation. In terms of spiritual development, her two dozen years were unbelievably compressed and efficient, as if she knew from the beginning that they would have to be.

We even have photographs. Some were pictures taken of her family by professional photographers, but many more were taken by her sister Celine in the Carmelite convent of Lisieux, for Celine brought a box camera into the convent with her when she joined Thérèse and her two older sisters there, and she was encouraged to photograph the community at work, at recreation, and, in Thérèse' case, in costume for a play presented by the novices on the life of Saint Joan. It is a stunning experience, when you come to Thérèse by way of lives so much more remote in time, to be able to look at the very eyes and the very smile, rendered in grainy black and white, of a young woman who in so many ways really could have *been* Julian of Norwich or Catherine of Siena. The smile itself becomes even more wondrous when you learn what lay behind it.

Thérèse Martin was born on January 2, 1873, in the town of Alençon, home of the famous *point d'Alençon* lace. She was the fifth daughter and last child of Zelie and Louis Martin. Madame Martin was forty-two when Thérèse was born, and she was unwell. She had been aware for eight years that something was wrong: four and a half years later she would die of breast cancer.

Thérèse herself fell ill soon after her birth and was sent to a farm to be under the care of a wet nurse. After several downward turns, she recovered at fifteen months and returned home, where she was by all accounts the special favorite of an exceedingly affectionate family. "My earliest recollections are of tender caresses and smiles," she would write later. "I was always cherished with the most loving care." And it does sound idyllic—long walks in the meadows carried on her father's shoulders when she tired, games and reading by lamplight in the evening, older sisters who adored her.

The family was extremely devout: Thérèse's mother and father attended the earliest mass every day and took communion four or five times a week. Ida Gorres, the most insightful of Thérèse's biographers, gives us an interesting perspective on the Martin family's religiosity. Reminding us that France was no longer an officially Catholic nation or a monarchy, she identifies the Martins as both "clericalist" and royalist in their leanings and refers to them as *emigrés de l'interieur:* "A phrase revived in the twentieth century as a political concept: exiles who have remained at home and who nevertheless have emigrated from the prevailing order, who are fugitives from the whole life of the nation, leftovers of a vanished era, quietly longing for a return to or restlessly bent upon reconquest of the past."[2]

To people like the Martins, "modern" represented one pole, and "Catholic" the other. When the Martin daughters speak of the "contempt for the world" their parents displayed, more is probably implied than simple detachment, and we realize that for Thérèse to become the beautifully balanced individual she was, she would have to outgrow some elements of the rather isolated and defensive piety that surrounded her early years.

Thérèse was four and a half years old when her mother died. It was a devastating blow to the whole family. Louis Martin moved them soon afterward to the town of Lisieux, where he meant to put painful memories behind them all. He also wanted to protect his daughters from the worldliness of their friends and relatives in Alençon. The way of life from which he removed them would seem by contemporary standards quite innocent, but to this intensely religious man halfway through his fifties, it spelled real danger. "They make compromises so easily," he explained.

Even the briefest overview of Thérèse's life requires that we say something more about her parents. Before they met, each of them had sought entrance into a religious order, and both had been turned away— he because he did not know Latin, and she for no certain reason. Denied admission to holy orders, Zelie Guerin vowed that, instead, she would bring children into the world for God. Many children. Meanwhile, to support herself and to set aside the dowry she would need, she became a professional lacemaker. Soon she had built up a home crafts industry that employed a number of other women whom she herself had trained.

Louis Martin, meanwhile, who was nine years older than Zelie, had dealt with his own disappointment by constructing a way of life that was very nearly monastic. A watchmaker and jeweler by profession, he took long walks, fished, and read a great deal, when he was not engaged in religious activities of one kind or another.

One day, as the two of them were crossing a bridge from opposite sides (she was about twenty-seven, and he was thirty-six), their eyes met. Certain immediately that this man was the father-to-be of all those children, Zelie found out who his family was and managed to meet him. They were married three months later. Louis did not come around immediately to what Zelie felt was his appointed destiny; the couple remained celibate for ten months until their spiritual director intervened. But it is clear that in time Zelie's strong sense of calling became her husband's as well: he applied himself to his children's upbringing with whole-hearted dedication. Zelie's business flourished, meanwhile, and her husband quit his own to help manage hers.

Louis was a dreamer, idealistic and introspective; Zelie was more extroverted, possessed of formidable energy and strength of will. She was generous and very affectionate. She gloried in motherhood, adoring each new child in turn. Her letters to Pauline, for example, away in boarding school, are filled with news about three year-old Thérèse: "She has a blonde little head and a golden heart, and is very tender and candid." Again, "She is going to be wonderfully good; the germ of goodness can already be seen." But also,

She is such a little madcap . . . not nearly so docile as her sister. When she says "no," nothing can make her change, and she can be terribly obstinate. You could keep her down in the cellar all day without getting a "yes" out of her; she would rather sleep there.[3]

Zelie never doubted that her daughters would all find their way into convents, but she had special intuitions about Thérèse. To her sister-in-law, shortly after the birth of Thérèse, she wrote as follows—with a high-hearted delight that astonishes us, considering she was running a business and a large household, caring for five daughters, and suffering all the while from a malignant tumor: "During the time I was carrying her, I noticed something that never happened before my other children were born: when I sang, she sang with me. I am telling you this, for no one else would believe it."

Zelie was decidedly the more forceful parent; her husband had a certain fragility about him that would become more pronounced as he grew older. Already now the girls began to speak protectively about him. As they stood about after their mother's funeral services, they arranged among themselves that the youngest two, Celine and Thérèse, would adopt the eldest two as their second mothers. Thérèse went to Pauline, Celine to Marie. (The middle child, Leonie, fifteen at the time, stands just to one side of this family grouping, unmentioned and we imagine, somewhat forlorn. Such would be the unfortunate Leonie's lot in this family of spiritual superstars.)

Pauline and Marie took full responsibility for the youngest two. Only sixteen and seventeen years old themselves, they ran the household (there were servants; Thérèse would recall later that she had never performed even the most minor household task) and guided both the intellectual and spiritual development of their charges. The first word Thérèse read was *heaven,* and her earliest reading lessons were from the Bible. She adored Pauline and obeyed her in everything.

Gazing into the Martin household through Thérèse's and her sisters' recollections is rather like peering into an antique dollhouse. It is all so dainty, so carefully turned out and so small in scale; just what you might expect of a lacemaker joined forces with a jeweler! Now Thérèse is in the garden brewing tisanes to serve in acorn cups to Papa; now she's feeling naughty for wanting blue silk hair ribbons or weeping incon-

solably for breaking the candy ring she was going to give Celine. With re
spect to spiritual instruction, too, the approach can seem lamentably precious and external: pretty strings of beads on which to record daily
"sacrifices," beautifully bound little books to hold "acts of virtue" (each
page decorated with a flower—roses for acts of love, violets for acts of
humility, and so on).

And yet no sooner do we acknowledge the somewhat claustropho-
bic atmosphere of all this than we have to recognize its strengths, too. In
one of their frequent theological discussions, for example, Thérèse asked
Pauline about fairness in heaven: Is glory distributed evenly or do the
spiritual giants get more? Here is Pauline's answer, recalled years later
by Thérèse:

> You sent me off to fetch one of Father's big glasses and had me
> put my little thimble by the side of it; then you filled them both
> up with water and asked me which I thought was the fuller. I had
> to admit that one was just as full as the other because neither of
> them would hold any more. That was the way you helped me to
> grasp how it was that in Heaven the least have no cause to envy
> the greatest.
>
> (*Story of a Soul* 45)

An accomplished Zen master could have done no better. Here is the
origin of that ardent celebration of diversity with which Thérèse com-
mences her memoirs: "I understood how all the flowers He has created
are beautiful, how the splendor of the rose and the whiteness of the lily
do not take away the perfume of the little violet or the delightful simplicity of the daisy" (*Story of a Soul* 14).

Writing about her life much later, Thérèse would see it as falling
into three periods. The first, supremely happy, ended when her mother
died. The second, a time of utter disequilibrium and struggle, would last
ten years. The third, beginning when she found her spiritual and emotional footing again at thirteen, would extend through the rest of her life.

The wildness Thérèse had displayed as a little girl was barely visible after her mother's death. Her stubbornness transmuted itself into a
will of steel. She became inordinately conscientious and unnervingly
self-controlled.

Sensing a certain desperation in Thérèse's desire to "be good," one wonders whether many of the "sacrifices" and "acts" she performed were not unconscious efforts to ward off any further blows of the sort life had just dealt her. In any event, the sensitivity that everyone had observed in her as a baby became extremely pronounced, subjecting her to fits of depression and what we would now call anxiety attacks.

At eight and a half, Thérèse started school—her lessons had all been at home up until now—and because she had been so well prepared, she was placed in a class of girls several years older. The experience was disastrous. She was timid and shy and never learned to enjoy the games or roughhousing that went on at recess. She would remark of herself later—in sharp contrast to Teresa—that she had never had the art of getting people to like her. Her family only found out later, when she wrote about it, how unhappy she had been; she confided in none of them at the time. Very likely, being able to return to their midst every evening was all that made school endurable: their ignorance of her misery probably allowed her to forget it when she was with them.

When Thérèse was nine (despite her nearly perfect grades in school and her painfully exemplary behavior), she received another stunning blow in the loss of her beloved second mother—not to death, but to the Carmel in Lisieux.

"In one instant, I understood what life was; until then, I had never seen it so sad; but it appeared to me in all its reality, and I saw it was nothing but a continual suffering and separateness" (*Story of a Soul* 58).

On the deepest level, she understood and accepted and even perhaps rejoiced, because there is a fierce kind of joy in discovering even the hardest truth so long as it *is* truth. But Thérèse was a nine-year-old girl, too, and on that level, she was absolutely unready to accept this appalling vision of things. She began now to have incessant headaches. Fits of shivering and tears would come over her and then high fevers and terrible convulsions. Her condition lasted for months.

The cure would come in a form that answered precisely the sense of abandonment that underlay her condition. Fearing for her life, her sisters knelt one night before a statue of the Blessed Virgin. Thérèse looked over, and "suddenly the statue came to life, and Mary appeared utterly lovely. Then all my pain was gone." She realized that she had a mother, after all, whom nothing could take away.

Thérèse recovered, and she more or less recovered her balance also. School continued to be sheer hell for her, though. She could not form friendships, not even, really, with her teachers. Nor did it help that her sister Celine flourished at the same school. Looking back, Thérèse sounds baffled still: "When I noticed Celine showing affection for one of her teachers, I wanted to imitate her, but not knowing how to win the good graces of creatures, I was unable to succeed" (*Story of a Soul* 80). She became increasingly more indrawn and isolated and more preoccupied with her spiritual state. Before her first communion, she wrote out three resolutions: "I will never lose courage. I will say a *Memorare* every day. I will take pains to humble my arrogance." Of her confirmation, soon afterward she wrote, "On that day I was given the strength to suffer." She would need an extra measure of courage to face what lay ahead.

> One would have to pass through this martyrdom to understand it well . . . All my most simple thoughts and actions became the cause of trouble for me, and I had relief only when I told them to Marie. This cost me dearly, for I believed I was obliged to tell her the absurd thoughts I had even about her. As soon as I laid down my burden, I experienced peace for an instant; but this peace passed away like a lightning-flash, and soon my martyrdom began over again.
>
> (*Story of a Soul* 84–85)

Thérèse had fallen victim to "the terrible sickness of scruples" (*Story of a Soul* 84). The word comes from the Latin *scrupulus,* which means, literally, a small sharp stone, something that "weighs" on the mind and hurts, like a pebble in the shoe. In the ordinary sense, a scruple is a qualm or misgiving, but in the special vocabulary of Catholicism, scruples are a serious affliction, symptomatic of an acute, paralyzing self-consciousness: self-will in its most deceptive camouflage (and a blight on any religious community).

Marie was of all the Martin girls the most down-to-earth and unflappable; it was she who would hold out longest against Thérèse's early entry into Carmel, opposing Pauline and even the prioress. She took Thérèse in hand now with breathtaking competence. She allowed Thérèse to tell the priest only two or three imagined sins at each confession, and she specified which ones. Thérèse's affliction continued but did not deepen.

Tears and agitation, oversensitivity and diffidence—it sounds familiar to anyone who has been close to twelve- and thirteen-year-olds. But in Thérèse's case, all of this was exacerbated by what we can only see as an obsession with *being good*. One reads with some dismay that Celine said later of this period, "She kept a grip on herself at every moment, and in the smallest things." Again, she fell ill, not seriously, as before, but enough to persuade her father she should be withdrawn from school and complete her education (such as it was) with private lessons.

In October of that year, Marie followed Pauline into Carmel, and Thérèse slipped into deepening solitude. "I was really unbearable because of my extreme touchiness. . . . If I caused someone some little trouble, I cried like a Magdalene, and then when I began to cheer up, I cried for having cried . . . " (*Story of a Soul* 97). That Christmas, though, the turning point came. It is wonderfully typical of Thérèse, this mystic who admits as a professed nun to having slept through virtually all of her appointed hours of prayer, that the transformative moment of her life came not as a dazzling visionary experience, but in the context of a perfectly innocuous domestic episode that could have been related by Charles Dickens in one of his more sentimental moods.

In France at that time gift giving took place on New Year's Day, but in the Martin home the children would find their shoes filled with candy and small gifts on Christmas Eve. Even Thérèse was technically too old for this tradition by now, but the family had continued to carry it out. ("You can see I was still treated as a baby.") On this particular Christmas, Papa and the three youngest girls arrived home from mass, and while Thérèse was upstairs removing her coat, about to run down and make a fuss over her gifts, she heard her father say to Celine in a rare moment of irritability that he hoped this would be the last year they would be doing this. Since Thérèse had really only put her shoes out to entertain him anyway, she was acutely mortified. Celine urged her not to go down yet; she might cry if she tried to open her presents in front of her father just then.

But something happened. Thérèse felt an influx of strength and clarity that she could only assume was a gift from the Child Jesus. "I felt charity slip into my soul, and the need to forget myself and to please others. I descended the stairs rapidly; controlling the poundings of my heart, I took my slippers and placed them in front of Papa, and withdrew the objects joyfully." That night, she wrote, "began the third period of my life, the most beautiful and the most filled with graces from heaven" (*Story of a Soul* 98).

It sounds so trivial, yet Thérèse's biographers identify this event confidently as her "second conversion," comparing it in effect to Teresa's experience at the Incarnation before the bust of Christ, or to Catherine of Genoa's when she met her sister's confessor. In such instances, the external form is not important. It is merely the "outward and visible sign" of a transformation that we are to understand has been building for years and that, if genuine, will go on bearing fruit across the years to come. And indeed, from this moment on, thirteen-year-old Thérèse was able to shed the overwhelming diffidence and self-consciousness that had marred most of her childhood. She blossomed in every way, and everyone recognized it. An honor student all along, she only now discovered a real passion for learning and read science and history with enormous delight. There arose in her at this moment a passionate desire "to save souls."

Her great struggle to be good was behind her, though. There would still be effort, but it was clear to Thérèse now that it is not our own strivings, finally, that bring us closer to God. We must, rather, accept our limitations and trust in God to remove them—must open ourselves to God's transforming grace. In fact, for the rest of her life, the whole focus of her practice would be to put herself entirely at God's disposal until at last she could say, "Now abandonment alone guides me—I have no other compass!" (*Story of a Soul* 178).

Thérèse had first become aware of her vocation as a Carmelite nun when she was just nine. Now, at fourteen, "the divine call was becoming so insistent that had it been necessary for me to go through flames to follow Our Lord, I would have cast myself into the flames" (*Story of a Soul* 106). The Carmelite order itself did not have a formal age limit, but in France church authorities would not normally permit anyone under twenty-one to enter. Pauline and Celine both supported Thérèse's desire for early entrance, but Marie felt she was much too young. The real concern, though, was what the news might do to their father. He was sixty-three and had already suffered his first stroke; his doctors were sure there would be more. Thérèse was his dearest companion. How could she ask him to let her go?

She did ask, finally, and her account of their conversation is one of the most moving episodes in the *Story of a Soul*. The two of them wept together, walking with their arms about each other in the garden while she told him about her vocation. Convinced that it was genuine, "he cried out that God was giving him a great honor in asking his children from him." An honor, we are to understand, by assuming that he could bear their loss. They talked for a long time. He raised no real objection to her early entrance, and after a while he picked a tiny white flower from the moss growing over the garden wall. "He gave it to me explaining the care with which God brought it into being and preserved it to that very day." As she accepted it, she realized that he had plucked it without disturbing its roots, as if to suggest that it was "destined to live on in another soil more fertile than the tender moss where it had spent its first days" (*Story of a Soul* 108).

We could be forgiven, I think, for having reservations about the Martin family structure, specifically the girls' unstinting adoration of "Papa" and the enormous solicitousness they displayed toward him. But as one becomes increasingly familiar with the story, the real quality of the man and his plain goodness become more and more apparent, particularly here, where he is sending off his best-beloved child. He could so easily have said the obvious—that she was much too young—but instead he supported her fully. In fact, he threw himself now into the effort to overcome official resistance. He was a true renunciate, this man who had been perfectly content as a bachelor, a monk by temperament who must have found family life more than a little stressful at times. Thérèse tells us that she and her sisters were able to confirm what their mother had told them about him—that he had never said an unkind word to anyone.

There is a picture of Thérèse taken when she was fourteen, right at the time when she and her father were approaching the authorities who could, if they chose, get her permission to enter Carmel at fifteen. Her hair is piled on top of her head to make her look older, and her expression is decidedly plucky.

The prioress said yes, but the father superior said no, not until she was twenty-one. The bishop said not yet, and the pope was noncommittal.

That's right, the pope. In the fall of 1887, Thérèse went with Celine and her father to Rome, ostensibly on pilgrimage, and as they passed before the Holy Father, she threw herself at his feet and begged him to approve her admission to Carmel. "Well, child!" he answered, "well, you will enter if it be God's will!" She returned home bitterly disappointed, but on New Year's Day she received a letter from the mother superior. The bishop had approved her immediate entry into Carmel. The mother superior herself, though eager to receive Thérèse at once, had decided that she should not enter during the rigorous Lent, but right afterward.

On March 9, 1888, at fifteen years and three months, Thérèse entered the Carmelite convent at Lisieux:

> My soul experienced a peace so sweet, so deep, it would be impossible to express it. For seven years and a half that inner peace has remained my lot, and has not abandoned me in the midst of the greatest trials. . . . Everything thrilled me; I felt as though I was transported into a desert; our little cell,[4] above all, filled me with joy . . . With what deep joy I repeated those words. "I am here forever and ever."
>
> (*Story of a Soul* 148)

The convent was indeed "more fertile soil" than the household where Thérèse had spent her childhood, but not in all the ways we might imagine. For in many regards the Martin home more closely approximated the ideal Carmelite community than did the Lisieux Carmel, with the qualities that Teresa of Avila had specified: love for one another, detachment, and humility. The "fertility" of the Carmel, its conduciveness to spiritual growth, had to do of course with its complete enclosure, its inherited disciplines, its mandatory silence, but even more, perhaps, with the tremendous number of opportunities it offered its members for the practice of self-naughting. I refer not so much to the physical hardships of the place, though they were considerable, as to the Carmelites themselves.

The community in which Thérèse took her place numbered, usually, between twenty-one and twenty-five. The majority of the women were over fifty years old. The Martin girls and a cousin of theirs were the youngest members: not until Thérèse's third year in the convent did more young girls enter. One biographer familiar with all the pertinent documents describes them vividly and disappointingly.

> All, without exception, bore the mark of the *emigré de l'interieur*. Raised behind artificial walls, cut off from the intellectual life of the age and from the shaping forces of ordinary reality, even before they entered the convent reared in an atmosphere of monastic, or rather puritanical, narrowness and timidity, they unconsciously suffered from intellectual and cultural undernourishment.[5]

With a few exceptions, she continues, they were "quite average, well-intentioned, unimportant; among them were a surprising number of queer, stunted, or sick personalities." Inevitably, therefore, the Martin girls (four, after Celine joined them) formed a visible and powerful presence in that community. Radiant, healthy, "they were gifted and capable," Gorres reminds us, and "knew how to get their way."[6]

The prioress herself stood out from the other nuns dramatically. She was a most complex figure. Hagiographers who present her as a blend of the thirteenth fairy and the wicked stepmother are exaggerating her flaws, but she was decidedly neurotic, and the community suffered under her leadership. Unlike most of the nuns, who had come from the petty bourgeois and artisan class, she came from a noble family, from whom she never really broke off as a Carmelite would have been expected to do. Her sister, "the Countess," would bring her family for extended visits, during which the entire community was drawn into her service, embroidering linens with the family crest, preparing special foods, and so on.

Arbitrary and domineering, subject to fits of childlike gaiety followed by darkest depression, capable of being incredibly tender in her consideration for others and just as incredibly rude, the prioress would issue complicated rules and, within a few days, forget them, leaving the nuns themselves quite at a loss to determine where obedience lay. If her cat caught a bird, the cook was asked to boil it up for him, and if he did not come home on time, all the sisters were sent running around to find him.

Her peculiarities are well documented. And yet, this woman was elected prioress for not one or two, but *seven* three-year terms, and many of her nuns would say later that their affection for this manifestly charismatic individual had been the single most tenacious attachment they had had to sever. Plainly, there was much more to her than her obvious excesses. Thérèse was apparently alert to the woman's real potential and tried all along to help her realize it.

The ongoing drama that played itself out across the nine years Thérèse spent at the Lisieux Carmel arose primarily out of the complex relationship between her own younger group, with Pauline as its natural leader, and the older women who supported Mother Marie de Gonzague. In fact, the circumstances under which *Story of a Soul* was written were closely shaped by that drama.

But we are getting ahead of ourselves.

Thérèse maintained that she had had no illusions about life at Carmel: "I found the religious life to be exactly as I had imagined it." Her childhood had prepared her well. The book in which she had recorded her acts of love and her sacrifices had trained her to see meaning—opportunity, even—in the smallest things. Soon after she arrived at the Carmel, for example, there was the time when she was returning to her cell after compline and could not find her oil lamp. Another sister had taken it from the shelf by mistake. A mild wave of pique would have been forgivable—no one likes to grope through darkness—but for Thérèse the mishap was a piece of spiritual instruction, for it taught her that real poverty consists "in being deprived not only of agreeable things but of indispensable things too" (*Story of a Soul* 159). For a sheltered child of the bourgeoisie, this was no trivial insight.

It is this attitude—this unblinking alertness to the meaning of each moment—that probably accounts for the intense compression of Thérèse's spiritual development. She just didn't miss a beat. As a novice, she was exerting special effort not to excuse herself ("I will take pains to humble my arrogance"). She could not bear to be criticized. So when she was wrongly blamed for breaking a vase (no great fuss was made, she was just asked to be more careful), and she managed not to protest or excuse herself, it does not seem trivial at all. We concur when she says, "Here was my first victory, not too great, but it cost me a lot" (*Story of a Soul* 159). (We concur, and we realize, suddenly, that our own lives are filled with just such opportunities. Teresa has already told us how much hangs on "small things," but only with Thérèse do we learn just *how* small!)

The worst suffering Thérèse underwent in terms of the living conditions at the convent had to do with the cold, and she characteristically made no compromises with her discomforts. She could not easily digest the food, either, and her family worried that she was not eating enough. On the other hand, we read with great amusement in the letters that relatives received—far more than a Carmelite would normally write, but then this was an odd Carmelite convent in several ways—expressions of gratitude for the baskets of fruit, and fish, and pastries that "Papa" and the aunts and uncles were sending—little luxuries of every kind meant to be sure the teenaged renunciate would not starve.

Her probationary period over, Thérèse took the habit as a Carmelite in January 1889 and received the name Thérèse of the Child Jesus. A month after this her father suffered his second stroke and had to be taken to a mental institution. Leonie and Celine followed him to Caen and boarded at an orphanage there to be near him. Thérèse tells us that while she had felt when he first fell ill that she could bear still more suffering, she knew now that she was at her limit imagining the bitterness and humiliation her father must be enduring.

In September 1890, Thérèse took her vows and added to her name in religion, "and of the Holy Face." When she took the veil, a few weeks after making her final vows, she was in a state of complete spiritual aridity, as she would be, she tells us, at every subsequent retreat. "Jesus was sleeping as usual in my little boat," she remarks bemusedly. He is, after all, "so fatigued with always having to take the initiative and attend to others" that she is glad to offer him some rest. Perhaps she should blame herself for this situation, she reflects, since she herself has slept through her prayers for seven years running, but no—her years of self-reproach are long gone—now she is all trust, all acceptance: "Well, I am not desolate. I remember that little children are as pleasing to their parents when they are asleep as well as when they are wide awake; I remember, too, that when they perform operations, doctors put their patients to sleep" (*Story of a Soul* 165).

In December 1891 an epidemic of influenza broke out in the convent. "My nineteenth birthday," she announces, "was celebrated by a death." It is continually touching to see in this young woman, so near perfection in so many ways, recurring bouts of the absolute solipsism of adolescence. But in fact it must have been an extraordinary reversal for her, "the little one," who had always been cared for, to find herself now one of only three nuns still on their feet. For weeks she helped nurse the others—and helped prepare three of them for burial.

In February 1893, Mother Marie de Gonzague completed her term as prioress and the community elected Pauline Martin—Sister Agnes of Jesus—to take her place. Almost immediately, Pauline assigned to the twenty-year-old Thérèse the post of assistant to the novice mistress. In effect, Thérèse would gradually become novice mistress. (In 1896, Mother Marie de Gonzague would be reelected as prioress, and at that time she combined the offices of prioress and novice mistress, but Thérèse actually served in that capacity without the title.) In this role she began to reveal her tremendous gifts. The fact that she was younger than most of her novices and that she was not officially novice mistress placed her at something of a disadvantage, but she proceeded with complete confidence. She let her novices say what they liked about her, and they did chafe, for she was merciless. She reveled in their diversity and in the resourcefulness it called up in her:

> With certain souls, I feel I must make myself little, not fearing to humble myself by admitting my own struggles and defects; seeing I have the same weaknesses as they, my little Sisters in their turn admit their faults and rejoice because I understand them *through experience*. With others, on the contrary, I have seen that to do them any good I must be very firm and never go back on a decision once it is made . . . God has given me the grace not to fear the battle.
>
> (*Story of a Soul* 240)

To Pauline one day she laughed ruefully and said, "Some I have to catch by the scruff of the necks, others by their wingtips." Thérèse's favorite novice, Marie of the Trinity, testified during the process of Thérèse's beatification: "She never tried to win my affection by natural means, and still she won it entirely. I felt that the more I loved her, the more I loved God, and when I sometimes felt my love for her grow rather cool, I felt my love for God diminishing too."[7] In other words, Thérèse never made things easy. As long as Marie's own zeal for the religious life was intense, that was fine, and she felt affection. If she weren't feeling fond of her novice mistress, it would have been because she wasn't in the mood to exert herself spiritually. One can imagine Teresa exulting over this description of what she would have called "spiritual friendship."

In July of 1894, Thérèse's father died, and Celine was at last free to enter the Carmel Lisieux. Briefly, the community resisted, apprehensive that four sisters (plus a cousin) might constitute something of a faction, but by September she was admitted.

Soon after this, Pauline, Marie, and Thérèse were talking one day about certain episodes from Thérèse's childhood. At Marie's suggestion, Pauline ordered Thérèse to write down her memories of those early years. Thérèse completed it in a year and gave it to Pauline in January 1896. This is the first part of the *Story of a Soul* (chapters one through eight). Pauline did not get around to reading it, which seems odd to us, until after the elections that spring. When she did, she was disappointed to find it did not contain as much as she had hoped about Thérèse's religious life. By this time, though, her term as prioress was over, and Mother Marie de Gonzague had been reelected. The prioress' idiosyncrasies were more and more visible now. Increasingly, during Pauline's term as prioress, Mother Marie had challenged Pauline's authority openly, and to ensure her own reelection she had carried out an embarrassingly political campaign. She had even tried to postpone Celine's profession until after the election: she was certain of her reelection and wished to preside at the ceremony. Even Thérèse, normally loathe to pass judgments on anyone, found the prioress's behavior scandalous, and said so before the other nuns, making it clear that the scandal lay in the disrespect the older nun was showing to the office of prioress itself. Thérèse's own reverence for that office would have prevented her continuing to write her memoirs without an express order from whoever held it. Pauline would have to bide her time, therefore, and hope the prioress would enter a more benign frame of mind.

Meanwhile, though, a new development altered the whole tenor of life at the Lisieux Carmel when it became apparent that Thérèse was very, very ill. She had not looked well for several years. Some, testifying later, spoke of the rigors of the life itself; there was no heating anywhere in the convent except for a fire in the chapter room, where nobody spent much time. Others have observed, though, that a remarkable number of these nuns lived to be quite elderly. Her sister Marie was eighty when she died. Pauline died in 1951 at ninety and Celine in 1959, also ninety.[8]

In any case, on the eve of Good Friday 1896, Thérèse coughed blood, the first symptom of the tuberculosis that would take her life eighteen months later. She rejoiced in believing it to be a call from Jesus. Again, that night, she received "the same sign that my entrance into eternal life was not far off."

It is of the utmost importance, when we see her joy at that juncture, to realize it was not death she was embracing, but eternal life, in which she had absolute faith. She said as much to her friend Marie of the Trinity, who had remarked one day during her illness that life is very sad.

> But life is not sad," Thérèse insisted. "If you had said 'the exile is sad,' I could understand. People make the mistake of calling what must come to an end 'life,' but it is only to heavenly things, to what will never end, that one should really apply the word. And in this sense, life is not sad; it is gay, very gay.
>
> (*Last Conversations* 265)

The significance of the unquestioning faith she expressed at this point will be clearer in a moment.

The *Story of a Soul* is composed of three manuscripts. The first is what Thérèse gave Pauline in January 1896. The second is a letter she wrote to her sister Marie, at Marie's request and authorized by Mother Marie de Gonzague, in which she explains her particular vocation. It was written in September 1896 with the express understanding that Thérèse would not live much longer. It is a deeply moving piece and interesting in terms of a motif that recurs in the writing of women mystics—the sudden restlessness that seizes them when, with the deepening of their life of prayer, they feel they could do or be almost anyone. Thérèse is tormented by the pull of multiple vocations: warrior, priest, apostle, doctor, martyr. At last, rejoicing, she finds the solution. Realizing that "love comprises all vocations," she cries out,

I have found my place in the Church. In the heart of the Church I shall be love. Thus I shall be everything, and thus my dream will be realized.

(*Story of a Soul* 194)

For Thérèse, as for Teresa, the enclosure of Carmel had come to represent genuine freedom.

The third manuscript represents the happy outcome of Pauline's having approached Mother Marie de Gonzague with supreme diplomacy in June 1897, when she knew time was running out:

Mother, it is impossible for me to sleep until I confide a secret to you: When I was Prioress, Sister Thérèse wrote down the memories of her childhood in order to please me and through obedience. I read this over again the other day; it's very good, but you will not be able to obtain much information to write her circular [obituary notice] after her death, for there is almost nothing in it about her religious life. If you were to tell her to do so, she could write something of a much more serious nature, and I don't doubt that you will have something better than I do.

(*Story of a Soul* xiv)

We catch something here of the delicacy and constraint that governed the relationships between these women who had lived so long together, in such isolation, and so continuously at odds. The ploy worked. The prioress asked Thérèse the very next morning to continue writing, and she did, working just two hours a day, while she had strength. This last manuscript is only about a third as long as the first. We observe a distinct shift in tone, and we can trace that to more than one source. One of course is Thérèse's awareness of her imminent death. But it also seems probable, as Gorres has observed, that this last section, addressed to the prioress, forms "a single urgent, veiled lesson. Here is detailed, infinitely tactful, modest and extremely earnest instruction on all the things which the Prioress had to learn or re-learn: on true charity, on patience with the weaknesses of others, on selfless kindness, on consideration, sympathy, lenient judgment, true penance, self-control, and the high art of guiding souls. . . chapters that hold up a mirror to the older woman."[9]

When the *Story of a Soul* was published just a year after Thérèse's death, Mother Marie de Gonzague insisted that the three manuscripts be combined in such a way as to suggest they were all addressed to her. Many older editions of the work preserve this structure. Only because we know the real history of the text, as we do now, can we understand the marked differences in tone between the first and the third sections. The early chapters, as full of sentimentality as they are of spiritual insight, were written for her family, and they were never intended for a wider audience. Thérèse is much more fairly judged by her later writings, and even then, we must realize that she thought she was writing simply to give her prioress information for her obituary.

During the first week of July 1897, Thérèse collapsed completely and was placed in the infirmary. She received last rites at the end of that month, but it would be two more months before she died: months of torment as her lungs quite literally dissolved. She died, in effect, of a long drawn-out suffocation.

She wrote no more, but her sisters sat with her each day and wrote down everything she said. Thérèse had never really spelled out the "little way" of which she had spoken in her memoirs, but to Pauline, one afternoon in the infirmary, she did.

"Mother, it is the way of spiritual childhood, it's the way of confidence and total abandon. I want to teach them the little means that have so perfectly succeeded with me, to tell them there is only one thing to do here on earth: to cast at Jesus the flowers of little sacrifices, to take Him by caresses; this is the way I've taken Him, and it's for this that I shall be so well received" (*Last Conversations* 275).

Shown a photograph of herself, she said, "Yes, but this is only the envelope. When will we see the letter? Oh, how I want to see the letter!" (*Last Conversations* 46).

With something remarkably like merriment, she assured her sisters that she would spend her heaven doing good on earth. "From heaven?" they asked her. Absolutely not. No. "I'll come *back!*"

The last entries form a harrowing record, much of it only broken off utterances. Urgently, she told them never to leave dangerous medicines around someone who was that ill, one's reason is so close to the breaking point. And, toward the end, "I am . . . I am reduced . . . no, I would never have believed one could suffer so much" (*Last Conversations* 230).

Thérèse died September 30, 1897, surrounded by the members of her community. Her death was preceded by what can only be called agony in the full, traditional meaning of the word. She had had premonitions and had warned her sisters in June that they should not be troubled if at the end she made no sign of joy, for Christ too had died a victim of love, and "see what his agony was." Nonetheless, at the very end, her face cleared as she went into a final ecstasy. The other nuns had just left, but a bell called them back.

"Open all the doors," ordered the prioress.

Thérèse gazed intently at her crucifix and said distinctly and finally, "Oh, I love him. . . . My God, I love you."

I HAVE already drawn upon *The Story of a Soul* to convey something of Thérèse's life, and I have acknowledged the difficulties those early chapters present. Among the passages that we read with full attention, though, is the very end of that book, where Thérèse described her state just weeks before her death. She knew finally from experience that the kingdom of God is within, for she felt Jesus' presence within her, "guiding and inspiring me with what I must say and do." It was given to her that summer to understand "how much Jesus desires to be loved," and that inspired her to make her "great Act of Oblation to Divine Mercy." Others offered themselves up as victims of God's justice "in order to turn away the punishment reserved to sinners and bring it down upon themselves." But justice did not attract her. Instead, she offered herself up to God's love. The result was precisely what Catherine of Genoa described: "Since that happy day, it seems to me that love penetrates and surrounds me . . . renews me, purifying my soul and leaving no trace of sin within it, and I need have no fear of purgatory" (*Story of a Soul* 181). It is understood implicitly that the love to which she is offering herself is synonymous with limitless suffering.

When her novice Marie of the Trinity asked her about the Act of Oblation, she explained, "People must not think that our "little way" is a restful one, full of sweetness and consolation. It's quite the opposite. To offer oneself as a victim to love is to offer oneself to suffering, because love lives only on sacrifice; so, if one is completely dedicated to loving, one must expect to be sacrificed unreservedly."[10]

On another occasion, speaking about her work as novice mistress, she said, similarly, "It is prayer, it is sacrifice, which give me all my strength." When Thérèse opened herself to suffering, then, in the million-and-one small ways that she had learned as a child, it was never gratuitously: in every tiny act of resistance to self-will, she was strengthening her capacity to love—confirming herself in love. And love, for her, was indistinguishable from her enormous desire to "win souls" and "save sinners."

As an example of the small sacrifices Pauline had helped her learn to make as a little girl, Thérèse recalled coming in from playing one day and announcing that she was very thirsty. Pauline asked whether she would be willing to forego her drink of water "to save a poor sinner." Deep sigh, shoulders squared, yes, she would. In a moment Pauline gave her the glass of water. What about the sinner? Pauline assured her that she had given him the merit of her sacrifice, now she could also help him by her obedience.

By the standards of contemporary childrearing practice, this may not be the most appealing vignette, but what it does convey is that in Thérèse's upbringing, sinners were perceived not in terms of wickedness, but of forlornness and despair. Indeed, it was understood that despair—failure to experience God's love—can be the motive for sin as much as its result. Sinners are essentially outcasts, yearning to be received again at the table of life, but despairing at the likelihood, and their despair holds them in more serious thrall than whatever sins they might have committed in the first place. For Pauline, it was very natural to associate thirst with sinners: relieving the thirst of Lazarus is imperative to Christ's followers. When Thérèse made one of her "sacrifices" she understood the need to align herself with sinners by experiencing something of their pain herself.

Soon after her Christmas Eve transformation, thirteen-year-old Thérèse had looked at a picture of Christ crucified and been suddenly overwhelmed by the sight of blood flowing from his hands. "I resolved to remain in spirit at the foot of the Cross and to receive the divine dew. I understood I was then to pour it out upon souls. The cry of Jesus on the Cross sounded continually in my heart: 'I thirst!' I wanted to give my Beloved to drink, and I felt myself consumed with a thirst for souls" (*Story of a Soul* 99).

Soon afterward, she adopted as her "first sinner" (later her "first-born"!) a man named Pranzini, with a long criminal record, who had been found guilty of murdering a woman, her maid, and her child. It was the most sensational crime of the day, and the man's refusal to receive a priest as he awaited his execution was played up in all the papers. Feeling the full horror of his estrangement from his fellow creatures as well as from God's mercy, Thérèse determined through her prayers to bring him around. He went to the scaffold unshriven, but at the last instant, he turned to the priest, seized the crucifix, and kissed the wounds of Christ three times. Thérèse was certain her prayers had been answered, and she perceived the whole episode in terms of thirst: Pranzini had relieved his thirst by drinking Christ's blood, but Christ's thirst for souls was satisfied at the same instant—and it was all her doing, prompted by her own deep thirst. Driven by the same essential thirst, she, Christ, and Pranzini become one—a configuration we have seen before with Julian.

We have in these early episodes, then, the genesis of the logic that culminates in the Oblation to God's Mercy. Love will "consume" her in the sense of annihilating the last border between her and the other—the other whom she sees as clearly in the hardened criminal, locked in despair, as she does in her Beloved: "For inasmuch as ye have done it unto the least of these."

We begin to see, I think, why a lifelong advocate for social justice like Dorothy Day would find Thérèse so appealing—why, too, when people ask Mother Teresa of Calcutta whose name she had taken, she smiles and says "The Little One"—Mother Teresa, who insists always that it is not enough to give bread to the poor, we must open our hearts to them, see Jesus in them.

We can begin to understand, too, and this is most interesting, what lay beneath Thérèse's complex relationship with Mother Marie de Gonzague.

The third section of *Story*, the part addressed to Mother Marie de Gonzague, is to my mind the finest of all: first-time readers of the book are well advised to begin with this section. It does not suffer from the overly intimate, somewhat cloying tone of the early chapters. The vignettes she presents in the last section are drawn from her adult life, and they have a universality that makes them irresistible. We feel with her the small but wildly debilitating annoyance of kneeling in prayer next to a sister who makes, as she prays, an odd clicking noise, day after day after day. And we are grateful to her for admitting to feeling more possessive over her own bright ideas than over any of the material things she has renounced: "If on a free day I tell a sister about some light received during prayer and shortly afterwards this same sister speaking to another, tells her what I confided to her as though it were her own thought, it seems as though she were taking what does not belong to her. Or else if during recreation one sister whispers to her companion something that is very witty and to the point, if her companion repeats it aloud without making known its source . . . " (*Story of a Soul* 233).

To the consternation of her sisters, Thérèse addresses the prioress throughout these chapters with easy affection and with every evidence of deep understanding between the two. (This woman had indeed said of Thérèse, "A soul of such mettle must not be treated like a child; dispensations are not made for her sort. Let her be. God supports her.")

Thérèse saw clearly the full extent of the prioress's spiritual decline and her resulting isolation. When she wrote that final section to her story, she gives every appearance of reaching out to her and drawing her toward her, just as she was accustomed to do with her novices. With consummate tact and generosity, Thérèse speaks of her own shortcomings, her failures in patience, and the almost absurd "littleness" of the measures she has taken to overcome them. One guesses that she saw the prioress was too proud and too jealous of her position to confide in anyone her awareness of her own shortcomings: the loneliness at the top! And as if to address that loneliness in particular, Thérèse opens what must have been a particularly painful wound, the prioress's jealousy of Thérèse's bonds with her sisters. Speaking of what it means to live in a spiritual community with one's own family members, Thérèse defends the privilege vigorously:

How can anyone say it is more perfect to separate from one's blood relatives? Has anyone ever found fault with brothers who were fighting on the same field of battle? . . . Undoubtedly, as some have rightly judged, they are a source of encouragement to one another, but still the martyrdom of each becomes the martyrdom of all. . . . When the human heart gives itself to God, it loses nothing of its innate tenderness; in fact this tenderness grows.

(*Story of a Soul* 216)

Then, in a brilliant stroke, as if in passing, she reaches out an arm and sweeps the prioress into that envied family unit: "I love you, dear Mother, with this tenderness, and I love my sisters, too. I am happy to combat as a family for the glory of heaven's King (*Story of a Soul* 216).

But Thérèse goes even further in her effort to draw the older woman to her. Describing her first intimation of death and the clear, living faith in heaven that had sustained her and made the thought of death so happy a prospect, she tells us that "during those very joyful days of the Easter season, Jesus made me feel that there were really souls who have no faith."

For Thérèse, at this stage in her life, to recognize a form of human suffering would have been, instantaneously, to open herself to it, and indeed: "He permitted my soul to be invaded by the thickest darkness, and that the thought of heaven, up until then so sweet to me, be no longer anything but the cause of struggle and torment" (*Story of a Soul* 211).

This trial did not last a few days or weeks, she explains. It would not end until God willed it to, "and that hour has not yet come." Quietly, in a tone of deep sadness, she explains the "dark tunnel" into which she has come.

> I imagine I was born in a country which is covered in thick fog. I never had the experience of contemplating the joyful appearance of nature flooded and transformed by the brilliance of the sun. It is true that from childhood I have heard people speak of these marvels, and I know the country in which I am living is not really my true fatherland.
>
> (*Story of a Soul* 212)

She finds herself seated now at a "table filled with bitterness at which poor sinners are eating"—those who have no faith, that is—and hopes by her own patient waiting to bring "the bright flame of faith" to them, if God so wills.

She breaks off, falters, apologizes for the fact that her "fairy tale" has turned into a prayer, but she goes on to depict her situation even more pathetically. "When I want to rest my heart fatigued by the darkness which surrounds it by the memory of the luminous country after which I aspire, my torment redoubles." Voices mock her. "You are dreaming!"

She goes on to insist to the prioress, "my dear Mother," that she must believe this to be true despite the fact that "I must appear to you as a soul filled with consolations."

It is an incredible revelation, and it would strike any reader so: but one wonders whether it was not meant to touch the prioress with special force. One wonders, that is, whether Thérèse suspected that the older woman was undergoing her own crisis of faith, that she was locked into a form of exile made all the more painful by her position of leadership.

It is interesting that in fact, this is not the first time in Thérèse's life that she has been in a "dark tunnel." Before her profession, her "wedding" with Christ, she had written to Pauline, "Before our departure my Bridegroom asked me to what land I wished to travel, and which path I preferred to take."

"The mountain of love," she replied, but he could choose the way.

And our Lord took me by the hand and made me enter a subterranean way where it is neither cold nor warm, where the sun does not shine and where rain and wind may not enter; a tunnel where I see nothing but a half-veiled glow from the downcast eyes in the face of my spouse. . . *I gladly consent to spend my entire life in this underground darkness to which he has led me; my only wish is that my gloom will bring light to sinners.* (Italics mine)[11]

The land of eternal fog in which Thérèse finds herself now is familiar to us, and it is directly related to her having yielded herself up to God's will. The echoes of Mechthild of Magdeburg are unmistakable.

In what we see of the interactions between a Thérèse and a Mother Marie de Gonzague—perhaps even between a Teresa and a John of the Cross—there is considerable mystery. One thinks of icebergs scraping past one another in deep seas and great slabs of ice falling into the water unwitnessed. Thérèse will thank the prioress on several occasions with something like ferocity for having understood that indeed her soul did *not* seek the dispensations her gentler sisters would have given her. She is moved, one suspects, by gratitude, as well as pity, to try to give the older woman the benefit of her own insight.

From the entire story of Thérèse, which we get in so much more complete a form than we do with any other mystic I know of, we keep being struck by the endless ways in which these individuals shaped one another. A model of spiritual development emerges that is remarkably *collective.* It began with her family; Gorres describes it as a "compound organism": the parents devoted so single-mindedly to the spiritual formation of their children, and the daughters themselves so extraordinarily watchful over one another and so deeply joined in love. They evolve *together,* prompting one another, correcting, consoling . . . and we see the same process in the convent itself, of individuals "working out their salvation," but *together.*

Western culture has always been so attuned to the heroic individual that we are not well prepared to recognize this version of spirituality, but it is not without precedent. The *Imitation of Christ,* for example (which Thérèse knew by heart) had an authorship that was essentially collective, reflecting the ideal of mutual edification that permeated the movement.[12] The literature that emerged from the first Franciscans has a similar quality. A single individual is very much at the center in these accounts of spiritual growth, but the presence of his or her companions is seen as deeply meaningful, and the warmth of their relationship to one another is continually underscored. ("See these Christians, how they love one another!")

Thérèse wrote:

> Just as a torrent, throwing itself with impetuosity into the ocean, drags after it everything it encounters in its passage, in the same way, O Jesus, the soul who plunges into the shoreless ocean of your love, draws with her all the treasures she possess. Lord, you know it, I have no other treasures than the souls it has pleased You to unite to mine.
>
> (*Story of a Soul* 254)

After her death, the community underwent a dramatic transformation. It was as if Thérèse really had "come back," in that eight nuns whom she had molded and shaped by her "little way"—among them her own three sisters—stepped forward and established the entire community on a new footing altogether.

With the story of Thérèse, and only with her story, we see a fully realized mystic and saint portrayed as someone living at the center of a web of intense relationships: embedded, that is, in an intimate personal context within which everyone is continually affecting everyone else. Theoretically, of course, a Carmelite does not retain relationships with her family members. Thérèse never stopped caring intensely for her sisters, though, and felt no need to, because she was relating to them as friends in the spirit, in precisely the terms Teresa of Avila had set forth. (Indeed, once she became a Carmelite, she stonewalled every attempt her sisters made to draw her back into a "special" familial configuration.)

Is it coincidental that this new twist on hagiography should emerge from a collective authorship that was entirely feminine? One can scarcely think so. And indeed, how many lives of saints might not look very much like this one if women had been the chief chroniclers, saving the mother's letters, persuading one another to write down memories some might think trivial, *telling stories* about the children of a family to themselves and one another exactly as Sarah Ruddick describes—and, yes, taking photographs of a decidedly odd-looking group of nuns as they do their laundry and cut their hay and sit stiffly "at recreation," and seeing them as aglow with significance. For women understand the deeply collective and communal side of human experience. They see the incandescent superstar for what it is, but they see the constellation in which it has come into being, too, the reverent and loving care that has surrounded and nourished it. They see how much we have to do with one another, how profoundly we require one another.

Conclusion

BEFORE this book was anything but a faint outline of a vague idea, its title barrelled up out of nowhere, so right that it felt like a gift or an encouraging shove from a friend. It worked nicely enough on the most literal level: the valor and the charm of these women does go on making itself felt down through time. *Their* grace endures. But its real strength is in what it conveys about the mystical experience itself. For as soon as we begin to look closely at Teresa, the Catherines, Thérèse, we realize that grace did not just enter their lives, it came on like an avalanche. Grace is not so much received, we come to understand, as it is weathered—like the embrace of a lover who is rougher than he means to be.

For these are not gentle stories. You can emphasize the moments of humor and the lyrical passages, and I've gone out of my way to do so, but the essential feature of all these narratives is the awakening of spiritual awareness, and that seems never to take place without stirring up antagonism: the family and community may be thrown into turmoil, but so, quite often, is the mystic herself. We may smile at the "dancing demons" who tried to derail Catherine of Siena, or the "fiend" with the livid face and long sidelocks who tried to unsettle Julian, but the violence of the Mitigated Carmelite brothers who nearly killed John of the Cross is all too comprehensible and all too familiar. And when Catherine of Siena visits Avignon, hoping to talk the pope into returning to Rome, we are horrified but not altogether surprised that a hostile lady of the court should "test" Catherine's absorption in prayer by sticking a long needle into her foot. (Catherine in fact did not move—she was only aware of her pain later.) Mechthild had enemies, and so did Teresa. And yet they would have been quick to insist that their most formidable opponents were within, longstanding habits and attachments that waged their own quiet war of resistance.

It is surely not a coincidence that so many of these women should have experienced illnesses, mysterious in origin, so severe that they were thought to be dying or even dead. This happened to Julian, to Catherine of Siena, to Teresa, and to Thérèse as a little girl. In Julian's case, the experience was consciously willed as a way of purging herself of worldly attachments. Catherine of Siena did not ask to experience death, but she wept bitterly at what she had lost in having to return to the body. In Teresa's case, and in Thérèse's, one has the feeling the experience had a very different significance, that a kind of war was taking place within the will itself, the body and mind being the battlefield, and the truce, when it came, an uneasy one.

Turbulence, in any event, and sorrow of a great many kinds, commonly pervade the mystic's life from beginning to end: ill health, overwork and exhaustion, political opposition, alienation from friends or loved ones, spiritual aridity. Mechthild chronicled it all more assiduously than most, but I suspect she spoke for all of them when she wrote, "If thou wouldst drink the unmingled wine, thou must ever spend more than thou hast." All of these women were in a sense "overdrawn" most of the time. (If Julian, for example, seems an exception with her ebullient "all manner of thing shall be well," remember that it was also she who said firmly, "This place is prison, this life is penance.")

And yet the very reason I have emphasized here the grief and turmoil of their lives is that the impression they leave with us is ultimately one of joy and transcendence. The mystics knew sorrow and disappointment inside and out, but they had also made their peace with them. Each words it differently—Teresa, for instance, speaks hesitantly with regard to the "seventh dwelling place" of the "interior castle," saying that it is as though she were both Mary and Martha now, that "despite the trials she underwent and business matters she had to attend to, the essential part of her soul never moved from that room" (*Interior Castle* 7.1.10). Catherine of Genoa marveled in her final days, that "as for the spirit, I sense such peace and joy that it goes beyond words; with respect to humanity, the deepest suffering a body can feel is nothing to what I am experiencing" (*Spiritual Dialogue* 139). Thérèse, Julian, Catherine of Siena, Mechthild: each will say essentially the same thing in her own way, and of course it is a mystery, a truth one can only grasp by experiencing it oneself. And yet the very fact that this *same* mystery keeps getting discovered and stated by one mystic after another brings it closer, gives it substance. For this—because all of us are struggling with some form of turmoil or suffering—we are consummately grateful.

EVERYONE who has written this book before (insofar as it resembles the collected "Lives of Women Saints" traditionally handed out to little girls at confirmation) has been Catholic. I am not: my spiritual home is elsewhere and it suits me. I *have* wanted the book to be useful to Catholics, though, and to that end I have had some Catholic friends look over the manuscript for obvious false steps—not exactly a *nihil obstat*, but a sincerely well-intentioned gesture toward the sensibilities of members of a tradition not my own.

Not my own, and yet held in great regard. To be perfectly honest, I've nursed a small but genuine apprehension that at some point in my relationship with these seven women I might find myself wanting to become, as they gloried in being, "a daughter of the Church." Those who grew up as I did in the fifties and sixties perhaps will understand: the popular culture of the period was obsessed with Catholicism. We soaked up *The Nun's Story* and a whole slew of novels whose plots hinged upon dramatic and soul-stirring conversions. Perhaps I got a stronger dose than most impressionable teenagers; my first boyfriend's mother was a converted Catholic who gave me Thomas Merton's *The Seven Storey Mountain*—at age fourteen, for pity's sake!

I remain, however, stolidly unconverted. I am one of those women of whom it has been said, "we piece together what we will believe in." I think this is true of a great many contemporary women. We are slow to take in, or take *on*, the great handed-down monolithic doctrines or credos. We know too much about the strengths of *all* religions, and too much about the weaknesses of these religions as well, particularly where women are concerned. Our personal experience counts for a lot, and so do the carefully recounted experiences of individuals who have won our trust. We find these individuals, women and men alike, in every religious tradition, and we feel they belong to all of us.

In an effort to bring greater objectivity to the research and writing of this book than has characterized similar books of the past, I have worked mostly with primary sources: the mystic's own writings or those of her contemporaries. But I realized early on that I was not going to be able to provide a truly balanced view of any of them, no more than I could of my husband, my son, or my mother. I did not choose these particular subjects because they were representative of feminine mysticism, but quite simply because I loved them, and I have written about them accordingly, celebrating their strengths and passing more lightly over their foibles or idiosyncrasies than consistent objectivity would dictate.

In her preface to *Holy Feast and Holy Fast,* historian Caroline Walker Bynum thanks friends who "never let me forget that the medieval women I studied sounded decidedly peculiar to modern ears." There are indeed a great many social and cultural assumptions we must lay aside before we can draw up close to a Mechthild or a Catherine of Siena, and I may not have underscored these adequately. With regard to sexuality, for example, a particularly wide gulf stretches between us. All seven of my subjects were celibate, even the "married saint" Catherine of Genoa, thanks to her husband's conversion. Are we to think, then, that sex and spirituality are mutually exclusive? For contemporary women, this isn't obvious. We are not as likely as our medieval counterparts to die in childbirth, after all, or to die exhausted after too *many* births. We might think it possible to raise children and still maintain a genuine spiritual practice of one kind or another; we might even think that raising children can be central to our practice. We suspect that the relationship between spirituality and sexuality is both subtle and profound. How would Julian have felt about all this, or Teresa? Unfortunately, they did not say. This particular gulf will continue to separate us.

We write what we want to know, just as we teach what we wish to understand. The two years I have spent writing this book have been a continuous revelation to me. My reasons for picking this particular set of subjects have only become clear after the fact. At the outset I could only say that I felt drawn to them and that each had left enough of a textual basis to assure that the latent scholar in me could feel herself on sure footing. Now the deep kinship of these seven women is patently clear—one will complete a line of inquiry that another had begun, or expand and clarify the same metaphor. Sometimes they sound really like only one voice, after all. Their relevance to contemporary spiritual endeavors is equally clear.

I was not prepared, however, for the degree of *personal* relevance they would turn out to have. All along the way, as I took up each new life, I found something in that life that would bring into sharp focus an issue surfacing in my own life. Some of these I spoke of in my introduction, others I did not: issues such as community, maternality, friendship, political activism, and "dark nights," and how to regard them.

Pervading the entire inquiry, central to it at nearly every point, has been the whole vexed topic of gender. Ultimately, as I have reiterated, mystics of every tradition assure us that gender is absolutely irrelevant, for as we move toward the highest levels of spiritual awareness, we gradually "dis-identify" ourselves from everything that normally constitutes identity—mind, body, intellect, ego. By the time we reach the threshold of full spiritual awareness, all dualities are behind us: we are no more male or female there than we are black or white, old or young, learned or ignorant, you or me. All is one, hence the expression "unitive consciousness."

In the earlier stages of spiritual awareness, however, the foothills where most of us are struggling, gender is, or can be, intensely relevant. (Hindu philosophers have a clever way of accounting for the seeming anomaly: one's difficulties are "real" with respect to the level of consciousness you have currently attained, and "unreal" with regard to the clear air of the higher slopes. As long as something is even relatively real to us, we have to reckon with it.)

Historians of medieval spirituality concur that with the spread of affective piety, many monks came to feel comfortable worshiping God with tears, tenderness, and a new delight in Christ's humanity. At the same time, *women* religious were displaying a marked new assertiveness—taking charge of their own lives, founding and reforming communities, chastising the clergy—in ways that took them well beyond conventional notions of appropriate feminine behavior, and they did so with the active, respectful encouragement of men like Francis of Assisi, Mechthild's "Heinrich," and Catherine of Siena's beloved Raymond of Capua.

In other words, among men and women alike, one sees here and there a new measure of freedom from the intensely gender-specific roles that life would otherwise have imposed upon them. Quite without seeking it, some of them seem to have stumbled into a kind of "safe zone" where they could live as more fully rounded and balanced human beings. We see in their writings a fresh kind of ease and fluidity where gender is concerned, and I have found it to be contagious: my own thinking about gender has been loosened up considerably. I feel more and more inclined to believe that the "maleness" and "femaleness" we assign to one another and to whole categories of experience is arbitrary, at bottom simply a projection of the painful feelings of dividedness we all carry around inside of us. We feel split up inside, for reasons every religious tradition will articulate in its own way, and in response we have formed the habit of dividing everything around us in two. The mystics have healed that division; everything about them conveys wholeness, and inclusion. The word *holy* is in fact cognate with the words *whole* and *hale.*

Here, as so often, Hinduism offers a fresh and somewhat whimsical perspective: suppose that with each new incarnation, the human being reverses gender? This seems to me—piecing together, once again—a thoroughly reasonable proposition that may explain a great deal. Now a girl, now a boy, now a man, now a woman, I pass through aeons of time experiencing each version of life in turn, taught all along that they are two different worlds until at last I wake up, laughing deeply, understanding that they are merely two halves of the one world.

It is just such an awakening we seem to see in a Mahatma Gandhi or a Teresa of Avila. As they come into their own, that "Berlin Wall" in consciousness falls, and the banished parts of them are called back out of exile. Strength, tenderness, delicacy, courage, artistry, passion, endurance: every human capacity is available to them. They do not deny the existence of gender, but they wear it lightly, even with a sense of humor.

The long, slow process of awakening that we see in individuals may well be trying to take place in the culture at large as well. The parallels I have found between aspects of mystical thought on the one hand and what Sara Ruddick calls "maternal thinking" on the other hand would suggest this. It is as if throughout most of human history a certain *kind* of truth has hovered about on the outer edge of things, trying to make itself heard. It is not an inherently feminine truth, but it is a truth, or set of truths, more familiar to women because the birthing and nurturing of children is almost universally in our hands. It is the truth that emerges whenever women are actively encouraged to speak their minds in a context that genuinely (if only momentarily) reveres "the feminine." And those contexts do arise. At rare intervals, a specific thirst builds up, an aridity that seems to call up a Clare, a Julian, a Mother Teresa, someone who lives close to the wellsprings of life and can guide the rest of us back to them.

All of this gives to the term *feminism* a somewhat specialized meaning, and with regard to that meaning I would suggest that women like Clare and Teresa are among the true proto-feminists. Roughly four hundred years before Virginia Woolf wrote *A Room of One's Own*, which maintained that women would certainly prove the equal of men in creativity once they had the privilege of doors they could close, Teresa of Avila insisted in her "Rule" that every nun should have a cell that no one could enter without permission. And if contemporary feminists are correct in believing that finding one's voice is the critical initial step women must take toward establishing a personal identity, then Teresa's own preoccupation with language, voice, and "conversation" was right on the mark. She defended as god-given her spiritual daughters' right to inwardness itself—and to living situations, mentors, and books that facilitated it—because nothing else would permit the "still small voice" from within to be heard.

I HOPE that readers will recognize the chapters of this book as introductory sketches only —as thresholds, built as invitingly as I could, but meant to be crossed. I am happy to think that some readers will be content with the book as it stands, seizing on the odd anecdote or the riveting one-liner like talismans, and will make good use of them. But I hope others will be moved to go on and read the mystics' own words, as scholars (and I envy anyone who is just now undertaking scholarly work in the field, for fascinating things are happening there), but even more, as seekers. My greatest hope is that some will find in these lives the inspiration to deepen their commitment to their own spiritual path, whatever that may be.

Notes

PREFACE

1. M. F. K. Fisher, foreword of *The Gastronomical Me,* reprinted in *The Art of Eating* (NY: Vintage, 1976).

2. Interested readers may see *The Making of a Teacher* (Petaluma, CA: Nilgiri Press, 1986), co-authored by me and my husband Tim Flinders, for a portrait of Easwaran's grandmother, whose full name was Eknath Chippu Kunchi Ammal.

3. I like what Alice Walker said about the differences between black and white writers: "It is not the difference between them that interests me, but rather the way black writers and white writers seem to me to be writing one immense story—the same story, for the most part—with different parts of this immense story coming from a multitude of different perspectives." (Alice Walker, *In Search of Our Mother's Gardens* (San Diego: Harcourt Brace Jovanovich, 1983), 5.

4. Heilbrun, *Writing a Woman's Life,* 20–21.

5. From the "Brihadaranyaka Upanishad," 4, 21, trans. Eknath Easwaran in *The Upanishads* (Petaluma, CA: Nilgiri Press, 1987), 45.

INTRODUCTION

1. Peter Dronke, *Women Writers of the Middle Ages* (Cambridge: Cambridge Univ. Press, 1984), 203.

2. Lamprecht von Regensburg, cited in *Women Mystics in Medieval Europe,* by Emilie Zum Brunn and Georgette Epiney-Burgard, xiv.

3. "Life of the Blessed Aldobrandesca," cited by Elizabeth Alvilda Petroff in *Medieval Women's Visionary Literature,* 19.

4. Petroff, *Medieval Women's Visionary Literature,* 19.

5. "As we have listened for centuries to the voices of men and the theories of development that their experience informs, so we have come more recently to notice not only the silence of women but the difficulty in hearing what they say when they speak. Yet in the different voice of women lies the truth of an ethic of care, the tie between relationship and responsibility, and the origins of aggression in the failure of connection . . . " Gilligan, *In a Different Voice,* 173.

6. Ruddick, *Maternal Thinking: Toward a Politics of Peace,* 93.

7. Ruddick, *Maternal Thinking,* 95.

8. Ruddick, *Maternal Thinking,* 96.

9. Ruddick, *Maternal Thinking,* 186.

10. Ruddick, *Maternal Thinking,* 119–20.

Chapter One: SAINT CLARE OF ASSISI

1. One guesses that leafy branches might well have been used in place of palm fronds (I don't recall seeing any palm trees growing around Assisi!), which would in turn lead us to guess that before the region was Christianized, some kind of ritual might have been enacted each spring having to do with beautiful virgins—Persephone returning after winter's darkness—and the leafy young branches poets love to compare them with.

2. The Testament of Saint Clare, *Early Documents* 55. This prophecy appears in two other early accounts of Francis's life (*Early Documents* 262 and 268), but Clare alone uses the word *again,* suggesting San Damiano may have been a convent in the past.

3. Clare herself spoke only of "sisters" and "poor sisters." In time the order was known as "Sisters of Saint Clare" as well as "Poor Ladies" and "Poor Clares." Today "The Order of Saint Clare" is the official designation (hence the initials "O.S.C.").

4. "Mirror mysticism" was relatively widespread during Clare's time. It is interesting that in South India, on the morning of "Vishu," the holiday that celebrates the arrival of spring, devout Hindu households practice their own form of mirror mysticism. Each member of the family is told to close her eyes and is then escorted to the family altar, where the mother or grandmother has put together an arrangement of flowers and fruit, grains, legumes, and a few coins, with a mirror at the center. "Repeat your mantram," she instructs each member of the family, "then open your eyes and see the Lord."

5. In the summer of 1224, Francis went to Mount La Verna and gave himself over to forty days of fasting and praying, which culminated in his petition to God to feel, first, the suffering Christ had endured on the cross and second, the love that had inspired him to accept it. Francis received both and came away with wounds on his hands, his feet, and in his left side. Blood would flow out of these wounds from time to time for the rest of his life.

6. From the *Mirror of Perfection,* retold in *Saint Francis of Assisi,* by Johannes Jorgensen (New York: Image Books, 1955), 192.

7. Pertinent to this episode is Caroline Walker Bynum's discussion in *Jesus as Mother* of the profound deference that male religious figures often displayed during the twelfth and thirteenth centuries toward contemplative women like Hildegard of Bingen and the nuns of the Cistercian abbey at Helfta. Observing that the church itself was consciously elevating the role of the priest and the eucharist at this time, she adds that many clergymen felt uncomfortable with their new power, in contrast with "those who do not have power and may be purer for the lack." She concludes that "the mystical alternative flourished as a complement to, not a contradiction of, the clerical role—and this in two senses: first, the visions mystical women received from Christ show admiration for the priest's authority; second, the mystical alternative to the authority of the priest gave Christians of both sexes an opportunity to express an ambivalence about power that was part of the Christian tradition" (*Jesus as Mother,* 261–62).

8. One of a series of church councils held at the Lateran Palace in Rome between the seventh and eighteenth centuries, this was one of five extremely important ones ranked as "ecumenical." This particular council, in addition to forbidding establish-

ment of new religious orders, issued an official definition of the doctrine of the eucharist in which the term *transubstantiation* was first used, and it enacted mandatory annual confession for all Christians

9. *Oxford Dictionary of the Christian Church*, ed. F. L. Cross (London: Oxford Univ. Press, 1957), s.v. "Rule of Saint Benedict."

10. This reference to the serving sisters does alert us to the fact that even in the relatively democratic atmosphere of these early communities of Poor Ladies, certain class distinctions were still observed.

11. I have specified "voluntary poverty," but in fact Mother Teresa of Calcutta describes situations in her work among the city's most hopeless people—people who have certainly not chosen to be poor—that mirror the ideal one we are imagining. She has told of a destitute Hindu family in Calcutta to whom she brought a little food, and described her astonishment at seeing the mother of the family divide everything in half. Asked what she was doing, she explained she would take it to a nearby Muslim family, because "they are hungry, too."

Chapter Two: MECHTHILD OF MAGDEBURG

1. Saint Augustine addressed this same theme in one of the most lyrical passages in all of mystical writing:

> What now do I love, whenas I love thee? Not the beauty of any corporal thing; not the order of times, not the brightness of the light which we do behold, so gladsome to our eyes; not the pleasant melodies of songs of all kinds; nor the fragrant smell of flowers, and ointment, and spices: not manna and honey; nor any fair limbs that are so acceptable to fleshly embracements. I love none of these things whenas I love my God: and yet I love a certain kind of light, and a kind of voice, and a kind of fragrance, and a kind of meat, and a kind of embracement, whenas I love my God. . . .
> Where that light shineth into my soul, which no place can receive; where that voice soundeth of which time deprives me not; and that fragrance smelleth, which no wind scatters; and that meat tasteth, which eating devours not; and that embracement clingeth to me, which satiety divorceth not. This it is which I love, whenas I love my God. (From *Confessions*, trans. William Watts [Cambridge: Harvard Univ. Press, 1912], 10.5.)

2. A historian of German mysticism discovered the full manuscript in 1860 in the library of a convent high in the Alps. Even this was not Mechthild's own manuscript, but a High Middle German translation of the Low Middle German original, which has never been found. The work was transcribed and published in German in 1869. Evelyn Underhill translated excerpts from the book into English and included them in her classic study, *Mysticism*. She gave a copy of the book to Lucy Menzies, who in 1953 published an English translation.

3. The rejection of permanent vows is an interesting feature of several grass-roots spiritual movements of the time. The Brethren and Sisters of the Common Life, the movement that nurtured Thomas à Kempis, are an example. Groups like these wished to set aside all the "trappings" of the spiritual life—habits, vows, enclosure,

etc.—and demonstrate that one could lead a Christlike life in any situation. They may have felt, too, that the idea of making a permanent vow is a bit presumptuous.

4. R. W. Southern, *Western Society and the Church in the Middle Ages* (Middlesex, England: Penguin Books, 1970), 329.

5. Southern, *Western Society*, 330.

6. Elizabeth Alvilda Petroff suggests, "Mechthild badly needed the serenity of Helfta, but it seems equally clear that Helfta was in need of her experience, too, in order to become a home not just for learned women, but for women writers" (*Medieval Women's Visionary Literature*, 211).

7. Ruddick, *Maternal Thinking*, 96.

8. Belenky, Clinchy, Goldberger, and Tarule, *Women's Ways of Knowing: The Development of Self, Voice, and Mind* (New York: Basic Books, 1986).

9. Bynum, *Holy Feast and Holy Fast*, 289. She adds a few pages later, "Recent feminist psychological theory has suggested that the profoundly asymmetrical patterns of child-rearing in Western culture may influence female children toward a less acute sense of binary oppositions and of "otherness" (293).

10. In several regards, the female body was seen by medieval men and women as "transformative." This was chiefly because of woman's reproductive role—the food she eats becomes the flesh of the child in her womb, and her very blood, supposedly, changes into breast milk—but it probably had to do also with her many roles in food production—the "magic" by which wheat becomes bread, cream becomes butter, grape juice wine, and so forth.

11. James Franklin, *Mystical Transformations* (Cranbury, NJ: Associated Univ. Presses), 144.

12. Only in recent years have writers of nursing manuals and baby books been able to be as comfortable as Mechthild was in evoking this motif. I recall being delighted to read sometime in the seventies about the first scientific research demonstrating that hormones secreted in a nursing mother and her infant promote bonding by lowering irritability, and so forth. I remember thinking, too, how poignant it is that we need scientists to tell us this. Today's La Leche League manuals speak with delightful aptness of "the nursing couple."

13. Since Mechthild presents God here as male lover of a soul presented as a young woman, the male pronouns for God will have to stand. When she speaks of being "wounded" by love, she is invoking the language of courtly love, but the motif is universal. The poems of the North Indian princess-troubadour Mira Bai, for example, include the same lament.

14. Dante may have known of Mechthild and her writings. Some scholars believe that the fair maiden Matilda, whom Dante places in Earthly Paradise atop Mount Purgatory, "singing and plucking flowers," might have been she. Considering that her mentor, Heinrich Halle, was a student of Albertus Magnus and therefore one of a network of Dominican scholars residing throughout Europe, and that he could well have sent her writings, proudly, to some of them, it is possible that Dante may have read them.

15. One is reminded here of the *Bhagavad Gita* and its teachings on evenness of mind—that come pleasure or pain, gain or loss, heat or cold, the mind of the illumined woman or man is unaffected.

16. The source of this fascinating observation is a review, written by the renowned neurologist Oliver Sacks, of John M. Hull's *Touching the Rock* (*New York Review of Books,* April 11, 1981):

> The receding visual world is the vanishing light behind him as he advances through the tunnel, the deathlike tunnel which has no light at the other end, the tunnel from which he can never hope to emerge. We travel with Hull farther and farther into the world, or nonworld, of blindness, until finally he comes to a point where he can no longer summon up memories of faces, of places, even memories of the light. This is the bend in the tunnel: beyond this is "deep blindness." And yet at this deepest, darkest, most despairing point, there comes a mysterious change—no longer an agonized sense of loss, of bereftness, of hopelessness, of mourning, but a new sense of life and creativity and identity. "One must recreate one's life or be destroyed," Hull writes, and it is precisely re-creation, the creation of an entirely new organization and identity, which is described in the closing pages of his astonishing book. At this point, then, Hull wonders if blindness is not "a dark, paradoxical gift" and an entry—unsought, surely horrific, but to be received—into a new and deep form of being. "Deep blindness" now shows its other side, and Hull becomes, as he puts it, "a whole-body-seer."
>
> "Being a Whole Body Seer," he writes in his post script, "is to be in one of the concentrated human conditions. It is a state, like the state of being young, or of being old, of being male, or female; it is one of the orders of human being.". . . After sinking hopelessly into a bottomless ocean, he discovers, in his deepest depths, his anchor and soul: this, for Hull, is "touching the rock."

17. This is an exceedingly complex topic, best approached by reading Bynum's *Holy Feast and Holy Fast,* particularly chapter 9, "Woman as Body and as Food."

18. With regard to the striking reciprocity of all this, it is useful to recall an earlier situation when Mechthild was denied communion and had a dream-vision wherein John the Baptist himself gave her the Host.

> Then the maid went up to the Altar with great love and a widely opened soul. John the Baptist took the white Lamb with the red Wounds and laid it on the mouth of the maid. Thus the pure Lamb laid itself on its own image in the stall of her body and sucked her heart with its tender lips. The more it sucked, the more she gave herself to it. (2.4)

19. See Belenky et al., *Women's Ways of Knowing,* chap. 6.

20. Contemporary feminist theologian and psychotherapist Sister Madonna Kolbenschlag took the same inclusive position in a recent interview. Asked whether she believed in a transcendent God, she replied:

I think our concept of God is a product of our own dualistic thinking, which is that things are either transcendent or immanent. And I don't believe that anymore. Spirit and matter are not split in the manner that we have stereotypically thought of it. My experience of God is of being transcendent and immanent all at once. . . I no longer believe that God is up there, and I don't believe that God is only within me, and I don't believe that God is merely out there in history. I think we are actually in God at all times. (*Sojourner* [May 1991], 28)

Chapter Three: JULIAN OF NORWICH

1. As a graduate student, I became so intrigued by the differences between Julian's two texts that I made them the subject of my doctoral dissertation. No critical edition of the *Showings* was available then. I had to work with photocopies (white on black, barely legible, library-use-only) of the Middle English manuscripts. It was heavy going, but amply rewarded, for not long after I'd started, Julian began rapidly to come to life for me. Perhaps because I was spending so much of my own time writing and rewriting, I could almost feel her at work, inserting a phrase here, a sentence there, suppressing one kind of detail and enhancing another.

2. Grace Jantzen's *Julian of Norwich, Mystic and Theologian* (New York: Paulist Press, 1987) is the source of the description of anchoritic life I have sketched out here.

3. Brant Pelphrey, *Christ Our Mother: Julian of Norwich* (Wilmington, DE: Michael Glazier, 1989), 44.

4. Thomas Merton writes, from a perspective much wider and more inclusive than mere scholarship:

Julian is without doubt one of the most wonderful of all Christian voices. She gets greater and greater in my eyes as I grow older. . . . I think that Julian of Norwich is with [Cardinal] Newman the greatest English theologian. She is really that. For she reasons from her experience of the substantial center of the great Christian mystery of redemption. She gives her experience and her deductions, clearly, separating the two. And the experience is of course nothing merely subjective. It is the objective mystery of Christ as apprehended by her, with the mind and formation of a fourteenth-century English woman. (From *Seeds of Destruction* [New York: Farrar, Straus & Giroux, 1965], 275.)

5. Carolly Erickson, *The Medieval Vision* (New York: Oxford Univ. Press, 1976), 218.

6. Erickson, *Medieval Vision*, 30.

7. Erickson, *Medieval Vision*, 214.

8. Today, no one wishing to compare the Short and Long Text of the *Showings* has to camp out in the university library, because the two texts have been published in an excellent translation under one cover by scholars Edmund Colledge and James Walsh (see select bibliography).

9. In *Psyche and Symbol*, Carl Jung describes the situation in psychoanalysis that typically precedes the emergence in dream or fantasy of the so-called child archetype.

Julian's state of mind prior to her discovery of the parable of the servant and master bears a remarkable resemblance to that situation. See *Psyche and Symbol*, ed. Violet de Laszlo (New York: Doubleday, 1958), 132–33.

10. The parable of the servant and the master is barely mentioned in the Short Text. This is understandable, for Julian had not yet raised the question to which the parable supplied the answer. Later in her life, however, in the context of her deepening anxiety over the question of sin and evil, she took it up.

11. Carolly Erickson tells us of Julian's time period that "it was a cultural habit to endow individual things with multiple identities" (*Medieval Vision,* 8). Julian, like Mechthild, illustrates this predilection beautifully.

12. Jung speaks in *Psyche and Symbol* of the "redemptive significance" of "uniting symbols." Clearly this parable was precisely such a "uniting symbol" for Julian.

13. This detail occurs only in the Gospel according to John (19:34).

Chapter Four: SAINT CATHERINE OF SIENA

1. I find *The Dialogue* to be very hard going. Only in recent years has its real structure been recognized. Suzanne Noffke, translator of the Paulist Press edition (see select bibliography), explains it interestingly, but even so the work is daunting in its unrelenting intensity and its impersonal tone. I feel much closer to Catherine when I read her letters, which are currently being translated and published in English by Dr. Noffke, but even more so, oddly enough, when I read the biography of Catherine written by her confessor, Raymond of Capua.

2. (See *Life* 37.) Alert students of myth and fairy tale will recognize the Cinderella motif here. Some may remember, too, that in the story of Iron John, which Robert Bly has interpreted, the young hero is compelled to work out his time in the kitchen, a situation that Bly links to the observation that in early Nordic cultures, young men were commonly understood to need a kind of dormancy before they stepped out into manhood and that often this would entail their lying about for months at a time near the hearth in a "ritual lethargy" or quasi hibernation, quite literally rolling about in the ashes. It is intriguing to recall that when Catherine fell asleep at the spit, as noted above, she, too, rolled into the ashes (*Life* 114).

3. Western mystics have rarely shed much light on the subject of sexuality. Eastern mystics, on the other hand, talk openly about sexual desire as a force in consciousness. It is not good or evil in itself, they insist, any more than an electric storm is. Rather, it is energy, raw power, and our task as human beings is to come to terms with that power—not to try and destroy it or suppress it, but to claim it and draw upon it for the good of all life. The Eastern tradition maintains that the individual who succeeds in tapping into that force will have superhuman vitality, on the one hand, and tremendous magnetism as a teacher, on the other. It is interesting to reflect that Catherine of Siena was notable in both regards.

4. The blunt and earthy quality of Catherine's language can be disconcerting and might seem to be inconsistent with her horror at the "coupling figures" described above. But there it is. One is reminded at times of the equally earthy discourse of the great Bengali saint of the nineteenth century, Sri Ramakrishna—earthy, and unutterably innocent.

5. For a full and fascinating exploration of a very complex question, I refer readers to Caroline Walker Bynum's *Holy Feast and Holy Fast.* No one who has followed the lines of her inquiry carefully can fall into the error of glibly equating the *inedia* of women like Catherine with the anorexia or bulimia of contemporary women, but they will glimpse some of the deeper, more mysterious connections between the food practices of medieval and contemporary women.

6. R. W. Southern, *Western Society and the Church in the Middle Ages* (Middlesex, England: Penguin Books, 1970), 133.

7. One is reminded of descriptions of Mahatma Gandhi's travels around India—the crowds that would swarm up over his railway car at every stop, hungry for his *darshan,* the simple sight of a man or woman of God that, for the devout Hindu, is in itself an influx of grace. Indeed, the comparison holds well, for the last days of our own century's greatest exponent of nonviolence were lurid with the bloodshed of Hindu-Muslim conflicts, just as Catherine's own were defined by mounting violence on all sides and by the realization that almost everything she had set out to achieve had failed.

8. Cited by Alice Curtayne, *Saint Catherine of Siena,* 187.

9. Curtayne, *Saint Catherine,* 196.

10. The Carthusians were a contemplative order of extreme austerity; only as a deathbed promise could Catherine have been sure her vacillating disciple would accept such a command!

Chapter Five: SAINT CATHERINE OF GENOA

1. When I cite Catherine's *Life,* I will hereafter be citing the translation by Mrs. George Ripley (see select bibliography). This particular passage, though, taken from Evelyn Underhill's classic *Mysticism* (441), has always seemed to me particularly well translated—has become, in fact, a personal talisman for me.

2. For a fascinating glimpse of the political, social, and ecclesiastical motives that can influence the canonization process, see *Making Saints: How the Catholic Church Determines Who Becomes a Saint and Who Doesn't,* by Kenneth Woodward (New York: Simon & Schuster, 1990).

3. Friedrich von Hugel, *The Mystical Element of Religion as Studied in Saint Catherine of Genoa and Her Friends* (London: Dent, 1908), 1:189. Baron von Hugel was spiritual and intellectual mentor to Evelyn Underhill, whose masterwork, *Mysticism,* remains one of the very best studies of mysticism ever written.

4. See *Medieval Women's Visionary Literature,* by Elizabeth Alvilda Petroff, 136ff.

5. Dante Alighieri, *Inferno,* trans. Allen Mandelbaum (New York: Bantam, 1980), canto 7, vv. 121–24.

6. See *The Changing of the Gods,* for instance, by Naomi Goldenberg (Boston: Beacon Press, 1979).

7. The contemporary "centering prayer" movement, initiated by Father John Keating and others, does entail the use of the single word *Maranatha,* which is Aramaic for "Come, Lord," and also the use in more pressed circumstances of an "action word," a single word like *love* or *hope.*

8. From the Latin hymn "Dulcis Jesu Memoria," which is generally attributed to Bernard of Clairvaux. This translation appears in Bynum's *Holy Feast and Holy Fast*, 66.

9. *The Cloud of Unknowing*, trans. Augustine Baker (London: Burns & Oates, 1924), chap. 7.

10. From Padre Umile Bonzi's two-volume study *Santa Caterina da Genova* (Turin: Marietti, 1962), vol. 1, p. 37 (translation of these lines is my own).

Chapter Six: SAINT TERESA OF AVILA

1. "A Satirical Critique," for example, is treasured because it gives us a glimpse of Teresa's most playful side. In prayer, late in the year 1576 (which would make her about sixty-one), she heard the words "seek yourself in me." Moved and curious, she told her brother Lorenzo, who in turn consulted with several of their friends as to what the words might mean. Teresa was in Toledo at the time, and her friends back at Avila were missing her heartily, so they gathered together at Christmas and considered the problem together. Each of them wrote down his or her response and mailed it off to Teresa. In her written reply, her "critique" of their answers, she imitates a kind of satirical ceremony, which candidates for the doctoral degree in Spanish universities had to undergo, and teases them quite without mercy. This is the source of her famous words to John of the Cross, who was one of the "contestants": "God deliver me from people so spiritual that they want to turn everything into perfect contemplation, no matter what." (The "Critique" is included in volume 3 of Teresa's collected works in the Kavanaugh/Rodriguez translation; see select bibliography.)

2. Indeed, the ironies of history are marvelous. Within the last few years, it has been recognized that in remote villages of Mexico, many families have practiced Judaism in secret for nearly five hundred years. Conquistadors who happened also to be *conversos* settled there in the sixteenth century and, far from converting the local population to Catholicism, resumed their own inherited faith instead.

3. St. John of the Cross, *The Ascent of Mount Carmel*, 1.1.11.

4. Auclair, *Saint Teresa of Avila*, 242.

5. Auclair, *Saint Teresa*, 385.

6. Bilinkoff, *The Avila of Saint Teresa*, 114.

7. Spain was first invaded by Muslim military forces in 711. The Christians of northern Spain managed to "reconquer" the country by the early thirteenth century, except for the kingdom of Granada, which would take more than two hundred years to recapture. Thus the phrase "during the Reconquest" is an exceedingly vague designation of time.

8. One winces over certain passages from Teresa's writings that reiterate the misogyny of her time and culture. With regard to endearments used sometimes among the sisters, for example, she says, "There's no reason for using them. They are very womanish, and I would not want you, my daughters, to be womanish in anything, nor would I want you to be like women, but like strong men " (*Way of Perfection* 7.8). On the other hand, just to keep things in perspective, from the same book:

"Nor did you, Lord, when you walked in the world, despise women. Rather, you always, with great compassion, helped them." The lines that followed, censored from the first published versions, read like this:

> And you found as much love and more faith in them than you did in men. . . . Is it not enough, Lord, that the world has intimidated us so that we may not do anything worthwhile for you in public or speak some truths that we lament over in secret, without your also failing to hear so just a petition? I do not believe, Lord, that this could be true of your goodness and justice. . . . These are times in which it would be wrong to undervalue virtuous and strong souls, even though they are women. (*Way of Perfection* 3.7)

Chapter Seven: SAINT THERESE OF LISIEUX

1. Dorothy Day, *By Little and By Little* (New York: Knopf, 1983), 197. Dorothy Day wrote a biography of Thérèse, which is rather hard to come by, but excerpts from it were published in this anthology of her writings.

2. Gorres, *The Hidden Face*, 27.

3. All of these quotations are from the collected letters of the Martin family, cited in Gorres's *The Hidden Face*, 44–45.

4. A Carmelite nun refers to the cell she lives in and everything she uses—lamps, pencils, even the habit itself—as "ours," in keeping with her vow of absolute poverty.

5. Gorres, *The Hidden Face*, 193.

6. Gorres, *The Hidden Face*, 196.

7. *Saint Thérèse of Lisieux By Those Who Knew Her*, ed. Christopher O'Mahony, 231.

8. In 1944, when Allied planes bombed German-occupied Lisieux, and the convent was evacuated, Celine and Pauline were among the evacuees. I can never quite take this in—that they were still there at Lisieux during the lifetimes of so many of us.

9. Gorres, *The Hidden Face*, 220.

10. O'Mahony, *Saint Thérèse of Lisieux*, 236.

11. Letter 91, cited by Gorres, *The Hidden Face*, 226.

12. The Brethren and Sisters of the Common Life, which together formed the milieu that produced the *Imitation of Christ,* were founded by a saintly individual named Geert Groote, but this spiritual movement was so deeply committed to the ideal of mutual edification that no one individual emerges as its "saint." Their literature is composed of *florilegia*, notebooks into which they jotted inspiring bits and pieces from scripture and also beautifully devotional obituary pieces written about one another. The *Imitation* itself appears to have evolved from Groote's own *florilegium* supplemented by the writings of Thomas à Kempis, to whom the book is usually credited. Thomas himself made no claim of authorship, merely signing it as a copyist would have.

Select Bibliography

WOMEN MYSTICS

Bynum, Caroline Walker. *Holy Feast and Holy Fast: The Religious Significance of Food to Medieval Women.* Berkeley and Los Angeles: Univ. of California Press, 1987. A brilliant scholarly investigation of the food practices of medieval religious women, too closely argued and too fully supported to begin to summarize, but essential reading for anyone wishing to understand the subject. An anthropologist's deep respect for other cultures informs the study, a woman's for other women, and, carefully concealed beneath impeccable scholarship, a seeker of living truth for others who have sought.

Petroff, Elizabeth Alvilda. *Medieval Women's Visionary Literature.* New York: Oxford Univ. Press, 1986. Excerpts from twenty-eight visionary writings spanning the period from late antiquity to the fifteenth century, each introduced very informatively by Petroff. The general introduction deserves close attention: its analysis of the stages of visionary mysticism is most interesting.

————. *Peace Weavers: Medieval Religious Women.* Volume II. Cistercian Studies Series, 72. Kalamazoo, MI: Cistercian Publications, 1987. Occupying an important middle ground between scholarship and devotional writing, this wide-ranging anthology includes essays by twenty-four scholars, including some of the best in the field. The designation "medieval" is taken loosely; Teresa of Avila and Jeanne de Chantal are among the subjects. Highly recommended.

ON MEDITATION AND MYSTICISM

Easwaran, Eknath. *Seeing with the Eyes of Love.* Petaluma, CA: Nilgiri Press, 1991. By way of commenting upon a widely cherished chapter of Thomas à Kempis's *Imitation of Christ,* Sri Easwaran introduces the practice of meditation and the allied disciplines from a perspective that is as comfortable for practicing Christians as it is for audiences more familiar with his commentaries on Hindu and Buddhist Scriptures and his basic introductory book, *Meditation.* All of Easwaran's books on the spiritual life are highly recommended. For information, write to Nilgiri Press, P.O. Box 477, Petaluma, CA 94952.

GENDER STUDIES

Bateson, Mary Catherine. *Composing a Life.* New York: Atlantic Monthly Press, 1989. Drawing upon conversations with four of her closest friends, the author has drawn a fascinating picture of "complex lives, where energies are not

239

narrowly focused toward a single ambition but rather are continually refocused and redefined." She concludes that "life is an improvisational art form, and that the interruptions, conflicted priorities, and exigencies that are a part of all our lives can, and should be seen as a source of wisdom."

Gilligan, Carol. *In a Different Voice: Psychological Theory and Women's Development.* Cambridge: Harvard Univ. Press, 1982. Demonstrating that psychology has built virtually all of its developmental theories on observations of men's lives, this is the groundbreaking work toward constructing models that illuminate the experience of women. A truly wonderful book.

Heilbrun, Carolyn G. *Writing a Woman's Life.* New York: Ballantine, 1988. Not only psychologists, but also biographers and even *auto*biographers of female subjects have worked with "scripts" drawn from men's lives: Heilbrun introduces us to several exceptional women whose lives have not been adequately understood because they did not fit those scripts, and she makes intriguing suggestions as to what some of the central concerns of a woman's biographer should be: overlooked themes like friendship between women, the female physical experience, and the richness that can characterize a woman's later years.

Ruddick, Sara. *Maternal Thinking: Toward a Politics of Peace.* New York: Ballantine, 1989.

Tannen, Deborah. *You Just Don't Understand.* New York: Morrow, 1990.

SAINT CLARE OF ASSISI

EDITIONS

Early Documents. Edited and translated by Regis J. Armstrong, O.F.M., Cap. New York: Paulist Press, 1988.

Francis and Clare: Complete Works. Edited by Regis J. Armstrong and I. C. Brady. New York: Paulist Press, 1982.

MECHTHILD OF MAGDEBURG

EDITIONS

The Revelations of Mechthild of Magdeburg, or *The Flowing Light of the Godhead.* Translated by Lucy Menzies. London: Longmans, Green, 1953. This remains my preferred translation, though it has been out of print for decades now and though printing costs forced the translator/editor to omit a considerable amount of material. The citations I have made here from *Flowing Light* are all from this translation unless otherwise noted.

Mechthild von Magdeburg, Flowing Light of the Divinity. Translated by Christiane Mesch Galvani; edited and with an introduction by Susan Clark. New York: Garland Publishing, 1991. One volume in a "library" of medieval literature, this book includes the only complete English translation of

Mechthild's writings. It is quite expensive, though, and less than wonderfully printed.

STUDIES

Brunn, Emilie Zum, and Georgette Epiney-Burgard. *Women Mystics in Medieval Europe.* New York: Paragon House, 1989. This is a fine introduction, sensitively written, to Hildegarde of Bingen and the chief Beguine mystics, including Mechthild of Magdeburg.

JULIAN OF NORWICH

EDITIONS

Julian of Norwich: Showings. Translated and with an introduction by Edmund Colledge, O.S.A., and James Walsh, S.J. New York: Paulist Press, 1978.

STUDIES

Erickson, Carolly. *The Medieval Vision: Essays in History and Perception.* New York: Oxford Univ. Press, 1976. This excellent book does not deal directly with Julian but with the subject of visions and visionaries.

Jantzen, Grace. *Julian of Norwich, Mystic and Theologian.* New York: Paulist Press, 1987.

SAINT CATHERINE OF SIENA

EDITIONS

Catherine of Siena: The Dialogue. Translated and with an introduction by Suzanne Noffke, O.P. New York: Paulist Press, 1980.

The Letters of St. Catherine of Siena. Vol. 1. Translated and with an introduction by Suzanne Noffke, O.P. Binghamton, NY: Medieval and Renaissance Texts and Studies, 1988.

STUDIES

Curtayne, Alice. *Saint Catherine of Siena.* Rockford, IL: Tan Books and Publishers, 1929.

Jorgensen, Johannes. *Saint Catherine of Siena.* Translated by Ingeborg Lund. London: Longmans, Green, 1939.

Raymond, of Capua. *The Life of St. Catherine of Siena.* Translated by George Lamb. Chicago: P. J. Kenedy & Sons, 1960.

SAINT CATHERINE OF GENOA

EDITIONS

Catherine of Genoa. *Purgation and Purgatory, The Spiritual Dialogue.* Translated by Serge Hughes. New York: Paulist Press, 1979.

Life and Doctrine of Saint Catherine of Genoa. Translated by Mrs. George Ripley. New York: Christian Press Association Publishing, 1896.

SAINT TERESA OF AVILA

EDITIONS

Teresa of Avila. *The Collected Works.* 3 vols. Translated by Kieran Kavanaugh, O.C.D., and Otilio Rodriguez, O.C.D. Washington, D.C.: Institute of Carmelite Studies, 1980. I prefer this relatively recent translation a great deal over the more widely available one by Allison Peers, but I have been careful to make my citations to chapter and section numbers rather than page numbers so that readers can find them easily in either translation.

STUDIES

Auclair, Marcelle. *Saint Teresa of Avila.* Petersham, MA: St. Bede's Publications, 1988. A reprint from 1953 Pantheon edition translated by Kathleen Pond. This is one of the loveliest spiritual biographies I know of, and I recommend it highly. It was, however, written more than forty years ago: one would love to see a new and comprehensive biography of Teresa that makes full use of the wealth of historical materials and perspectives that are available now.

Bilinkoff, Jodi. *The Avila of Saint Teresa.* Ithaca, NY: Cornell Univ. Press, 1989. A fine introduction to the kind of historical background that can light up our understanding of Teresa: scholarship at its best.

Clissold, Stephen. *St. Teresa of Avila.* London: Sheldon Press, 1979. A fine start toward that more heavily "contextualized" telling of Teresa's life, but only a start.

Green, Deirdre. *Gold in the Crucible.* Dorset, England: Element Books, 1989. Green looks at the possibilities of influence on Teresa's thought of Jewish mysticism and "Christian Kabbalah," but has interesting things to say, too, about the whole issue of women's spirituality.

SAINT THERESE OF LISIEUX

EDITIONS

Thérèse of Lisieux. *The Story of a Soul: The Autobiography of St. Thérèse of Lisieux.* Translated by John Clarke, O.C.D. Washington, D.C.: Institute of Carmelite Studies, 1972.

Thérèse of Lisieux: Her Last Conversations. Translated by John Clarke, O.C.D. Washington, D.C.: Institute of Carmelite Studies, 1977.

St. Thérèse of Lisieux: Testimonies from the Process of Beatification, by Those Who Knew Her. Edited and translated by Christopher O'Mahony, O.C.D. Huntington, IN: Our Sunday Visitor, 1975.

STUDIES

Beevers, John. *The Storm of Glory: The Story of St. Thérèse of Lisieux.* Garden City, NY: Image Books, 1955.

Gorres, Ida. *The Hidden Face: A Study of St. Thérèse of Lisieux.* New York, Pantheon, 1959. This extraordinarily sensitive and insightful book was translated from the original German by Richard and Clara Winston. It was originally published in Freiburg by Herder Verlag in the year (think about this) 1944. In that same year, Allied planes bombed German-occupied Lisieux, forcing the Carmelites to evacuate. The convent itself was undamaged. Among the evacuees were Sisters Agnes of Jesus and Genevieve of the Holy Face— Pauline and Celine Martin.

Index

Act of oblation, Thérèse of Lisieux's, 212

Adorna, Caterina. *See* Saint Catherine of Genoa

Adorno, Giuliano: conversion of, 146–48; death of, 150–51; marries Catherine of Genoa, 135–37

Agnes of Jesus. *See* Pauline Martin

Agnes of Prague, 16–18, 23

Agnes (sister of Clare of Assisi), 21

Ahumada, Beatriz de, 160–61

Ahumada y Cepeda, Teresa de. *See* Saint Teresa of Avila

Aldobrandesca of Siena, 4–5

Ammal, Eknath Chippu Kunchi, 229n.2

Anchoritic enclosure, 80–81

Attentive love, 8

Auclair, Marcelle, 173

Augustine, Saint, 176, 231n.1

Autobiography (Teresa of Avila), 157, 175

Beguines, 2–3; decline of, 50; movement described, 48–49

Belenky, Mary Field, 54

Benedict of Nursia, Saint, 35

Benincasa, Catherine. *See* Saint Catherine of Siena

Bernard of Clairvaux, Saint, 1–2

Bhagavad Gita, 9–10, 233n.15

Book of Showings to the Anchoress Julian of Norwich, A (Julian of Norwich), 78, 86–98, 101, 234nn.1 and 8. *See also* Long Text (Julian of Norwich); Short Text (Julian of Norwich)

Brethren and Sisters of the Common Life, The, 231–32n.3

Bruno of Olmutz, Bishop, 50

Bynum, Caroline Walker, 224, 230n.7, 233n.17, 236n.5

Canticle of the Creatures (Francis of Assisi), 31

Carmelite Order: founded by Teresa of Avila, 157; Primitive Rule of the, 163; reform of the, 172–73

Catherine of Genoa, Saint: conversion of, 131, 138–39; early life of, 134–38; last years of, 151–54; religious service of, 130–33, 146–51; sufferings of, 140–45; teachings of, 133–34, 148–49

Catherine of Siena, Saint: appeal to Gregory XI, 121–23; becomes a *mantellata*, 110–12; force of personality, 126; last days of, 124–27; life of, 103–10; relationship with Christ, 113–14, 116–17; religious service of, 114–21; self-esteem of, 110–11; tormented by demons, 112–13

Catholic Church: canonization process, 236n.2; conflict with Julian's revelations, 89; conflict with the "Tuscan League," 121–23; Great Schism (1377), 82, 123; Mechthild's attacks on, 51; on *scrupulus*, 199; suffers Great Schism (1377), 82; views on mental prayer, 167–68; vow of poverty, 25–26. *See also* Religion; Spanish Inquisition; Virgin Mary

"Centering prayer" movement, 236n.7

Cepeda, Alonso de: allows daughter to join convent, 163; conversion of, 167–69; death of, 169; early life of, 160–61. *See also* Saint Teresa of Avila

Christianity: current visibility of women in, 8; perception of femininity by medieval, 2–3; reflection of feudal structure in, 1–2; spread to Spain, 158–59

Christina of Markyate, 136

Cisneros, Ximenes, 159

Clare of Assisi, Saint: death of, 38–39; early life of, 15–21; Francis of Assisi and, 23, 25–33; miracles performed by, 39–40; religious service of, 21–27, 41–42. *See also* Poor Ladies convent

Clement V, Pope, 120

Clement VII (of Avignon), 124

Cloud of Unknowing, The (anonymous), 145

Confessions, The (Augustine), 176

Connective thinking: described, 53–54; on God and soul relationship, 54–55, 67; Mechthild's use of, 74

Constitutions (Teresa of Avila), 156

Convents: description of medieval, 47. *See also* Carmelite Order; Poor Ladies convent

Conversos, 160, 237n.2

Council of Vienne (1312), 50

Cruz, Juan de la. *See* John of the Cross

Dante, 63, 65, 68, 232n.14. *See also* Mechthild of Magdeburg

Dejados, 177

Detachment: concept described, 149; Teresa of Avila on, 182–83

Dialogue (Catherine of Siena): described, 104, 123–24; English translation of, 235n.1; on the protective covering of truth, 109; transformation process described in, 114

Difference feminists, 53–54

Dillard, Annie, 79

Discretio, 36

Divine Comedy (Dante), 63

Divine inspiration. *See* Revelations

Divine Mother, 4–6. *See also* God

Doctrine of atonement, 93–95

Dominican friars, 49

Easwaran, Eknath, xiv, xv

Enclosure (anchoritic), 80–81

Erasmus, 159

Erickson, Carolly, 83–84

Fasting, 118–19

Feminine character: Catholic Church model of, 54; Francis of Assisi's expression of the, 31–33; modern concept of, 6–7; of mysticism, 3–4, 226–27; and aspect of God, 96–97; warming of

masculine by, 67–69. *See also* Masculine character; Women

Feminists: connectedness as key concept, 53–54; female mystics as proto, 227

Flesh, The: Mechthild's description of the, 70–71; medieval view of women's, 232n.10; mystics revile, 69–70

Flinders, Tim, 229n.2

Flowing Light of the Godhead, The (Mechthild of Magdeburg), 45–46, 51

Fonte, Tomaso della, 108

Fourth Lateran Council, 34

Francis of Assisi: Clare of Assisi and, 15, 17–21, 23, 25–33; renunciation of, 29–30

Franciscan friars, 26–27, 29, 49

Friendship, 12, 119, 181–82

Gandhi, Mahatma, xv–xvii, 29, 189, 236n.7

Gender. *See* Feminine character; Masculine character

Gift from the Sea (Lindbergh), 79

Gilligan, Carol: describes connection concept, 53–54; on the feminine character, 6, 34

God: Augustine writes of love of, 231n.1; belief in divine inspiration, 35–36; Catherine of Genoa's love for, 132–33, 144; Catherine of Siena's charge from, 117; hearing the "still small voice" of, 227; Julian describes, 89–91, 96–97; Julian on motherhood of, 94–95, 97–98; Mechthild describes, 44, 54–55, 61–64, 67–68; referring to, 10–11; transcendent vs. immanent, 74; worshiped as Divine Mother, 4–6. *See also* Jesus Christ; Love

Gorres, Ida, 194, 218

Great Schism (1377), 82, 123

Gregory XI, Pope, 121–23

Groote, Geert, 238n.12

Halle, Heinrich, 48, 50–51, 232n.14

Holy Feast and Holy Fast (Bynum), 224, 233n.17, 236n.5 (chap. 4)

Hugolino, Cardinal, 35

Humility, 183, 205–6

Il Poverello. *See* Francis of Assisi
Illuminism, 160
Imitation of Christ, 218, 238n.12
In a Different Voice (Gilligan), 6
Inferno (Dante), 63
Innocent III, Pope, 34, 36–37
Innocent IV, Pope, 35, 39
Interior Castle (Teresa of Avila), 186–87
Interior prayer. *See* Mental prayer

Jesus Christ: Catherine of Genoa's identification with, 135; Catherine of
Siena's relationship with, 113–14,
116–17; Julian on doctrine of atonement, 93–95, 98–99; maternality of, 5,
32; Thérèse of Lisieux's identification
with, 21–14; women's identification
with, 168. *See also* God
Jesus as Mother (Bynum), 230n.7
John of the Cross: imprisoned by
Mitigated Carmelites, 175; relationship
with Teresa of Avila, 173–74, 189–90; on
temptations of triviality, 164
Judaeo-conversos, 159, 237n.2
Julian of Norwich: anchoritic enclosure
of, 81–83; describes God, 89–92; on
doctrine of atonement, 93–95; liberating impact of teaching, 78–79; "showings" (revelations) of, 86–98, 101; on
Trinity, 95–96; visionary writing of,
79–80, 83–84
Jung, Carl, 234–35n.9

Keating, Father John, 236n.7 (chap. 5)
Kempe, Margery, 83, 100
Kempis, Thomas à, 231n.3, 238n.12
Kolbenschlag, Sister Madonna, 233–34n.20

Ladies of Mercy, 146
"La Madre Fundadora." *See* Teresa of Avila
"La Santa." *See* Teresa of Avila
Letrados, 175–76
Life (Catherine of Genoa), 148, 151, 236n.1
Lindbergh, Anne Morrow, 79
Little Flowers of Saint Francis, 27
"Little way," 205–6, 212, 215, 218. *See also*
Saint Thérèse of Lisieux

Lollards, 82
Long Text (Julian of Norwich): described,
78, 85–87; on motherhood, 98; on
motherhood of god, 96; parable from,
92–93; on seeking spirituality, 100–101;
on temptations, 99
Love: attentive, 8; Augustine on, 231n.1;
between Francis and Clare of Assisi, 33;
Catherine of Genoa on, 132–33, 144,
148–49; Catherine of Siena on, 117;
Julian on, 94–95; Mechthild on God's,
54–59, 67–68; Pure and Simple, 141–42,
150; Teresa of Avila on, 188; Thérèse of
Lisieux on, 209–10, 212, 214. *See also* God

Maconi, Stefano, 124–26
Magnus, Albertus, 232n.14
*Making Saints: How the Catholic Church
Determines Who Becomes a Saint and
Who Doesn't* (Woodward), 236n.2
Making of a Teacher, The (Flinders and
Flinders), 229n.2
Mantrams, 145
Marabotto, Don Cattaneo, 151–52
Marie de Gonzague, Mother, 205, 207–11,
214–17
Marie of the Trinity, 207–8, 212
Martin, Celine: death of, 209; early life of,
196, 208; enters Carmel Lisieux, 208;
evacuated during W.W. II, 238n.8;
supports Thérèse's decision, 201
Martin, Louis, 193–95, 200–203, 208
Martin, Marie, 196, 199–200, 209
Martin, Pauline: becomes prioress, 207–8;
death of, 209; evacuated during W.W.
II, 238n.8; leadership of, 205; on power
of obedience, 213; raises Thérèse after
mother's death, 196–97
Martin, Thérèse. *See* Saint Thérèse of
Lisieux
Martin, Zelie, 193–96
Mary Magdalene, 105, 113
Masculine character: arbitrary assign-
ment of, 226; Catholic Church model
of, 54; integration with the feminine,
31–33; modern concept of, 6. *See also*
Feminine character

Maternal practice, 7–9

Maternal Thinking: Toward a Politics of Peace (Ruddick), 6–9

Mechthild of Magdeburg: character of, 43–45; death of, 52; early life of, 46–49; moves to Helfta, 51–52; on power of prayer, 40; sufferings of, 60–66, 74–75; writings of, 44–46, 50–51, 52–62

Meditation, 10

Mental prayer: Catholic Church views on, 167–68; "four waters" stages of, 177–79; Teresa of Avila resumes, 169–70; Teresa of Avila's practice of, 157–58, 160, 165–67, 181–82; vs. vocal prayer, 184. *See also* Prayer

Menzies, Lucy, 231n.2

Merton, Thomas, 223

Mirror mysticism, 230n.4

Mirror of Simple Souls (Porete), 50

Mortification, 23

Moslem religion, 158–59

Mysticism: fasting and, 118–19; impact of nuptial, 2; mirror, 230n.4; sexuality in Eastern, 235n.3; Spanish, 158–60; tendency to revile body in, 69–70; women and traditions of, 1–6, 34

Mysticism (Underhill), 231n.2

Mystics: family and friend connections of, 97–98; and grace, 221–22; relationship with religion, 77–78; self-esteem of female, 110–11; suffering of the, 126; as true proto-feminists, 227

Noffke, Suzanne, 235n.1

Order of Saint Clare, The. *See* Poor Ladies convent

Osuna, Francisco de, 159

Pammetone Hospital, 147–48, 151, 153–54

Paul, Apostle, 113

Petroff, Elizabeth Alvilda, 232n.6

Philip II, King, 160

Pilgrim at Tinker Creek (Dillard), 79

Poor Ladies convent: currently Order of Saint Clare, 230n.3; establishment of, 21; Fourth Lateran Council on, 34–35; life of poverty, 23, 25–26, 34–35, 38; ongoing relationship with brethren, 26–27; Rule of, 35–37. *See also* Saint Clare of Assisi

Porete, Margaret, 49–50

Poverty: Clare of Assisi's version of, 25–26; Poor Ladies life of, 23, 25–26, 34–35, 38; Teresa's commitment to, 156; Thérèse of Lisieux on, 205

Pranzini, 214

Prayer: "centering prayer" movement, 236n.7; meditation as, 10; mental vs. vocal, 184; *recogidos* on, 177; Teresa of Avila's teachings on, 177–82. *See also* Mental prayer

Primitive Rule of the Carmelite order, 163

Protestant Reformation, 159–60

Psyche and Symbol (Jung), 234–35n.9

Pure and Simple Love, 141–42, 150

Purgation and Purgatory (Catherine of Genoa), 133

Raptures, 156, 172, 188

Raymond of Capua: on Catherine of Siena's struggles, 113, 116–17, 119, 122; on Catherine's teachings, 111; meets Catherine, 119

Recogidos, 177

Religion: illuminism movement, 160; Julian of Norwich's examination of, 78–80; Moorish, 158–59; mystic relationship with, 77–78. *See also* Catholic Church

Revelations: Julian of Norwich's, 86–98, 101

Room of One's Own, A (Woolf), 227

Ruddick, Sara: describes connection concept, 54; describes maternal practice, 7–9, 226; on the feminine character, 6–7, 34; on "histories of flesh," 70

Rule of Saint Benedict, 35–37

Saints: canonization process, 236n.2; defining, 10

Sanchez, Alonso. *See* Alonso de Cepeda

Sanchez, Juan, 159

San Damiano, 21–22

Saracini, Alessia, 115

"Satirical Critique, A" (Teresa of Avila), 237n.1

Seven Storey Mountain, The (Merton), 223

Sexuality, 224, 235n.3

Short Text (Julian Norwich), 78, 85–86, 89

Schreiner, Olive, 8

Sin: Catherine of Genoa's repentance of, 138–39; Julian of Norwich's revelations on, 89–90; "occasions of," 166–67; Thérèse's despair and, 213; Thérèse's "terrible sickness of scruples" and, 199-200

Southern, R. W., 50

Spanish Inquisition: dangers of the, 156–57; members described, 168, 175–76; rise of the, 159–60. *See also* Catholic Church

Spiritual Dialogue, The (Catherine of Genoa), 133, 152

Story of a Soul, The (Thérèse of Lisieux), 202, 209–12, 214

Tannen, Deborah, 6–7

Tauler, John, 24

Teresa of Avila, Saint: character of, 155–57; early life of, 161–63; enters the Incarnation, 163; foundations established by, 174–75; "four waters" treatise, 177–79; reform of Carmelite Order, 172–73; second conversion of, 169–71; spiritual teachings of, 158, 175–90

Teresa of Jesus. *See* Saint Teresa of Avila

Thérèse of the Child Jesus and of the Holy Face. *See* Saint Thérèse of Lisieux

Thérèse of Lisieux, Saint: death of, 212; early life of, 193–200; enters convent, 203–6; illness of, 209; second conversion of, 200–202; spiritual service of, 214; takes her vows, 206–8; teachings of, 192, 211; writings of, 208–19

Third Spiritual Alphabet, The (de Osuna), 159, 165

Thomas of Celano, 28–29

Trinity, 55, 67, 95–97

Tuchman, Barbara, 82

"Tuscan League," The, 121–23

Underhill, Evelyn, 231n.2

Urban VI, Pope, 123–25

Vigne, Raymond delle. *See* Raymond Capua

Virgin Mary: Julian's description of, 94–98; Mechthild's description of, 71–72; Thérèse and, 198; worship of, 5. *See also* Catholic Church

Visionary literature, 79–80, 83–84

Walker, Alice, 229n.3

Way of Perfection (Teresa of Avila), 162, 171, 180–81, 186–87

Women: approach to moral choices by, 6–7, 229n.5; connected ways of knowing by, 53–54, 74; detachment concept and, 149; identification with Christ, 168; language and power connection, 171–72; maternal practice of, 7–9; medieval view of body of, 232n.10; mysticism traditions and, 1–6, 34. *See also* Feminine character

Women's Ways of Knowing, 53

Woodward, Kenneth, 236n.2

Woolf, Virginia, 227

Wycliffe, John, 82

You Just Don't Understand (Tannen), 6